Current Approaches in the
Cognitive Science of Religion

Current Approaches in the Cognitive Science of Religion

Edited by Ilkka Pyysiäinen and Veikko Anttonen

continuum
LONDON • NEW YORK

CONTINUUM

The Tower Building, 11 York Road, London, SE1 7NX

370 Lexington Avenue, New York, NY 10017-6503

First published 2002 by Continuum

British Library Cataloguing-in-Publication Data
A catalogue record for this book is available from the British Library.

    ISBN 0-8264-5709-6 (hardback)
        0-8264-5710-X (paperback)

Library of Congress Cataloging-in-Publication Data
Current approaches in the cognitive science of religion / edited by Ilkka Pyysiäinen and
Veikko Anttonen.
    p. cm.
   Includes bibliographical references and index.
   ISBN 0-8264-5709-6 (hb) — ISBN 0-8264-5710-X (pbk.)
    1. Psychology, Religious. I. Pyysiäinen, Ilkka. II. Anttonen, Veikko.
  BL53 .C787 2002
  200′.1′9—dc21   2001047579

Typeset by CentraServe Ltd, Saffron Walden, Essex
Printed and bound in Great Britain by
Biddles Ltd, Guildford and King's Lynn

Contents

Contents

Contributors

Veikko Anttonen Professor of Comparative Religion, Department of Cultural Studies, University of Turku, Finland
veikko.anttonen@utu.fi

Justin L. Barrett Research Investigator in the Institute for Social Research, Visiting Assistant Professor in the Psychology, Culture and Cognition Program, University of Michigan, Ann Arbor, USA
JustinLB@umich.edu

Pascal Boyer Henry Luce Professor of Individual and Collective Memory, Washington University in St Louis, USA
pboyer@artsci.wustl.edu

Stewart Guthrie Professor of Anthropology, Fordham University, New York, USA
guthrie@fordham.edu

Jeppe Sinding Jensen Senior Lecturer, Department of the Study of Religion, University of Aarhus, Denmark
pangolin@post9.tele.dk

Matti Kamppinen Senior Lecturer in Comparative Religion, Department of Cultural Studies, University of Turku, Finland
matti.kamppinen@utu.fi

E. Thomas Lawson Professor of Comparative Religion, Department of Comparative Religion, Western Michigan University, Kalamazoo, USA
lawson@wmich.edu

Contributors

Robert N. McCauley Professor of Philosophy, Department of Philosophy, Emory University, Atlanta, USA
philrnm@emory.edu

Ilkka Pyysiäinen Associate Professor of Comparative Religion; Researcher, University of Helsinki Collegium of Advanced Studies, Department of Comparative Religion, University of Helsinki, Finland
ilkka.pyysiainen@pp.inet.fi

Pertti Saariluoma Professor of Cognitive Science, Department of Psychology, University of Yräskylä, Finland
psa@utu.fi

Jesper Sørensen Assistant Professor, Department of the Study of Religion, University of Southern Denmark, Odense
js@filos.sdu.dk

Harvey Whitehouse Reader in Anthropology, School of Anthropological Studies, Queen's University of Belfast, Northern Ireland
h.whitehouse@qub.ac.uk

1 Introduction: Cognition and Culture in the Construction of Religion

ILKKA PYYSIÄINEN

The cognitive approach

One of the basic ideas in the *cognitive science of religion* is that religious thought and behaviour are made possible by evolved cognitive capacities which are the same for all humans and which thus can explain certain recurrent patterns in religious representations (see Tooby and Cosmides 1995; Boyer 1994; 1998). One important point is that the human mind is understood not as an all-purpose problem-solver but as a collection of subsystems carrying out content-specific operations. The mind operates differently in such domains as folk biology, folk psychology and naive physics (Karmiloff-Smith 1992; Hirschfeld and Gelman 1994: 3–4; Cosmides and Tooby 1994; Tooby and Cosmides 1995; Sperber 1994; Mithen 1998; Atran 1998; Boyer 1998; Medin and Atran 1999). Religion is based on cognitive processes in which the boundaries between these ontological domains are violated (Boyer 1994; Mithen 1998: 198–202).

Explanations of religious thought and behaviour can therefore only be based on independent knowledge about the human mind (Boyer 1993). Such knowledge cannot be deduced from religious materials alone, such as ancient texts or anecdotal observations by anthropologists. We need to explain religious materials in a systematic manner by a coherent theory of the human mind. Religion need not be separated from other domains of knowledge as a *sui generis* phenomenon which requires special methods of gaining knowledge.

Yet religion does not consist of ideas alone. Religions also participate in social and cultural processes, a fact which has made many anthropologists argue that religion can be defined simply as a symbolic expression of the social. This, however, is counter-productive. If 'religious' simply equals 'cultural', then the concept of 'religion' becomes superfluous. Yet we can identify distinctive recurrent patterns of

1

thought and behaviour that form a specific subset of the wider set of cultural thought and behaviour, and which can be conceptualized as 'religious' (McCauley and Lawson 1996; Boyer 1994). It would thus seem necessary to steer a middle way, basing our explanations of human thought and behaviour on the one hand on proper knowledge concerning the human mind/brain, on the other on social reality. Minds always operate in some context, and the boundary between a mind and its environment is in a sense a negotiable one. We cannot understand the mind/brain apart from the reality of which it is a part (see Clark 1997). This takes us towards connectionist models of cognition rather than functionalism/cognitivism, a move which the various authors of this volume are in varying degrees willing to make.

One way of expressing the difference between these two research traditions is to say that while for the functionalist the mind is a computer program, for the connectionist it is the programs (the so-called 'neural nets') that imitate the brain. According to functionalists, cognition consists of computations on the syntactical relations between mental representations. As cognition (and consciousness, if such there be) are based on certain kinds of functional organization of matter, the biological brain is not essential for them to emerge. Such organization can be supported by any kind of matter (see Dennett 1993; Chalmers 1997; cf. Varela et al. 1996: 6–8, 37–57).

Connectionists, for their part, maintain that cognitive abilities are based on the formation and strengthening of connections between neural units, not on individual neurons. These processes can be simulated by artificial neural nets in which several processors compute distributed inputs in parallel fashion. The brain is a parallel processor, not a serial one, and thus for example a single damaged unit does not necessarily make the whole system collapse. It is the connections between groups of neurons that enable us to represent the world; individual neurons are no smarter than any tiny bit of living tissue. No symbolical tokens are needed for the representation of information (see Varela et al. 1996: 85–103; Churchland 1995; Clark 1997; Elman et al. 1998: 47–106; McLeod et al. 1998).

From the connectionist perspective, the basic error of classic rule-and-symbol-based artificial intelligence is that combinations of human cognitive powers and manipulation of external reality are regarded as an inherent property of the human mind alone. Although ultimately it is our brains that make it possible for us to use external reality as an external memory store, there is no sharp dividing line between the brain and the external world. We can for example write things down, and we use all kinds of material tokens, including computers, to improve our capacity to remember and carry out mental processes such as calculation (Clark 1997: 45–69, 179–218). 'External memory aids' are even more effective than various internal mnemonics (Harris 1982). Beginning to extend the mind by exploiting material culture and social structure as means of augmenting the mental capacities of the brain has been considered a key event in the evolution of the modern mind (Mithen 2000). It made it possible for each new generation to start from what previous generations had done and achieved, rather than starting from scratch; in other words, it made possible the transmission of culture (Tomasello 1999).

Recent developments and criticisms

The cognitive approach in the study of religion has developed mostly in the 1990s, although its first incentive, Dan Sperber's *Rethinking Symbolism*, was published as far back as 1974 (see Malley 1996). In 1980 Stewart Guthrie published an article, 'A Cognitive Theory of Religion', in which he extends the suggestions of such authors as Melford E. Spiro, Robin Horton and Ernest Gellner, arguing that religious thought and behaviour should be understood as a form of anthropomorphization and on a par with nonreligious thought and behaviour. Religious beliefs are based on attempts at explaining perceptual ambiguity by postulating humanlike but nonhuman beings behind otherwise unexplainable events.

It was not until the 1990s that Sperber's ideas really started to influence the scientific study of religion. In 1990 two important books were published: Pascal Boyer's *Tradition as Truth and Communication*, and E. Thomas Lawson and Robert N. McCauley's *Rethinking Religion*. Boyer subsequently found out about the work of Lawson and Mc-Cauley when he was writing the second version of his second book, *The Naturalness of Religious Ideas* (1994), and for a time he was horrified at the idea that someone had just produced a book 'on exactly the same topic seen from the same angle' (Boyer 1994: xiv). On closer examination, however, these two books turned out to be rather different, despite the shared interest in cognitive science. In due course, Boyer, Lawson and McCauley began a collaboration which turns out to have had some far-reaching repercussions for the study of religion.

There are at present four interrelated areas of study: the application of psychological theories of theories of mind and of agent causality in explaining the social use of religious beliefs and the representation of

3

ritual structures; 'epidemiological' models of the cultural success of religious representations; the role of the different memory systems in the transmission of religious ideas; and the role of emotions in the adoption and transmission of religious beliefs (Andresen 2001; Barrett and Nyhof 2001; Boyer 1994; 1996; 2001; Boyer and Ramble 2001; Guthrie 1993; Lawson 2001; Lawson and McCauley 1990; in press; Pyysiäinen 2001a,b; Sperber 1995; 1996; Whitehouse 1995; 1996; 2000). In the summer of 1997, E. Thomas Lawson, Pascal Boyer, Veikko Anttonen and I were once talking, after a Finnish sauna, and started to discuss the possibility of arranging a small-scale workshop on religion, cognition and cultural context. Two years later, in June 1999, the workshop was in due course held at the archipelago research station of the University of Turku, on the island of Seili in south-western Finland.

When planning the event, we did not know that Jensine Andresen was engaged in a similar project at the University of Vermont. In the summer of 1998 she organized an interdisciplinary workshop on religious experience and cognitive science. The aim was to initiate dialogue between scholars of religion and neuroscientists and cognitive scientists. Two publications emerged from the workshop: *Religion in Mind* (Andresen 2001) presents cognitive scientific perspectives on religious belief and ritual, while *Cognitive Models and Spiritual Maps* (Andresen and Forman 2000) focuses on neuroscientific perspectives on religious experience.

The articles of the present volume are based on the papers read at the Seili workshop. Of the authors, only Barrett, Guthrie, Lawson, McCauley and Pyysiäinen attended both workshops. Their contributions to the respective volumes, however, are rather different. The present volume is, among other things, more clearly focused on relating cognitive scientific perspectives to the traditions of comparative religion. The concept of 'religion' receives much more attention than it does in *Religion in Mind*, and the relationship between cultural analysis and cognitive science is discussed in detail. As most of the authors have known each other for quite some time, and have been in continuous collaboration, this book is not just a collection of separate papers; it presents to the reader a coherent line of enquiry, with a certain cumulative pay-off. We hope it can serve as a useful guide to the cognitive science of religion for those not yet familiar with this approach, and also as an important update for those who follow the ongoing discussion on a regular basis.

The cognitive science of religion is characterized by scholarly co-operation to a much greater extent than is usually the case in the social sciences and especially in the humanities. Each scholar is not just developing his or her own idiosyncratic ideas, but contributes to the development of a larger programme of mapping the cognitive basis that makes religion as a phenomenon possible. Thus research can be considered truly cumulative: our knowledge of the phenomenon of religion grows with empirical studies, the results of which always provide a starting point for further study. Many humanistic studies of religion are different, in the sense that they are the projects of a single scholar, intimately tied to that scholar as an individual. One scholar cannot continue what another has initiated, new studies of old materials always starting more or less from zero.

Some, however, have been highly critical of the cognitive approach, arguing that as it does not say anything about the meaning of religion it is a futile enterprise (e.g. Levine 1998). This is not valid criticism, however; the cognitive approach is not meant to contribute to the interpretation of meanings, and thus should not be evaluated in the light of what it can contribute to this kind of research. All approaches fail to contribute *something*; what is important is what they *do* contribute. It even seems that much of the criticism directed against cognitive study is based on a lack of knowledge of what the cognitive science of religion is all about, not on a careful consideration of the arguments. It is the validity of the cognitive approach as such, not any specific individual arguments, that has been called into question. This seems to be reflective of the fact that religion is a sensitive subject; many think it can only be studied by empathetic participation in the religious experience. We shall not here enter into the philosophical discussion concerning hermeneutical understanding and its relation to explanation. It is sufficient for our purposes to point out three things: (1) empathetic understanding itself always involves the drawing of inferences and thus a cognitive element; (2) a metaphysical interest in such matters as the 'meaning of life' has not been shown to be a universal concern of humans; and (3) even if gods do exist, and reveal themselves to humans, the knowledge revealed will become known through ordinary cognitive and communicative processes, which can and should be scientifically explained (see Boyer 1994: viii–ix; Pyysiäinen 1999: 118–19).

The cognitive science of religion has also been seen as scientistic, reductionist and generally detrimental from the point of view of humanistic values. Our reply to these charges is twofold. On the one hand, we have to distinguish between the scientific study of religion and its practice; on the other hand, a purely scientific study of religion can also contribute to human self-understanding and cultural development. We argue that religion can and should be studied scientifically as natural forms of human thought and behaviour, without any explicit or implicit theological agenda. The cognitive approach, understood in a broad sense, including neuroscience and evolutionary psychology, offers possibilities for scientific work on the way religious ideas are adopted, represented and communicated. It thus enables us to explain how religion functions, irrespective of whether religions embody certain revealed truths or not.

As to the charge that the cognitive approach does not help us to better understand the human condition: we feel that the scientific study of religion can, in the long run, deepen our general understanding of life and of ourselves, even though individual studies may not have this as an explicit goal. Science serves us best when scientists stay within the limits of science in their work, not attempting to force their results to fit any preconceived ideology. Notwithstanding such claims as for example John Dupré's (1999), that folk-biological knowledge is not easily changed by the progress of science, and that this is not even something we should strive towards, we think that in many domains the progress of science has changed the common-sense understanding of things, and that this has not always been for the worse. Although in online processing we usually have to have recourse to such intuitive assumptions as for example that the sun 'rises' (see Barrett 1999), we also often apply scientific knowledge in everyday life. We have no problems in understanding, without special reflection, how a thermostat works, that the mercury in the thermometer will not rise to a level above the actual body temperature no matter how long the thermometer is held in the mouth, or that firearms are not a manifestation of supernatural powers. In the domain of folk psychology, a good example is the change in our attitudes towards mental illness, although there still are many prejudices (Churchland 1998: 88).

Here we think somewhat analogously to Mark Johnson (1998), who has argued that moral psychology, in telling us what is involved in making moral judgements, cultivates in us a certain wisdom that comes from knowledge concerning the nature and limits of human understanding. The purpose of moral theory is the enrichment and cultivation of moral understanding, and moral psychology occupies a central place in this in providing us with moral insight into complex situations and personalities. Likewise the scientific study of religion, in telling us

6

what is involved in religious thought and behaviour, cultivates in us a certain wisdom that comes from knowledge concerning the nature of the phenomenon of religion. It enriches and cultivates religious understanding, even though there is no direct link between specific scientific results and one's outlook on life. Nor is there any preconceived ideal towards which scientific progress should proceed (see Johnson 1997; Churchland 1995: 143–50, 286–94; Boyer, this volume). Science offers us knowledge about reality and influences our thinking, but it is not the only thing that affects our ways of thinking. Religions, art and common sense also play a rightful role.

The contents of this volume

In this volume, Veikko Anttonen discusses problems in identifying mechanisms that generate religion. Claiming that answers to the enigma of religion can be found in the architecture of the human mind, he argues for the view that the debated issue of the origins of religion is not that of historical specificity. We need not try to locate the earliest possible forms of religion in a specific moment in human history, but should instead focus on the evolution of those cognitive mechanisms that make religion possible. He claims that the human capacity to theologize and sacralize is based not only on classifying objects and phenomena into categories, but on the ability to cross category boundaries and invest representations of boundary-points with special referential value and causal potential. However, scholars of religion should also be interested in the various socio-cultural factors according to which humans organize the knowledge of things in their environment, process strategically important information, and induce shifts of attention from one domain of knowledge or conceptual entity to another.

Stewart Guthrie outlines a cognitive account of the evolution of religion. According to his theory, the lowest common denominator of all religions is constituted by animism and anthropomorphism. Due to the ambiguity of all perception, people, and apparently also other hominids, tend to postulate humanlike (or, apelike) agents to account for things that would otherwise have no unambiguous explanation. These agents do not have to be counter-intuitive; it is enough that they are nonhuman, although humanlike. Thus, although religion as such might be a uniquely human phenomenon, it is nevertheless based on a phenomenon that is common to humans and other hominids, such as for instance chimpanzees. However, in this case too the question of the boundaries of religion emerges, and Guthrie's reply seems to be that in the last analysis we cannot distinguish between religion and non-religion.

Pascal Boyer argues that ideas about personal beings, such as gods and ghosts, pervade religion because we humans are endowed with a specialized cognitive mechanism dedicated to reasoning about the behaviour of agents. Representations about agents activate this mechanism, thus allowing important inferences to be made. It is for this reason that ideas about all kinds of counter-intuitive agents are culturally successful, i.e. easily become widespread. It is not important whether such agents really exist or not, as long as believers can make useful inferences about them. Belief in these agents thus emerges because the respective ideas are useful, not the other way around.

Justin Barrett argues that a cognitive science of religion can explain both regularities and variation in religious thought and behaviour. He presents experimental evidence to support two hypotheses: (1) that Christian believers are biased toward praying for God to act through psychological intervention (as opposed to mechanistic and biological intervention), because God is represented as a distant psychosocial being. In other words, the believer's intuitive expectations as regards the behaviour of intentional agents determine his/her expectations about God's behaviour. (2) Since religious rituals are represented using the same conceptual architecture as ordinary social causation, generally the intentions of a person performing a ritual are more important than the particular action performed. Only when God's knowledge is considered fallible, the particular action becomes more important, probably because it is regarded as indexical of the actor's intentions. These predictions follow from cognitive observations about how minds function, not from the specifics of a given culture. Religious cognition is thus spontaneously generated from ordinary natural and social cognition.

Ilkka Pyysiäinen claims that religion can be identified using counter-intuitive representations as a necessary but not sufficient criterion for religiousness. This way of understanding religion is substituted for the Durkheimian idea that whatever is an expression of the 'common conscience' is *ipso facto* religion. The reason for this is that such a concept of religion is too heterogeneous to form any coherent category, and that it cannot be supported by evidence. As believers themselves do not understand their religion to be about the social, we cannot say their *explicit* religious beliefs are only about the social. And, if the social function of religion is implicit, then some mechanism, responsible for the translation of ideas about the society into ideas about gods, would have to be posited. But no such mechanism has been indicated by Durkheimians. Furthermore, the occurrences of such counter-intuitive representations as 'god' clearly form an identifiable recurrent pattern of their own, which requires some explanation. But as not all counter-intuitiveness can be taken to be religious, the bounds of religion as a category are, after all, to some extent fuzzy.

Harvey Whitehouse outlines a new approach for understanding and explaining ritual behaviour, drawing from cognitive psychological studies of memory. He argues that frequently repeated rituals are governed by implicit, 'embodied' knowledge, not by explicit, declarative knowledge and exegetical reflection. Although they may be given exegetical interpretations, these interpretations do not constitute the knowledge that is needed for the performance of the rituals. Rarely performed, 'climactic' rituals, on the other hand, are governed by explicit knowledge preserved in episodic memory. Making use of psychological distinctions between types of memory and types of knowledge, Whitehouse puts forward a theory that is not only psychologically plausible but also anthropologically relevant, allowing us to track globally and historically recurrent correlations between patterns on the one hand of codification and transmission, on the other of political structure.

E. Thomas Lawson and Robert N. McCauley present a lucid summary of their cognitive approach to ritual form. They argue that the same cognitive apparatus that underlies action representation in general guides action representation in religious ritual as well. Religious rituals are special only in that they involve representations of agents with counter-intuitive properties which have certain effects on various characteristics of rituals. A number of these characteristics can be cognitively explained quite apart from the meanings that believers attribute to their rituals, and from culture- and religion-specific features of rituals. Such cognitive explanations refer to a tacit knowledge of which people are not consciously aware and which is the same in all cultures, enabling people to make predictions about ritual practices.

Jesper Sørensen provides a discussion of the cognitive basis of magical ritual action. He tries to account for the cognitive constraints on the morphology of magical rituals as well as the cognitive procedures involved in the creation of meaningful magical rituals. Employing theories of so-called 'mental spaces' and conceptual blending, he outlines the way in which basic-level categorization, image-schematic structures, and event-frames supply a large amount of the structure and implicit knowledge that organize the contents of mental spaces, and facilitate mapping between separate mental spaces. In magical rituals the ascription of magical agency is based on representations of perceptual similarity or psychological essentialism, which serve to create connections between what are understood as 'sacred' and 'profane' spaces.

Jeppe Sinding Jensen argues that cognition is conditioned 'not only by the constraints of what individual minds are able to process, but also by the ways in which that which is transmitted between minds is organized'. Cognition is part of a cultural process and culture is an intrinsic component of the 'human mind'. Thus, not only do cognitive studies contribute to an understanding of religion, but the study of religion may in turn contribute to the study of cognition. Cognition and culture are not like hardware and software, with no intrinsic relations between them, and the 'hardware' alone determining which 'software' it can run. The human 'hardware' may be capable of being (re-)configured by its own 'software', and that may 'turn religion into something more scientifically interesting than "just" spurious ripples on cultural surface phenomena high above the bedrock of cognition'.

Pertti Saariluoma argues that the actual contents of concepts such as 'god' cannot be approached by prevalent cognitive scientific theories of categorization, which focus exclusively on how concepts are used to sort entities into different categories. Instead, we need a content-oriented cognitive psychology, which will allow us to analyse the attribute structure of concepts, and thus can yield knowledge of the content of concepts. Explicating the content of a concept allows us to put forward predictions about the thought and behaviour of people who have this concept.

Matti Kamppinen first discusses the varieties of scientific explanation, from the classical deductive-nomological model to the contextualizations of cultural traits practised by postmodern anthropologists. He then goes on to argue that cognitive and evolutionary explanations are of more scientific value than pure descriptions or subsumptions. Cognitive and evolutionary explanations refer to different levels of reality, explain the observed in terms of the unobserved, and utilize lawful patterns that have been proven worthy in other fields of research. According to Kamppinen, the cognitive and evolutionary turn in the study of religion is happening right now. In future, much of the traditional descriptive and labelling work will be put in its proper place, to provide materials for cognitive and evolutionary explanations.

Acknowledgements

Veikko Anttonen and I would like to take the opportunity to thank all the authors for their contribution to this volume, as well as Janet Joyce and Continuum for accepting this book for publication. We are also very grateful to Ellen Valle for her help with copy-editing. Outi Fingerroos, Riku Hyppänen, Jouni Karvonen, Tiina Mahlamäki, Petri Männistö and Pirjo Virtanen provided a helping hand in organizing the workshop and in preparing the manuscript for publication. The workshop and this publication were made possible by the financial support of the Academy of Finland (Grant 45553 (Anttonen); Project 42719 (Pyysiäinen)). The workshop was also supported by the Foundation for the University of Turku and the Foundation for the Åbo Akademi University.

References

Andresen, J. (ed.) (2001) *Religion in Mind: Cognitive Perspectives on Religious Belief, Ritual and Experience*. Cambridge: Cambridge University Press.

Andresen, J. and R. K. C. Forman (eds) (2000) *Cognitive Models and Spiritual Maps: Interdisciplinary Explorations of Religious Experience*. Thorverton: Imprint Academic.

Atran, S. (1998) 'Folk biology and the anthropology of science: cognitive universals and cultural particulars'. *Behavioral and Brain Sciences* 21: 547–609.

Barrett, J. L. (1999) 'Theological correctness: cognitive constraint and the study of religion'. *Method and Theory in the Study of Religion* 11: 325–39.

Barrett, J. L. and M. A. Nyhof (2001) 'Spreading non-natural concepts: the role of intuitive conceptual structures in memory and transmission of cultural materials'. *Journal of Cognition and Culture* 1: 69–100.

Boyer, P. (1990) *Tradition as Truth and Communication*. Cambridge: Cambridge University Press.

Boyer, P. (1993) 'Cognitive aspects of religious symbolism'. In *Cognitive Aspects of Religious Symbolism*, ed. P. Boyer, 4–47. Cambridge: Cambridge University Press.

Boyer, P. (1994) *The Naturalness of Religious Ideas: A Cognitive Theory of Religion*. Berkeley: University of California Press.

Boyer, P. (1996) 'What makes anthropomorphism natural: intuitive ontology and cultural representations'. *Journal of the Royal Anthropological Institute* n.s. 2: 1–15.

Boyer, P. (1998) 'Cognitive tracks of cultural inheritance: how evolved intuitive ontology governs cultural transmission'. *American Anthropologist* 100: 876–89.

Boyer, P. (2001) *Religion Explained: Evolutionary Origins of Religious Thought*. New York: Basic Books.

Boyer, P. and C. Ramble (2001) 'Cognitive templates for religious concepts: cross-cultural evidence for recall of counter-intuitive representations'. *Cognitive Science* 25: 535–64.

Chalmers, D. J. (1997 (1996)) *The Conscious Mind.* New York: Oxford University Press.

Churchland, P. M. (1995) *The Engine of Reason, the Seat of the Soul: A Philosophical Journey into the Brain.* Cambridge, MA: MIT Press.

Churchland, P. S. (1998 (1986)) *Neurophilosophy: Toward a Unified Science of the Mind/Brain.* Cambridge, MA: MIT Press.

Clark, A. (1997) *Being There: Putting Brain, Body, and World Together Again.* Cambridge, MA: MIT Press.

Cosmides, L. and J. Tooby (1994) 'Origins of domain specificity: the evolution of functional organization'. In *Mapping the Mind,* ed. L. Hirschfeld and S. Gelman, 85–116. Cambridge: Cambridge University Press.

Dennett, D. C. (1993 (1991)) *Consciousness Explained.* Harmondsworth: Penguin.

Dupré, J. (1999) 'Are whales fish?' In *Folkbiology,* ed. D. Medin and S. Atran, 461–76. Cambridge, MA: MIT Press.

Elman, J. L., E. A. Bates, M. H. Johnson, A. Karmiloff-Smith, D. Parisi and K. Plunkett (1998 (1996)) *Rethinking Innateness: A Connectionist Perspective on Development.* Cambridge, MA: MIT Press.

Guthrie, S. (1980) 'A cognitive theory of religion'. *Current Anthropology* 21: 181–203.

Guthrie, S. (1993) *Faces in the Clouds.* New York: Oxford University Press.

Guthrie, S. (1996) 'Religion: what is it?' *Journal for the Scientific Study of Religion* 35: 412–19.

Harris, J. E. (1982 (1978)) 'External memory aids'. In *Memory Observed,* ed. Ulric Neisser, 337–42. New York: Freeman.

Hirschfeld, L. A. and S. A. Gelman (1994) 'Toward a topography of mind: an introduction to domain specificity'. In *Mapping the Mind,* ed. L. Hirschfeld and S. Gelman, 3–35. Cambridge: Cambridge University Press.

Johnson, M. (1997 (1993)) *Moral Imagination: Implications of Cognitive Science for Ethics.* Chicago: University of Chicago Press.

Johnson, M. (1998 (1996)) 'How moral psychology changes moral theory'. In *Mind and Morals: Essays on Ethics and Cognitive Science,* ed. L. May, M. Friedman and A. Clark, 44–68. Cambridge, MA: MIT Press.

Karmiloff-Smith, A. (1992) *Beyond Modularity: A Developmental Perspective on Cognitive Science.* Cambridge, MA: MIT Press.

Lawson, E. T. (2001) 'Psychological perspectives on agency'. In *Religion in Mind: Cognitive Perspectives on Religious Belief, Ritual and Experience,* ed. J. Andresen, 141–72. Cambridge: Cambridge University Press.

Lawson, E. T. and R. N. McCauley (1990) *Rethinking Religion: Connecting Cognition and Culture.* Cambridge: Cambridge University Press.

Lawson, E. T. and R. N. McCauley (In Press) *Bringing Ritual to Mind.* Cambridge: Cambridge University Press.

Levine, M. P. (1998) 'A cognitive approach to ritual: new method or no method at all?' *Method and Theory in the Study of Religion* 10: 30–60.

Malley, B. E. (1996) 'The emerging *cognitive* psychology of religion: a review article'. *Method and Theory in the Study of Religion* 8(2): 109–41.

McCauley, R. N. and E. T. Lawson (1996) 'Who owns "culture"?' *Method and Theory in the Study of Religion* 8: 171–90.

McLeod, P., K. Plunkett, and E. T. Rolls (1998) *Introduction to Connectionist Modelling of Cognitive Processes.* Oxford, New York: Oxford University Press.

Medin, D. and S. Atran (eds) (1999) *Folkbiology.* Cambridge, MA: MIT Press.

Mithen, S. (1998 (1996)) *The Prehistory of the Mind.* London: Phoenix.

Mithen, S. (2000) 'Mind, brain and material culture: an archaeological perspective'. In *Evolution and the Human Mind: Modularity, Language and Meta-Cognition,* ed. Peter Carruthers and Andrew Chamberlain, 207–17. Cambridge: Cambridge University Press.

Pyysiäinen, I. (1999) '"God" as Ultimate Reality in religion and in science'. *Ultimate Reality and Meaning* 22: 106–23.

Pyysiäinen, I. (2001a) 'Cognition, emotion, and religious experience'. In *Religion in Mind: Cognitive Perspectives on Religious Belief, Ritual and Experience,* ed. J. Andresen, 70–93. Cambridge: Cambridge University Press.

Pyysiäinen, I. (2001b) *How Religion Works: Towards a New Cognitive Science of Religion,* Cognition and Culture Book Series, 1. Leiden: Brill.

Sperber, D. (1995 (1974)) *Rethinking Symbolism.* Cambridge: Cambridge University Press.

Sperber, D. (1994) 'The modularity of thought and the epidemiology of representations'. In *Mapping the Mind,* ed. L. Hirschfeld and S. Gelman, 39–67. Cambridge: Cambridge University Press.

Sperber, D. (1996) *Explaining Culture: A Naturalistic Approach.* Oxford: Blackwell.

Tomasello, Michael (1999) *The Cultural Origins of Human Cognition.* Cambridge, MA: Harvard University Press.

Tooby, J. and L. Cosmides (1995 (1992)) 'The psychological foundations of culture'. In *The Adapted Mind: Evolutionary Psychology and the Generation of Culture,* ed. J. H. Barkow, L. Cosmides and J. Tooby, 19–136. Oxford: Oxford University Press.

Varela, F., E. Rosch and E. Thompson (1996 (1991)) *The Embodied Mind: Cognitive Science and Human Experience.* Cambridge, MA: MIT Press.

Whitehouse, H. (1995) *Inside the Cult: Religious Innovation and Transmission in Papua New Guinea.* Oxford: Clarendon Press.

Whitehouse, H. (1996) 'Jungles and computers: neuronal group selection and the epidemiology of representations'. *Journal of the Royal Anthropological Institute* n.s. 1: 99–116.

Whitehouse, H. (2000) *Arguments and Icons: The Cognitive, Social, and Historical Implications of Divergent Modes of Religiosity.* Oxford: Oxford University Press.

2 Identifying the Generative Mechanisms of Religion: The Issue of Origin Revisited

VEIKKO ANTTONEN

Directions in theory of religion

Throughout its academic history, scholars in comparative religion have extended not only the bounds of the unknown in religion the world over, but also the bounds of theories that help to identify that which it is important to know. Considering the range of types of representations in religious traditions in both Western and non-Western societies, however, a common conceptual foundation, on the basis of which phenomena in the category 'religion' can be discussed, theorized and analysed, has been hard to find. Comparative religion is still a field with multiple truths (Wiebe 1999a). Practitioners of the discipline are continuously faced with the problem of how to identify the characteristics on the basis of which people cross-culturally categorize recurrent cultural phenomena as religious and consider them to belong to the semantic sphere of the generic concept of 'religion'. The subject matter to be subsumed under the category is in principle boundless, causing great variance in the methodology according to which specific sets of cultural materials are chosen to cast light on 'religion' in different geographical, historical and social contexts.

The field has been differentiated into such major sub-fields as psychology, sociology, anthropology, phenomenology and history of religion. Although scholars participate in the debate on the politics and ideology of cross-cultural study from the standpoints of their academic training, theoretical refinements for improving the comparative methodology have been motivated by the effort to create a common ground on which the exponents of different sub-fields can meet and draw the boundaries of religion as a conceptual entity. The aim of the methodological considerations is to demarcate the subject matter in sufficiently general and at the same time sufficiently precise terms to allow them to serve the interests of divergent branches of enquiry. Some harmony has been achieved among practitioners in comprehending the location of the discipline within the academy, its composite nature in reference to principles of research methodology, and the fact that there is no theory- or culture-free notion of 'religion' available to provide a stage for analysis. (See Honko 1979; Lawson and McCauley 1990; Guthrie 1995; 1996a; McCutcheon 1997; Wiebe 1999a,b; Martin 2000; Saler 2000a; Braun and McCutcheon 2000; Geertz and McCutcheon 2000.)

Problems in identifying phenomena for study

According to the established academic view, comparative religion gains its scientific rationale from the conceptualization of the religious ele- ment in human thinking and behaviour as an expression of manifest or hidden structures that are shared by individual members of a particular community, culture and society and that are rooted in their mentality by the force of various socio-cultural factors. In order to exist, religion does not need theological concepts, institutions or the notion of soteri- ology. In this view, religion, or – more precisely – tradition-specific systems of belief and behaviour, are seen as socio-cultural constructs on which both the mental worlds of individuals and the fabric of human society are built. The function of a religious tradition is to communicate – either directly or encoded in symbols – shared knowledge on the transcendental origin of the goals and ideals on the basis of which members of a community, a society or a nation are aware of themselves as an entity distinct from others. Whether religious ideas are transmit- ted in the flow of everyday social life or in specifically designated ritual contexts, the principal reason why human beings have them is to trigger emotions and other forms of representations by which to renew the conditions of day-to-day life. Religion has been seen as an integrative element in the sociopsychological construction of a culture and its traditions. As W. Robertson Smith (1894: 29) argued, it is not out there – and in there – for saving souls, but for the preservation and welfare of society, in other words to generate and maintain such highly charged notions as solidarity, nationality, ethnicity, identity, morality, i.e. values.

During the last few decades, however, the area of scholarly attention in comparative religion has grown much wider. The manner in which the analytical potential of the notion of 'religion' is or should be assessed, or whether the inherent content of the concept has become a burden and needs to be swept out of our terminological tool kit, has become an issue of critical discussion. Pascal Boyer has drawn attention to a methodological attitude that he calls 'inherent theologism' or 'theologistic bias'; by this he does not refer to an inside point of view from which religious materials are represented, but to assumptions according to which 'religious representations of a given group, "culture", or "society" constitute an integrated and consistent set of abstract principles' (Boyer 1996a: 202). According to Boyer, the assumptions of integrity and consistency are based on two erroneous premises by scholars: that connections between assumptions are a self-evident aspect of religious representations, and that connections form abstract social formations such as 'symbol-systems' or 'webs of meanings' (Boyer 1996a: 202; see also Boyer 1994: 50, 114–15). Calling into question the idea that certain domains of phenomena, such as cultural and religious orders, form a proper object for scientific analysis, Boyer raises an important methodological issue by asking whether 'the term "religious" denotes objects which have distinctive causal properties' and whether these objects can be 'explained in terms of causal generalisations that apply throughout the domain and would not apply outside it' (Boyer 1996a: 207; see also Boyer 1994: 30–4).

As analytical constructs, the notions of 'culture' and 'religion' have become almost unbearably light in content, thus running the risk of becoming empty of any scientific value. The emergence of cultural studies as a distinct academic field, with its own comprehension of what constitutes 'culture', has led anthropologists to take the notion much more seriously and to sharpen its analytical potential (Keesing 1994: 303; see also McCauley and Lawson 1996). As a scholarly concept, 'culture' cannot be reduced merely to the visible and invisible constructs, concrete or abstract, material or spiritual entities that human beings produce as members of a specific community, although as such the concept may have operational value as an analytical tool in social research. If the concept of 'culture' is used to refer only to the species-unique characteristics of human beings by which we build our social worlds, scholars should be able to identify the differences on the basis of which human cognition can be set apart from the cognition of other primates, our nearest relatives in the animal world. This can be done by studies in primatology. Exploring nonhuman behaviour helps us to track the evolutionary origins of the cognitive capacities that make human culture possible, and to define more closely the contents of the notion 'culture' and the prerequisites for its scholarly use. Michael Tomasello has argued for the view that even though human cognition is a special version of primate cognition, there is nevertheless a crucial difference between them. Just like humans, nonhuman primates also have their social worlds: language and other symbols, complex instrumental technologies, complex social organizations and institutions. And neither party is able to work out these characteristics as individual agents: cultural competence is a collective cognitive product (Tomasello 1999a: 512). What sets nonhuman primates apart from humans, however, is that they do not have an understanding of intentionality of conspecifics and the causality of inanimate objects and events. They do possess and use concepts and differentiate animate from inanimate objects, and employ insightful problem-solving strategies in their interaction with the environment; nevertheless, as Tomasello argues, 'they do not view the world in terms of the kinds of intermediate and hidden "forces", the underlying causes and intentional/mental states, that are so important to human thinking' (Tomasello 1999b: 18–19).

The ongoing theoretical and methodological discussion within the comparative study of religion clearly shows that not only the notion of 'culture' but also the concept of 'religion' needs a critical reassessment. Modernist and postmodernist theoretical reflection has dispelled attempts to set bounds to religion and has turned it into a phantom-like category (see Braun 2000: 3–18; McCutcheon 1997: 19–24; McCutcheon 1999: 91–2; Wiebe 2000: 352–3). The use of the notion varies from established religious traditions to such things as shopping rituals in supermarkets. While I agree with many of the comments made by Timothy Fitzgerald on the distortions in the scholarly use of the concept 'religion', presented in his book *The Ideology of Religious Studies* (2000), I cannot welcome his suggestion to abandon the concept altogether (see Fitzgerald 2000: 49). Conceptual cleansing will not alter our scholarly task if theology is eliminated along with the very concept of religion, and replaced by culture; nor will converting new emic categories into etic ones, or inventing a totally new rubric – let's say comparative numenology – under which to carry out research. We would still have to map the same territory. While describing 'religion' as a subject based on a chimera, Fitzgerald seems to be worried about something else than the lack of clarity in using scholarly concepts. As a scholar placing a greater emphasis on folk-religious traditions than on the traditions of theological religions, more on orally than on literally transmitted traditions, I strongly support the use of the category 'religion' and 'the religious' also in reference to systems of belief and practice in the context of all forms of culture, high or low, elite or popular. Although the notions of gravity, disease or causation are missing from the lexical systems of many indigenous peoples in the world, this does not mean that the phenomena themselves are missing and foreign to their experience.

I find Benson Saler's erudite conceptual refinement of the category, in his *Conceptualizing Religion* (2000), useful as a guideline. It provides, if not a cure, at least a sound theoretical and methodological consideration of the notion and the prerequisites for its use as a scholarly category. In a similar manner as the concept of 'gravity' or the concept of 'disease', religion needs to be worked out as a scientific concept that can be used for its classificatory purpose, i.e. to identify and sort out phenomena as objects of study (see Saler 2000a: 197–226). In conceiving religion in polythetic terms, Saler advocates the family-resemblance approach, in which the study starts out from the pool of elements that cluster together in varying degrees and to which different religious traditions in varying cultural contexts relate differently (Saler 2000a: 213). According to him there are no single distinctive or defining features to be abstracted from the possible pool of elements that can serve as the common denominator and thus as a standard according to which phenomena can be identified for study under the rubric 'religion' (see Saler 2000a: x–xi, 214). Since all of the abstracted elements are not predicable for all religious traditions, Saler suggests that we should not assume that the context will provide clues to determine whether an element can be interpreted as an indication of the presence of 'religion'. The scholar cannot draw a sharp line whereby a religious element can be set apart from an element that merely resembles religion. Saler, however, does not add to the phantom-likeness of the category, but points out that there are certain analytical purposes for which it makes sense to treat elements outside conventional religious contexts as religious (Saler 2000a: 216). According to him, 'identifying religious elements facilitates going beyond religion and attending to "the religious dimension" of much of human life' (Saler 2000a: 214; cf. Pyysiäinen, this volume). In following Saler's methodology, however, the scholar needs to remember that an element to be treated as 'religious' is not bounded by the category of 'religion', since the bulk of the methodology lies in its conceptualization without reference to boundaries.

The solution to the identification problem that Saler offers is prototype theory. This theory addresses questions concerning the inferential principles according to which human beings organize knowledge into categories. Cognitive psychologists and linguists have shown by empirical evidence that people do not assign category membership according to any particular feature that is seen as essential. In the classical theory of categorization it was stated that there is at least one necessary and sufficient criterion on the basis of which membership is determined. The present position (see Rosch 1978; Lakoff 1987; MacLaury 1991; Boyer 1994; Saler 2000a; Sperber 1996b: 143–5; Johnson 1999: 694–5) holds that people explore possible metaphorical and metonymical extensions from prototypical to nonprototypical cases and consider one member to be a better example of a category than another. George Lakoff and Mark Johnson characterize the notion of prototype as a neural structure that permits humans to perform some sort of inferential and imaginative task relative to a category (Lakoff and Johnson 1999: 19).

Saler suggests that as comparative religion scholars we should harness prototype theory to serve our analytical purposes, taking the most prototypical religions – Judaism, Christianity and Islam – as cognitive reference points 'for orientation, illustration and comparison' (Saler 2000a: xiv). Saler departs from the view that culture equips people with a common-sense notion of what counts as religious. As cultural knowledge forms the basis on which the discourse of the religious is constructed, whether speakers are believers or non-believers of theological or non-theological religion, it can serve the purpose of identification, categorization, systematization of cultural materials also as a scholarly concept. No sharp line is needed between scientific theories and folk theories of religion.

Methodical strife over ideology of enquiry

At the regional conference of the International Association for the History of Religions (IAHR) on method and theory held in Turku, Finland, in 1997, Donald Wiebe proclaimed that religion should be appropriated from the humanities to science and applied 'solely as a taxonomic device to differentiate and explain a peculiar range of human behaviour demonstrated in religious practices' (Wiebe 1999a: 255). Wiebe stresses the importance of organizing religious material on a strictly scientific basis and keeping any trace of theology outside of its confines. Wiebe regards religious studies, with its political and social agendas, as a pseudo-science, and recommends that it should be left 'to the humanists and religious devotees concerned with their place as public intellectuals in the life of society' (Wiebe 1999a: 261). In wishing to keep the academic study of religion scientific, Wiebe suggests that the field should be re-established, with an ideology of enquiry involving a twofold structure for the normative behaviour of practitioners: norms concerning methodology and norms concerning science policy. As his methodological position, Wiebe declares that scholars in the field should not condone polymethodism; it should be kept at bay at all costs in defence of 'the university as an institution dedicated to scientific research' (Wiebe 1999a: 267). As the majority of the scholars within the comparative study of religion seem to adhere to humanistic pluralism rather than to scientific rigour with respect to methodological considerations (see Lawson and McCauley 1993), Wiebe challenges the claim according to which religious phenomena should be approached by combining a multitude of scholarly strategies. Instead, he advises students to adopt the naturalist and materialist programme.

Even though Wiebe gladly accepts the call to treat religion in cognitive evolutionary terms, there does not need to be an ideological tension in the emerging cognitive science of religion between scientific and humanistic approaches. The cognitive scholar, like any fellow citizen, is free to locate him/herself at any of the ideological positions available in the academic or non-academic culture. From the perspective of cognitive methodology, all minds, scientific, theological and humanistic, are equal as objects in cognitive theorizing. In cognitive scholarship the aim is to unravel the mechanisms that are operative in the human mind whenever people acquire and organize cultural knowledge – thus also religious knowledge – and make that knowledge accessible (see Bloch 1994). As participants in specific culture- and ideology-bound discourses in their linguistic communities, human beings employ 'religion' within their daily concerns along with other designative labels that the lexical system offers for their use, such as art, literature, music, folklore, sexuality, politics or science. Actions, perceptions, experiences and feelings at specific times and in specific places, in reference to specific objects, persons, animals and phenomena, pertain to the category of religion according both to the interpretive frames of the symbolic-cultural systems where actions are performed and to the cognitive demands of the context. This concerns the conglomerate of beliefs and practices referred to either as 'institutional religion' or as 'folk religion'. Justin Barrett has argued that people are not so correct in matters of theology as one is easily led to believe from people's commitment to a religious institution or from their personal statements as believers. While not treating religious entities, concepts and ideas in a theologically 'correct' manner, people nevertheless report them as similar to the dominant theological dogma. In our explanatory preoccupations we employ parallel levels of understanding or representation of the phenomenon. We reflect and draw inferences as to things in the world and as to the causal relationships that govern them on the basis of naive intuitive knowledge (in basic-level conceptualizations) or employ more complicated, intuition-violating theoretical concepts (see Barrett 1999: 338). In real-time problem-solving, human beings are less concerned with the contents and meanings of theological (or scientific) concepts than with ways of acting in accordance with intuitive assumptions as to how the desired goal can be successfully achieved. Theology, like science, is a matter of experts. Both of them are institutionalized systems of cultural knowledge and presuppose the acquired ability to apply their refined and elaborate concepts, the authority of which is validated by reflective beliefs (see Barrett 1999: 326, 332–3; Barrett and Keil 1996: 243–4; Boyer 1999: 64–6; see also Sperber 1996a: 89).

In his systematic treatise on the distinction between religion and science, Robert N. McCauley wants to shake the cultural impressions established in our Western forms of thinking about religion. In consonance with the arguments put forth by Pascal Boyer, McCauley stresses that religion cannot be opposed to the rational and science to the irrational (see Boyer 1994: 50). In spite of their antagonism as ideological constructs, religion is, in McCauley's terms, a natural domain of knowledge while science is an unnatural domain. In defining 'natural' as familiar, obvious and self-evident, McCauley states the fact upon which all conservative politicians rely in their campaign strategies: religion has greater natural (publicity) appeal than science (McCauley 2000: 65). Since science must be taught, the role of cultural input is more significant in acquiring knowledge in the scientific than in the religious domain. The skills needed for the practice of science, and its systematic and sophisticated forms of assessing the importance of the evidence for the verification of propositions, presuppose elaborate cultural institutions. Religious systems can persist and religious ideas can be generated by naturally evolved cognitive capacities in human beings. In addition to cognitive input, such as perception, inferences and memory, religious systems, however, also presuppose cultural input, i.e. the possession of common codes on the basis of which shared knowledge of the physical world is transmitted. In discussing prehistoric hunter-gatherers, however, McCauley fails to valorize the cultural input needed for their religious representations; they do not come naturally. The contagiousness of religious ideas depends for instance on the significance of specific routes and paths for locating food, the appropriation of spatial categories to systems of economy, kinship and dwellings, and also on normative divisions based on gender or on observing the category-boundary between the living and the dead. Contributions on the metarepresentational nature of human cognition suggest that no sharp distinction can be drawn between cognitive and cultural input, between internal and external representations (see Wilson 2000: 49–50; Sperber 1996a; 2000). We need to ask how specific cognitive capacities for action representation (e.g. arithmetical or ritualistic) can emerge, unless certain cultural conditions are present that give rise to numerical systems or ritual systems, i.e. the setting apart of an event from other series of events and the repetition of that event (for instance sacrificing an animal) at a specific time and in a specific place.

A cognitive approach to the issue of origin

Theoretical treatments of the generative mechanisms of religion vary according to methodological considerations concerning the choice of level of description and explanation. As McCauley has said, 'the lower a science's analytical level, the more ubiquitous the entities it studies' (McCauley 1999: 612). Comparative religion scholars have tradition-ally combined research strategies and induced or deduced theories of generative mechanisms by integrating knowledge of lower-level entities that are identified in the disciplines of biology, physiology, psychology, sociology, anthropology, archaeology, linguistics, folklore and history.

In this combinatory enterprise, theoretical formulations concerning the building blocks and organizing principles of religion have not been free from the metaphysical concerns of their proponents. It was the nineteenth-century Victorian anthropologists who – as their major cultural paradigm – posited questions on the conjectural history of humankind, with the aim of revealing the evolutionary sources of such distinctive human characteristics as art, religion, ethics, moral ideas and marriage (see e.g. Voget 1975: 206–49). Theoretically, the primi-tive as an evolutionary construct was the product of the modernity that provided the motive and the context for fabricating origins (see M. C. Taylor 1999: 53; Masuzawa 2000). According to Mark Taylor, it was its polyvalence that made the primitive so fascinating: as simultaneously both attractive and repulsive, the primitive represented the desire of the modern – desire meaning the pulse of life (see M. C. Taylor 1999: 53).

For instance Sigmund Freud, as Samuel J. Preus posits, identified, from the ethnographic materials on totemism, two generative 'moments' of religion: the fulfilment of irrepressible wishes and the institutionalization of repression. Religious systems are an outcome of the urgent wishes (or illusions) of humankind: in the first place the oedipal wish to internalize the father and identify with him, in the second the instituting of the laws as sacred which prohibit men from fulfilling their repressed wish to murder the father and have an incestuous sexual relationship with the mother (Preus 1987: 190–1). Émile Durkheim conjectured that the natural, ever-present causes of religion are best identified in the most primitive human society. For Durkheim, ethnographic evidence of the totemic principle in the collective life of Australian aborigines was the earliest record of the categorical distinction between the sacred and the profane on which the social origin and the foundation of religion rests (Durkheim 1995: 207–41; see also M. C. Taylor 1999: 54–9; Masuzawa 2000: 217–19). While Freud and Durkheim did not postulate any crucial difference between the operation of the modern (Western) and the primitive mind, Edward Burnett Tylor, on the other hand, insisted on the animistic origins of human religious history and set the primitive or the savage mentality apart from the thought processes occurring among the civilized. According to Tylor, 'the supernatural' was implanted in the primitive mind through the experience of dreams, trance, visions, death and disease. This 'early' implantation is not, however, transmitted to religious representations in modernized societies. The linkage between the notion of soul and the dream life is absent from the institutionalized context of the supernatural (see Gell 1998: 121; Stringer 1999: 544–5).

Recently, Stewart Guthrie and Pascal Boyer have both developed their theories of religion to wrestle with this issue. In Guthrie's theory the issue of religious origins is approached from the perspective of perceptual strategy shared by human beings and other animals. According to this view, humans posit 'for nonhuman things and events the highest actual organisation we know: that of human beings and their society' (Guthrie 1995: 36). For Guthrie, religion is an accidental product of the evolutionary process that results from the inferential mechanism whereby human beings interpret while seeing and signify while interpreting (Guthrie 1995: 41; this volume). It is this interpretative quest – or, in the final analysis, a guess, based on perception – that according to Guthrie changes an entity from an inanimate to an animate category. The ontological change, however, basically concerns entities belonging to the same ontological tree: tigers and lions are changed into cats; wolves and chihuahuas into dogs (Guthrie 1995: 46). Although Guthrie does not pose explicit questions regarding conceptual change across ontological categories, it is dealt with in his theory of religion as animism, in which he makes the assumption that

religion is made possible and in the final analysis rests on the evolutionarily evolved strategy of humans to attribute life to non-human domains
(for a discussion of anthropomorphism in conceptualizing God see
Barrett and Keil 1996; Boyer 1996b).

Guthrie expands his theory beyond the religious domain, and – as
Alfred Gell has pointed out – succeeds in amassing copious examples
of anthropomorphic thinking in everyday perception and cognition, in
the arts and in the sciences (Gell 1998: 121). Guthrie's theory on
animism as attribution of life to inanimate objects does not, however,
according to Gell, explain what animacy entails. Gell argues that for
instance stones can be perceived as 'alive' and thus worshipped as
idols, but animacy does not explain their remarkable quality. Their
distinctiveness is due to the very fact that they are not alive. Gell writes:
'[t]he imputation of "animacy" to non-living things cannot, as Guthrie
seems to suggest, rest on people making category mistakes about
whether inanimate objects such as boulders are really biologically living
things, such as bears' (Gell 1998: 122).

The question of why anthropomorphic and animistic representations
are so widespread, and appear not only among children but also among
adults the world over, is answered in detail by Boyer: they violate our
intuitive expectations. Drawing from the work of Frank Keil and others
on ontological distinctions (Boyer 1994: 100–2), he argues that the
human mind is not a free-for-all of random associations, but the
combination of ontological categories (persons, artefacts, animate
beings, events and abstract objects) and domain-specific principles with
a set of specific expectations which constitute our intuitive ontology
(Boyer 1994; 2001). Intuitive ontology organizes our experience in
order to make sense of it. But the reason why the notion of intuitive
ontology is important for the comparative religion scholar is that, once
people have ontological categories, they also have violations that run
against the expectations and forms of natural explanations concerning
the properties and behaviour of members in the specific category. Boyer
refers to massive amounts of evidence of counter-intuitiveness in the
volumes of mythology, fantastic tales, anecdotes, cartoons, religion and
science-fiction. Persons can be represented for instance as having
counter-intuitive physical properties (ghosts or gods) or a counter-
intuitive biology (gods who never grow or die) (Boyer 2001: 63–71).
The notion of the 'counter-intuitive' is a technical term which Boyer
uses in the sense of information that contradicts some of the information provided by ontological categories (Boyer 2001: 65, 73). He
points out that 'the implicit ontological category "living kinds" carries

quasi-theoretical assumptions about underlying causal structure that makes animals different from, for instance, artefacts' and that 'these theoretical assumptions are also manifest in children's reactions to putative scenarios of transformation from one kind to another' (Boyer 1994: 106). The boundaries that place members in one ontological category apart from another are not fuzzy, but stable and clearly marked. This means that in attributing animacy to non-living things people do not make categorial mistakes: live things are not artefacts, persons and plants are not the same, events and the abstract are different (Boyer 1996b: 87). The inferential principles on the basis of which entities are assigned to a distinct ontological category evolve in human beings as the result of normal cognitive growth from childhood to adulthood. To produce religious representations does not require more than regular inferential principles, the very same ones that are also employed in non-religious domains. The answer to the issue of origin, then, does not, according to Boyer (1996b: 89), depend on the 'primitivist speculations according to which various features of religious or, more generally, symbolic, thought consist in a return to some early stages of cognitive development. There are no such things as early animism and anthropomorphism, and therefore nothing to "return" to.'

A cognitive approach to religion thus alters significantly the strategy needed to valorize the issue of religious origins. One does not need to engage in guesswork in order to discover the 'true' origins of religious ideas. The origin of religion is not an issue of historical specificity. It cannot be resolved by attempts to reconstruct a location in a specific historical moment at which the human capacity for religion is postulated to have first emerged. In order to explain representations in general and religious representations in particular, the scholar has to pose questions concerning the evolution of human conceptual capacities (see Boyer 1994; Sperber 1996a). As cognitive agents, humans are predisposed to the conceptual organization not only of visions, sounds, smells, tastes, objects, events, but also of notions of unseen agents and entities; and, moreover, of the properties of things and objects on the basis of which they are set apart from other similar things and objects. Whether these abstractions are labelled religious, sacred, or just in some way different, they are nevertheless integral elements of human cognition.

And so is the notion of origin itself. From childhood to adulthood, we expect and search for causes of events and regularities in things and phenomena. By means of folk-theoretical assumptions of religious entities and metaphysical concepts such as God, the Soul, the Self, Power or the Sacred, we explain the causes of occurrences and experiences in the course of our everyday interaction with the environment. In the scientific domain scholars pursue the same ends, although from diverse ideological positions. In the world of science, origins and the ways of managing the past are construed under such conceptual abstractions as Evolution, Descent, Genealogy, Heritage, History and Progress (see e.g. Masuzawa 2000; Anttonen, P. J., et al. 2000). The notion of origin becomes validated by reflective beliefs concerning the intellectual, religious or ideological benefits of this essentializing enterprise. By means of an awareness of causes and origins, human beings can embrace such abstract notions as Identity, Ethnicity, Equality, Freedom, Being, Reality and the Absolute, and can reflect upon the properties on which essences of things are based and by means of which they are preserved in spite of changes and transformations, whether biological, historical or socio-cultural (see Gelman and Hirschfeld 1999: 413–16).

'Sacred' as a mental concept: a category-theoretical approach to mechanisms in religion

Answers to the enigma of religion and the generation of its most identifiable characteristics thus do not need to be projected into the conjectural origin of human history, but are to be located in the architecture of the human mind and its systems of inference (see Boyer 2001). The explanatory potential of current approaches in the cognitive science of religion needs to be applied to various sorts of empirical materials. We already have access to a host of studies by cognitive or cognitively oriented scholars in which many of the fundamental mechanisms in religious representations are dealt with (see Boyer 1994; 2001; Guthrie 1995; Lawson and McCauley 1990; Mithen 1996; Pyysiäinen 2001; Whitehouse 1995; 2000). The mechanisms are approached and identified on varying theoretical grounds and levels of explanation. One of the pivotal mechanisms in the field of cultural analysis, as McCauley and Lawson argue (1996: 177, 180–1), is psychological.

In the following, I shall look briefly at the issue of generative mechanisms in religion from the category-theoretical viewpoint that has been developed to explain conceptual change within and across ontological categories. In cognitive science the issue of conceptual change is a topical one (see e.g. Chi 1992; Boyer 1994; Keil et al. 1999). Comparative religion scholars have not devoted much attention to questions of conceptual change, although the broader knowledge systems in which issues specific to the attribution of things as 'divine' or 'sacred' are embedded in them. The notions of 'kratophany', 'hierophany' or 'theophany' that Mircea Eliade coined for the ontological change were not adopted as technical terms to explore the formation of religious ideas, but to express and decipher the subjective meaning dimensions of 'religious showings' (see Ryba 2000: 181–4). As Stewart Guthrie posits, the Eliadean notion of the 'sacred' does not make the issue 'inaccessible to the intellect and to analysis' (Guthrie 1996b: 128).

For scholars, there is hardly a more serious task to wrestle with than that of identifying the mechanisms that generate religion; in other words, that make people assume that various material and visible entities can be reassigned to another category, and that bring about as an outcome of such reassignment that an entity ceases to be constrained by properties pertaining to a former material category. In the world of science, as Michelene T. H. Chi has put it, 'we find it difficult to change our belief that an entity that belongs to one ontological category (such as a human being) can be changed to an entity in another ontological category (such as a spiritual being)' (Chi 1992: 136). In the world of religion, on the other hand, adherents for instance of the Christian faith find no contradiction in the assertion that the son born to Joseph and Mary outside Bethlehem in an animal shed is the Son of God. But an assertion according to which in a specific context a car has been changed from a material entity into a non-material one, with special spiritual properties, arouses objections and is condemned as blasphemy, although there may be persons who consider the representations to be true. From the notion of a car, we can generate the inferences that it has an engine and that its motion is constrained by certain properties, but we are in trouble when we try to proceed from the notion of car to assumptions concerning its religious qualities. To validate the classification of the car as a religious entity, there has to be something more available to us than our intuitive understanding of the nature of entities in the ontological categories of living and non-living kinds (Saariluoma, this volume).

Although the notion of conceptual change can be observed in both the religious and the scientific domains, the mechanisms leading to transformations are understood and approached differently in the respective explanatory systems (see Boyer 1998: 882). In the religious domain, understanding the change from one ontological category to another, a theme dominant in miracle accounts, does not require

27

extensive learning: explanations are incorporated in the acquisition of religious knowledge. As Boyer argues, violation of ontological expectations explains much of the contagiousness of religious ideas. 'Religious representations', he writes, 'would probably not be acquired at all, if their counter-intuitive aspects did not make them sufficiently salient and "attention-grabbing". They would probably not be acquired and stored if their intuitive part did not give them sufficient inferential potential' (Boyer 1998: 881).

In reference to physics, Michelene Chi has argued that 'to achieve radical conceptual change . . . is to learn to differentiate the two ontological categories, and not to borrow predicates and properties of the material substance category to interpret events in the alternative category'. A scientist who needs to cross ontological boundaries with the aim of transforming a concept requires extensive learning in order to explain how one kind of thing can be changed into another. None of the cognitive mechanisms, such as deletion, addition, discrimination or generalization, according to Chi, can bring about the change (see Chi 1992: 132, 141, 180).

Approaches and avenues for theoretical reflection within the frameworks developed in the emerging cognitive science of religion do not concern only the hard sciences, but also include the study of both synchronic and diachronic aspects in religious traditions of the world. The issues specific to the cognitive approach, however, need to be applied differently when using ethnographic and historical texts instead of the methods of data collection, both qualitative and quantitative, used in psychology, anthropology and sociology. In my studies of the notion of the 'sacred', I have organized diverse linguistic, folkloristic and ethnographic texts, archival sources, and the scholarly literature on the attribute 'sacred' by viewing the data within the framework of cognitive semantics, most specifically against the principles of categorization (Anttonen 1996a). My intention has been to establish a theory to explain why the notion exists in the first place and what explains its universality and versatile attributions. I have paid attention to the properties on the basis of which various elements, among both living and non-living kinds, artefacts and events, have been designated over the course of history in cultures and geographical areas the world over by terms denoting 'sacred'.

As the scholarly literature on the subject indicates (see Anttonen 1996b; 1999; 2000a; 2000b; 2000c; Guthrie 1996b; Idinopulos and Yonan 1996; Paden 1991; 1992; 1994; 1999; 2000; Penner 1989; Smith 1987), there are multiple and controversial ways of assessing the analytical significance of the notion in comparative religion. The sacred can be adopted as a heading for the supramundane and for accounts of the kind of mental representations in which objects and phenomena are perceived and interpreted as mysterious and awesome. It can be postulated as a core element that has characterized religious thought throughout human history. The list of things classified and designated in world ethnography as sacred is endless. In my study I have concentrated on folklore materials from Finland and elsewhere in North-Eurasian cultures and to a certain extent on linguistic and ethnographic evidences among the Mediterranean culture area dominated by the Judaic, Christian and Islamic religious traditions. I have asked for instance why specific topographically exceptional places, especially along waterways or along paths out in the wilderness, such as springs, rapids, marshes, lakes and mountains, are designated as 'sacred'. How can we explore the distribution of place-names on a world-wide scale in which the attribute appears as an appellative designation for a place, and moreover, why is it that these places are located in uninhabited regions out in the wilderness and find their location amid settlements only after the rise and spread of Christianity? What were the properties that made a rowan tree and its red berries 'sacred'? Why was the bear held a sacred animal among Northern peoples? What are the 'cognitive' roots of the temporal systems, still valid, on the basis of which there are sacred days in opposition to non-sacred days? Why do the Mosaic laws assign the pig the status of a defiled (forbidden, tabooed, and thus sacred) animal, rules which Muslims, too, carefully observe? Why were women set apart during their menstruation period and in the late stage of pregnancy (see Anttonen 1996a)? Finding answers to these fundamental questions does not concern only ethnographers, anthropologists, sociologists and phenomenologists of religion, but also scholars of cognition.

In my cognitive framing of the issue I set out to explore the human mind and its capacity to generate types of representations and a special vocabulary for their communication. The fact that in human languages and cultures there have evolved over thousands of years both folk-theoretical notions and theological concepts such as 'god' and the 'sacred' indicates that human beings have some specific form of mental imagery, a pattern of thought, a cultural logic – or perhaps, as Boyer sees the issue, an obsession (Boyer 2001: 237) – on the basis of which certain events, objects, places and times, persons and animals are set apart and marked off as a class of their own. Within the framework of anthropology of religion, Lucien Lévy-Bruhl and Claude Lévi-Strauss approached the issue by formulating ideas to explain 'how natives think'. While Lévy-Bruhl paid attention to mystical participation, Lévi-Strauss postulated that sacred objects contribute to the maintenance of order in the universe of the ethnic cultures by occupying the places that are allocated to them. Once they are out of their place, people believe that it is an apt situation for generating power by carefully designed ritual. Or they become obsessed by beliefs and omens that concern their contagious, polluting properties (Lévi-Strauss 1966: 10; see Smith 1978: 147–51). Sigmund Freud, who thought that man is in the main a rule-following animal, held the terms denoting 'sacred' in various languages as primal words, in the sense that these terms have antithetical meanings. In Latin, for example, *sacer* means both holy and accursed. Antithetical signification implies that humans, according to Freud, not only follow rules, but are inclined to act in diametrical opposition to them (see Szasz 1984: 162).

Taking a step closer to cognitive theorizing, the issue of sacrality needs to be viewed against the dispositional properties of human beings in forming specific types of representations of some objects and things (especially the class of fantastic animals) as aberrant, marginal, paradoxical, different, exceptional, or 'wholly other'. Their position within specific taxa has been a heavily debated topic among scholars (see Sperber 1996b). While the criteria according to which various entities in the categories of living kinds and non-living kinds are made quite explicit and seen as less problematic, sentiments, as Sperber points out, are not classified into mutually exclusive and hierarchically organized categories: an emotion can be at the same time love, tenderness and esteem (Sperber 1996b: 151).

With regard to the category of the sacred, there are no definite criteria according to which membership inclusion can be determined. Within Western cultural history there are two metarepresentational options (second-order representations) that stand out as most common: things with exceptional qualities, showing intuition-violating properties, and things with perfect and ideal qualities. Both of these can be re-represented either as the presence of God or as non-God. In the latter case there are various options; the most extreme form of re-representation is expressed by the attribute 'cursed'. There is evidence that in specific religious institutions the line that separates the holy and cursed is thin. In a study dealing with parental concern about the imaginary companions of children, the scholar interviewed a fundamentalist Christian mother. She had become worried about her son, who had refused to join the other children in school in drawing Santa Claus on decorations for Christmas. When the boy was interviewed, he pointed out to the interviewer that 'Santa' was 'Satan' with the order of the letters changed (M. Taylor 1999: 55–6).

The 'sacred' as a notion in comparative religion can be conceptualized as a category-boundary. Human beings have the dispositional property to invest the boundary-points of categories of for instance time, space and the human body with special referential value and inferential potential. This capacity is activated in places set apart as sacred, such as temples, churches, cemeteries and other sanctuaries. But there are also other locations, circumstances and events in which the perceived properties extend beyond categorial constraints. Anomaly accounts in religious literature and folklore testify to the significance of boundary-points in human thinking and behaviour. Their inferential potential is triggered by metarepresentations of agents and powers that can be manipulated in the context of ritual for either good or bad purposes.

As an example of a type of representation in which the sacred as category-boundary becomes visible by the specific properties typical of religious representations (violation of intuitive expectations), I refer here to a study by the Swedish folklorist Barbro Klein. She offers an interesting view of an incident that took place in Södertälje, in Sweden, in 1992. A fifteen-year-old Syrian Orthodox girl named Samira Hannoch, a member of Saint Afram's Church and a recent immigrant to Sweden, was reported to have experienced in her apartment a series of visions of the Orthodox saint Mar Charbel. On Friday 20 March 1992, the day after her fifteenth birthday, after the girl had experienced a revelation of Christ on her balcony, she felt oil starting to emanate from her hands and arms. When she stepped back into the room, she noticed that oil was also running down the face of the saint in the picture on the wall. The saint announced that the girl had been chosen from among millions of young boys and girls for a mission: to unite the divided Churches of the Syrians and the Assyrians. After the miracle was made public, believers started to make pilgrimages to the apartment not only from Sweden but from other countries as well. Klein describes vividly how Channel Two of Swedish Television had the consistency of the oil examined in the Laboratory of Criminal Technology after the TV reporter had visited Samira and had received the sign of the Cross on her forehead with a ball of cotton that Samira had drenched in the oil. The laboratory test found that the oil contained fatty acids similar to those produced by the human body, but in different proportions. The source of the Holy Oil was thus outside the girl's body (Klein 2000).

Although the cognitive theory of religion does not address issues of truth and meaning, the incident in Sweden is a case in point, showing how cognitive theorizing can be utilized in explaining ethnographic accounts of religious phenomena within the field of comparative religion. In the incident, counter-intuitive properties are displayed: predicates that characterize the category of living kinds (emanating bodily fluids) are extended to a member of the category of an artefact (the portrait of a saint). Similar phenomena are often reported among Catholics: for example a statue of the Madonna is observed to bleed or to shed tears. To approach the incident in Sweden from the point of view of Boyer's cognitive theory, we need to make a distinction between two types of assumptions on the basis of which conceptual structures can be analysed. Boyer distinguishes between causal schema assumptions and non-schematic assumptions. In the causal schema type, there is a schematic core in a concept representation to which assumptions are causally linked; in the non-schematic representations, such causal linkage to a schematic core is absent. People can use various sorts of assumptions to generate inferences and expectations (Boyer 1994: 70). Contrary to the cognitive semantics approach developed by George Lakoff and Mark Johnson (see e.g. Lakoff and Johnson 1999: 45–73), Boyer argues that non-schematic representations cannot be conceptualized in terms of metaphor. According to Boyer, metaphor is a salient example of schematic representations (Boyer 1994: 71; n. 6).

A teenage girl became a marked-off, 'sacred' boundary zone which triggered metarepresentations of the ethnically bounded notions of the saint. The public response to the miracle benefited the Syrian and the Assyrian communities in their ethno-religious goals of achieving unity of their Churches in Sweden, and recognition of their members' position in multicultural society. The incident as such is an expression of the way in which modes of cognitive representations that are deeply rooted in religious traditions, and their distinct forms of communication and action representation, are employed by members both of the immigrant community and of the Swedish majority population, and what their cultural transmission involves in an environment where competing conceptual structures are available.

Even if these conclusions are external to cognitive theorizing *per se*, I am inclined to share the view of Harvey Whitehouse, according to whom 'certain "cutting-edge" theories in cognitive psychology have profound implications for social theory in general, and the comparative study of religion in particular' (Whitehouse 2000: 4).

References

Anttonen, P. J., in collaboration with A.-L. Siikala, S. R. Mathisen and L. Magnusson (eds) (2000) *Folklore, Heritage Politics and Ethnic Diversity: A Festschrift for Barbro Klein.* Botkyrka: Multicultural Centre.

Anttonen, V. (1996a) *Ihmisen ja maan rajat. 'Pyhä' kulttuurisena kategoriana* (The Making of Corporeal and Territorial Boundaries: 'The Sacred' as a Cultural Category). Helsinki: Finnish Literature Society.

Anttonen, V. (1996b) 'Rethinking the sacred: the notions of "human body" and "territory" in conceptualizing religion'. In *The Sacred and Its Scholars: Comparative Methodologies for the Study of Primary Religious Data*, ed. T. A. Idinopulos and E. A. Yonan, 36–64. Leiden: Brill.

Anttonen, V. (1999) 'Does the sacred make a difference? Category formation in comparative religion'. In *Approaching Religion*, part I, ed. T. Ahlbäck, 9–23, Scripta Instituti Donneriani, 17:1. Åbo: Donner Institute.

Anttonen, V. (2000a) 'Sacred'. In *Guide to the Study of Religion*, ed. W. Braun and R. T. McCutcheon, 271–82. London: Cassell.

Anttonen, V. (2000b) 'What is it that we call "religion"?: analyzing the epistemological status of the sacred as a scholarly category'. In *Perspectives on Method in the Study of Religion*, ed. A. W. Geertz and R. T. McCutcheon, 195–206. Leiden: Brill.

Anttonen, V. (2000c) 'The enigma of the sacred pillar: explaining the Sampo'. In *Ethnography Is a Heavy Rite: Studies of Comparative Religion in Honor of Juha Pentikäinen*, ed. N. Holm et al., 165–92, Religionsvetenskapliga Skrifter, 47. Åbo: Åbo Akademi University.

Barrett, J. L. (1999) 'Theological correctness: cognitive constraint and the study of religion'. *Method and Theory in the Study of Religion* 11(4): 325–39.

Barrett, J. L. and F. C. Keil (1996) 'Conceptualizing a nonnatural entity: anthropomorphism in God concepts'. *Cognitive Psychology* 31: 219–47.

Bloch, M. (1994) 'Language, anthropology and cognitive science'. In *Cultural Anthropology*, ed. R. Borofsky, 276–82. New York: McGraw-Hill.

Boyer, P. (1994) *The Naturalness of Religious Ideas.* Berkeley: University of California Press.

Boyer, P. (1996a) 'Religion as an impure subject: a note on cognitive order in religious representation in response to Brian Malley'. *Method and Theory in the Study of Religion* 8(2): 201–13.

Boyer, P. (1996b) 'What makes anthropomorphism natural? intuitive ontology and cultural representations'. *Journal of the Royal Anthropological Institute* n.s. 2: 1–15.

Boyer, P. (1998) 'Cognitive tracks of cultural inheritance: how evolved intuitive ontology governs cultural transmission'. *American Anthropologist* 100(4): 876–89.

Boyer, P. (1999) 'Cognitive aspects of religious ontologies: how brain processes constrain religious concepts'. In *Approaching Religion*, part I, ed. T. Ahlbäck, 53–72, Scripta Instituti Donneriani, 17:1. Åbo: Donner Institute.

Boyer, P. (2001) *Religion Explained: The Evolutionary Origins of Religious Thought*. New York: Basic Books.

Braun, W. (2000) 'Religion'. In *Guide to the Study of Religion*, ed. W. Braun and R. T. McCutcheon, 3–18. London: Cassell.

Braun, W. and R. T. McCutcheon (eds) (2000) *Guide to the Study of Religion*. London: Cassell.

Chi, M. T. H. (1992) 'Conceptual change within and across ontological categories: examples from learning and discovery in science'. In *Cognitive Models of Science*, ed. R. N. Giere, 129–86, Minnesota Studies in the Philosophy of Science, 15. Minneapolis: University of Minnesota Press.

Durkheim, É. (1995) *The Elementary Forms of Religious Life: A New Translation*, by K. E. Fields. New York: Free Press.

Fitzgerald, T. (2000) *The Ideology of Religious Studies*. New York: Oxford University Press.

Geertz, A. and R. T. McCutcheon (2000) 'The role of method and theory in the IAHR'. In *Perspectives on Method in the Study of Religion*, ed. A. W. Geertz and R. T. McCutcheon, 3–37. Leiden: Brill.

Gell, A. (1998) *Art and Agency: An Anthropological Theory*. Oxford: Clarendon Press.

Gelman, S. A. and L. A. Hirschfeld (1999) 'How biological is essentialism?' In *Folkbiology*, ed. D. Medin and S. Atran, 403–46. Cambridge, MA: MIT Press.

Guthrie, S. (1995 (1993)) *Faces in the Clouds: A New Theory of Religion*. New York: Oxford University Press.

Guthrie, S. (1996a) 'Religion: what is it?' *Journal for the Scientific Study of Religion* 35(4): 412–19.

Guthrie, S. (1996b) 'The sacred: a skeptical view'. In *The Sacred and Its Scholars: Comparative Methodologies for the Study of Primary Religious Data*, ed. T. A. Idinopulos and E. A. Yonan, 124–38. Leiden: Brill.

Honko, L. (ed.) (1979) *Science of Religion: Studies in Methodology*, Religion and Reason, 13. The Hague: Mouton.

Idinopulos, T. A. and E. A. Yonan (eds) (1996) *The Sacred and Its Scholars: Comparative Methodologies for the Study of Primary Religious Data*. Leiden: Brill.

Johnson, Mark L. (1999) 'Ethics'. In *A Companion to Cognitive Science*, ed. W. Bechtel and G. Graham, 691–701. Oxford: Blackwell.

Keesing, R. (1994) 'Theories of culture revisited'. In *Assessing Cultural Anthropology*, ed. R. Borofsky, 301–12. New York: McGraw-Hill.

Keil, F. C., D. T. Levin, B. A. Richman and G. Gutheil (1999) 'Mechanism and explanation in the development of biological thought'. In *Folkbiology*, ed. D. Medin and S. Atran, 283–319. Cambridge, MA: MIT Press.

Klein, B. (2000) 'The miracle in Södertälje, Sweden: mass media, interethnic politics, and a profusion of texts and images'. In *Thick Corpus, Organic Variation and Textuality in Oral Tradition*, ed. Lauri Honko, 401–16, Studia Fennica. Folkloristica, 7. Helsinki: Finnish Literature Society.

Lakoff, G. (1987) *Women, Fire and Dangerous Things: What Categories Reveal about the Mind.* Chicago: University of Chicago Press.

Lakoff, G. and M. Johnson (1999) *Philosophy in the Flesh: The Embodied Mind and Its Challenge to Western Thought.* New York: Basic Books.

Lawson, E. T. and R. N. McCauley (1990) *Rethinking Religion: Connecting Cognition and Culture.* Cambridge: Cambridge University Press.

Lawson, E. T. and R. N. McCauley. (1993) 'Crisis of conscience, riddle of identity: making space for a cognitive approach to religious phenomena'. *Journal of the American Academy of Religion* 61(2): 201–23.

Lévi-Strauss, C. (1966 (1949)) *The Savage Mind.* London: Weidenfeld & Nicolson.

MacLaury, R. E. (1991) 'Prototypes revisited'. *Annual Review of Anthropology* 20: 55–74.

Martin, L. H. (2000) 'Comparison'. In *Guide to the Study of Religion*, ed. W. Braun and R. T. McCutcheon, 45–56. London: Cassell.

Masuzawa, T. (2000) 'Origin'. In *Guide to the Study of Religion*, ed. W. Braun and R. T. McCutcheon, 209–24. London: Cassell.

McCauley, R. N. (1999) 'Levels of explanation and cognitive architectures'. In *A Companion to Cognitive Science*, ed. W. Bechtel and G. Graham, 611–24. Oxford: Blackwell.

McCauley, R. N. (2000) 'The naturalness of religion and the unnaturalness of science'. In *Explanation and Cognition*, ed. F. C. Kiel and R. A. Wilson, 61–85. Cambridge, MA: MIT Press.

McCauley, R. N. and E. T. Lawson (1996) 'Who owns "culture"?' *Method and Theory in the Study of Religion* 8(2): 171–90.

McCutcheon, R. T. (1997) *Manufacturing Religion: The Discourse on Sui Generis Religion and the Politics of Nostalgia.* New York: Oxford University Press.

McCutcheon, R. T. (1999) 'Of straw men and humanists: a reply to Brian Rennie'. *Religion* 29: 91–2.

Mithen, S. (1996) *The Prehistory of the Mind: The Cognitive Origins of Art, Religion and Science.* London: Thames and Hudson.

Paden, W. E. (1991) 'Before "the sacred" became theological: rereading the Durkheimian legacy'. *Method and Theory in the Study of Religion* 3: 10–23.

Paden, W. E. (1992) *Interpreting the Sacred: Ways of Viewing Religion.* Boston: Beacon Press.

Paden, W. E. (1994) *Religious Worlds: The Comparative Study of Religion.* Boston: Beacon Press.

Paden, W. E. (1999) 'Sacrality and the worldmaking: new categorial perspective'. In *Approaching Religion*, part I, ed. T. Ahlbäck, 165–80, Scripta Instituti Donneriani, 17:1. Åbo: Donner Institute.

Paden, W. E. (2000) 'Sacred order'. In *Perspectives on Method in the Study of Religion*, ed. A. W. Geertz and R. T. McCutcheon, 207–25. Leiden: Brill.

Penner, H. H. (1989) *Impasse and Resolution: A Critique of the Study of Religion*, Toronto Studies in Religion, 8. New York: Peter Lang.

Preus, J. S. (1987) *Explaining Religion: Criticism and Theory from Bodin to Freud*. New Haven: Yale University Press.

Pyysiäinen, I. (2001) *How Religion Works: Towards a New Cognitive Science of Religion*, Cognition and Culture Book Series, 1. Leiden: Brill.

Rosch, E. (1978) 'Principles of categorization'. In *Cognition and Categorization*, ed. Eleanor Rosch and B. B. Lloyd, 27–48. Hillsdale, NJ: Erlbaum.

Ryba, T. (2000) 'Manifestation'. In *Guide to the Study of Religion*, ed. W. Braun and R. T. McCutcheon, 168–89. London: Cassell.

Saler, B. (2000a (1993)) *Conceptualizing Religion: Immanent Anthropologists, Transcendent Natives and Unbound Categories*. New York: Berghahn Books.

Saler, B. (2000b) 'Toward a realistic and relevant "science of religion"'. Unpublished manuscript.

Smith, J. Z. (1978) *Map Is Not Territory*, Studies in the History of Religions. Studies in Judaism in Late Antiquity, 23, ed. J. Neusner. Leiden: Brill.

Smith, J. Z. (1987) *To Take Place: Toward Theory in Ritual.* Chicago: University of Chicago Press.

Smith, W. Robertson (1894) *Lectures on the Religion of the Semites*, First Series: *Fundamental Institutions.* London: Adam and Charles Black.

Sperber, D. (1996a) *Explaining Culture: A Naturalistic Approach.* Oxford: Blackwell.

Sperber, D. (1996b) 'Why are perfect animals, hybrids, and monsters food for symbolic thought?' *Method and Theory in the Study of Religion* 8(2): 143–69.

Sperber, D. (ed.) (2000) *Metarepresentations: A Multidisciplinary Perspective.* Oxford: Oxford University Press.

Stringer, M. D. (1999) 'Rethinking animism: thoughts from the infancy of our discipline'. *Journal of the Royal Anthropological Institute* n.s. 5: 541–56.

Szasz, T. (1984 (1961)) *The Myth of Mental Illness.* London: Paladin Books.

Taylor, M. (1999) *Imaginary Companions and the Children Who Create Them.* New York: Oxford University Press.

Taylor, M. C. (1999) *About Religion: Economies of Faith in Virtual Cultures.* Chicago: University of Chicago Press.

Tomasello, M. (1999a) 'The human adaptation for culture'. *Annual Review of Anthropology* 28: 509–29.

Tomasello, M. (1999b) *The Cultural Origins of Human Cognition.* Cambridge, MA: Harvard University Press.

Voget, F. W. (1975) *A History of Ethnology.* New York: Holt, Rinehart and Winston.

Whitehouse, Harvey (1995) *Inside the Cult: Religious Innovation and Transmission in Papua New Guinea.* Oxford: Clarendon Press.

Whitehouse, Harvey (2000) *Arguments and Icons: Divergent Modes of Religiosity.* Oxford: Oxford University Press.

Wiebe, D. (1999a) 'Appropriating religion: understanding religion as an object of science'. In *Approaching Religion*, part I, ed. T. Ahlbäck, 253–72, Scripta Instituti Donneriani, 17:1. Åbo: Donner Institute.

Wiebe, D. (1999b) *The Politics of Religious Studies.* New York: St Martin's Press.

Wiebe, D. (2000) 'Modernism'. In *Guide to the Study of Religion*, ed. W. Braun and R. T. McCutcheon, 351–64. London and New York: Cassell.

Wilson, R. A. (2000) 'The mind beyond itself'. In *Metarepresentations: A Multidisciplinary Perspective*, ed. D. Sperber, 31–52. Oxford: Oxford University Press.

3 Animal Animism: Evolutionary Roots of Religious Cognition

STEWART GUTHRIE

> There is no fundamental difference between man and the
> higher mammals in their mental faculties . . . the tendency in
> [humans] to imagine that natural objects and agencies are
> animated by spiritual or living essences, is perhaps illustrated
> by . . . my dog [which] was lying on the lawn during a hot
> and still day; but at a little distance a slight breeze occasion-
> ally moved an open parasol . . . every time that the parasol
> slightly moved, the dog growled fiercely and barked. He must
> [unconsciously have felt] that movement without any appar-
> ent cause indicated the presence of some strange living agent.
>
> Charles Darwin, *The Descent of Man*

> Permeated by [divine] power is everything that moves in the
> universe.
>
> First mantra, *Isa Upanishad*

Introduction

Despite Darwin, most scholars still see religion as marking a sharp
divide between humans and nonhuman animals. Religion, in their view,
involves symbolism, wishful thinking, explanation or some combination
of these activities, of which only humans are capable. Thus any
explanation of religion begins and ends with ourselves. A few writers,
however, root religion in a biological matrix shared by other animals. A
key part of this matrix is that we and other animals all inhabit
ambiguous environments that we must scan for hidden agents. In
scanning for such agents, we encounter false positives: we think we see
agents where none exist.

I hold, then, that nonhuman animals display the common denominator of religions: seeing more organization in things and events than

these things and events really have. Like us, other animals appear to attribute characteristics of life and agency to the inanimate world. In this sense, other animals are animists. This is because we all respond to perceptual ambiguity in a strategic way, produced by natural selection: when in doubt about whether something is animate or intentional, or is the result of action by something animate or intentional, we assume that it is. Because all perception is ambiguous and because natural and human deceptions increase this ambiguity, both we and other animals always must assume that there is more to the world than meets the eye.

Previously I have argued that religion is grounded in a general perceptual and cognitive strategy. I now am extending this argument by suggesting continuities and similarities between religious thought and action on the one hand and nonhuman animal perception and behaviour on the other. Far from requiring unique explanations, religious ideas are generated by cognitive mechanisms that are not only ordinary (Hume 1957 (1757); Darwin 1871; Tylor 1871; Horton 1960; 1993; Guthrie 1980; 1993; 1997a; 1997b; 2001; Lawson and McCauley 1990; Boyer 1994; Barrett 2000) but also broadly distributed in the animal world.

Religion doubtless has uses – 'functions' – that are typically human (McCutcheon 1997), but its existence cannot be explained primarily by such uses. It can be explained, however, as a byproduct of something else: a perceptual and cognitive strategy. As it arises, religion may well serve various purposes – just as do other accidental products of evolutionary process – and serving such purposes may encourage it.

The fundamental question is, however, *why* religion arises. (Jensen, this volume, remarks that this always has been the grand question; and Anttonen, this volume, writes that 'for scholars, there is hardly a more serious task'.) My answer is avowedly reductive. I find it in religion's continuities with other thought and action, including those in non-human animals, and in features of the natural environment in which such thought and action evolved. This approach agrees with recent assumptions in cognitive science about the fit between minds and the environments in which they have evolved, as well as with older assumptions in biology (e.g. Uexküll 1992). Cosmides and Tooby (1994: 103), for instance, write that because 'ancestral environments *caused* the design of psychological adaptations', investigating environments should guide 'exploration of our cognitive mechanisms'. That is, understanding the natural environments of our ancestors will help clarify how our own cognition works. Such clarification aims at what Sperber (1996: 4) calls the 'prototypical natural-scientific goal', namely, to 'discover some natural mechanism that explains a wide range of phenomena in a testable manner'.

What is at stake in my argument is not so much the question of what analogues to religion nonhuman animals may have, as what the answer can tell us about what humans have and why they have it. I have argued earlier (Guthrie 1980; 1988; 1993; 1996b; 1996c; 1997a; 1997b; 2001) that religion may best be considered cognitively, as a form of anthropomorphism (and of the related phenomenon of animism). I've argued moreover that the cognitive processes producing anthropomorphism and animism are deeply intuitive – as this term is used by Sperber (1996: 89), for example, who describes intuitive beliefs as 'typically the product of spontaneous and unconscious perceptual and inferential processes; in order to hold these intuitive beliefs, one need not be aware of the fact that one holds them, and even less of reasons for holding them'. This describes most anthropomorphism and animism very well indeed – and hence, in my view, most religious thought and action.

In contrast, however, Sperber himself (1996), Boyer (1994 and this volume), Pyysiäinen (this volume) and some others regard religion as in conflict with intuitive thought and action. Indeed, the latter two scholars find the explanation for the existence of religion in this very conflict. Thus although we all approach religion cognitively, we do so from quite different directions. Our diversity, however, is not unusual among theorists of religion, who, as Anttonen (this volume) notes, still are quite heterogeneous.

Is religion uniquely human?

The prevailing answer to the question whether religion is unique to us is yes (e.g. Lessa and Vogt 1979; Carey 1995; Atran 1995; Mithen 1999; Rappaport 1999). In this view, religion is different from anything in nonhuman animals. It is diagnostically and decisively human, and depends on capacities and preoccupations that set us off radically.

One familiar analysis of religion (Feuerbach 1972; Freud 1964; Malinowski 1948) that limits it to humans is that it consists of wishful thinking. Caught in various existential traps, not least our knowledge of our mortality, we fantasize ourselves rescued by gods and enjoying some comfortable post-mortem existence. Since only humans know that they will die, and only humans imagine something better, only humans have religions.

This wishful-thinking account (which appears as early as the Greeks and as recently as Stark and Bainbridge 1987) doubtless has some truth, but it appears insufficient. For one thing, many religious ideas picture a world we would not wish for, with demons, angry gods, or terrifying afterlives. Indeed, Burkert, noting that many religions are frightening, writes, 'to transmit religion is to transmit fear' (1996: 30–1). For another, we do not believe just anything we want. As Pinker (1997: 555) puts it, people freezing to death don't comfort themselves with a belief that they are warm. That is, even if all religious beliefs were comforting, we still would need to know why they are plausible. Thus the wishful-thinking theory is weak, and an absence of wishful thinking in other animals would not necessarily mean the absence of the basis for religion.

A second analysis of religion, often called intellectualist or, more generally, cognitivist, is that it constitutes explanation (Hume 1957 (1757); Tylor 1871; Horton 1993) and, of course, only humans explain. Again there is some truth here. Religions often do offer explanations, and these, as far as explanation is propositional, require language and symbols. But, as Lawson and McCauley (1990) argue, explanation is closely interwoven with interpretation and is hard to distinguish from it; and certainly other animals interpret the world, since all perception is interpretation, as Wittgenstein pointed out.

A recent cognitive account of religion that also seems to make it unique to humans is Boyer's (1994, partly adopted by Pyysiäinen and by Anttonen, both this volume). This account explains not how religious ideas arise, but why they persist. As in Darwinian selection, they persist because of a selective advantage: here, their memorability. Memorability is conferred by a combination of intuitiveness and counter-intuitiveness. Ideas with this combination are variously 'supernatural', 'non-natural' and 'extra-natural'. As this account relies heavily on the notion of the counter-intuitive, and as animals give little or no instruction (much less in metaphysics), we might conclude once more that animals cannot share the common denominator of religion.

Several problems with this theory arise, however, that are pertinent to my own argument. The most basic is that because the reproductive success of ideas is independent of the success of their bearers – unlike the relation of genes to their bearers – the theory is inconsistent with the Darwinian account of selection. Only by conceiving of ideas themselves as life forms (as does Sperber, see below) can this inconsistency be avoided. But such a conception, giving life to ideas, is both reifying and animistic and hence best avoided.

Another problem arises, as Talmy (1995: 647) and Guthrie (1996a) note, because Boyer describes the counter-intuitive components of religious ideas as generated randomly. Which ideas persist and which do not is determined solely by the need for some balance of intuitivity and counter-intuitivity. Thus, memorable non-natural ideas should encompass an endless range of combinations. But instead certain features, such as the frequent invisibility and intangibility of agents, in fact commonly recur while virtually limitless others, equally counter-intuitive, do not occur at all.

A third, related problem is whether invisibility and intangibility are indeed counter-intuitive or merely, as Talmy suggests, consistent with experience in natural environments. Ethology and human experience alike suggest that the latter is the case. First, animals in the wild not infrequently behave as though in the presence of unseen agents (for example, even with no predator in sight, they often act cautiously – though occasionally, as in the chimpanzee rain dance, with bravado). This behaviour is not surprising, since invisible agents are common in nature and in human experience, and intangible ones are not unusual (Guthrie 1993 and below). And it is, of course, in a natural context that human intuitions also have evolved.

Further, the ethologist Uexküll (1992: 377) recounts instances of animals from various phyla acting in *Umwelten* (subjective worlds of perception and action) that possess 'phenomena which, however, are visible to the subject alone and are bound to no experiences'. Such phenomena include search images triggered in the absence of any objective stimulus. One might call such phenomena 'imaginary', but Uexküll calls them, together with the consequent behaviour, 'magical'. For example, a pet starling, which never had caught or even seen a fly, one day was seen to 'suddenly rush toward an invisible object, catch it in mid-air, return with the object to its perch, peck away at it with its bill as any starling will do with a captured fly, and finally swallow the invisible thing . . . There was no doubt that the starling had had the apparition of an imaginary fly in its *Umwelt*. Evidently the starling's whole world had been so charged with the 'feeding tone', that even without the appearance of a sensory stimulus, the functional image of fly-catching, which was in readiness, forced the perceptual image to appear, and this released the entire action chain. This experience indicates that otherwise utterly puzzling actions by various animals should be interpreted magically' (Uexküll 1992: 378).

Moreover, in human experience, people commonly act at a distance, as through place markers, projectiles, land mines and other artefacts.

This produces what Gell (1998) calls the 'distributed person': the fact that persons, through their distributed artefacts, typically are agents in various places at the same time. They need be neither visible nor tangible to have a presence.

On the other hand, the invisibility and intangibility of most gods and spirits, like those of most animals, are neither complete nor intrinsic but only partial and contingent (Guthrie 1993). They are achieved by the Greek gods, for example, by producing a screen of fog or smoke. Burkert (1996, like Guthrie 1993) notes that dealing with gods we never see is little different from dealing with monarchs or distant trade partners we never see. In addition, many gods, such as those of the Hawaiians and Aztecs, not only have been perfectly visible and tangible but also have looked very much like humans – thus enabling Captains Cook and Cortez to be mistaken for returning deities.

Reports of agents who are invisible and intangible may demand our attention. As Burkert suggests, however, this probably is simply because these features make such agents more powerful – and sometimes more sinister – than agents without them. The same attention would be demanded by reports of camouflaged men in the woods or reports of invisible microbes on one's food. No 'supernatural' qualities are required.

This conclusion avoids a potential ethnological problem, moreover, since, as Hallowell (1960) and Saler (1977) argue, the very notion of supernatural is Western and culture-bound. As Horton (1993) observes, applying this notion to traditional African religions is no more useful than applying it to nuclear physics on the grounds that physics invokes invisible entities and powers. Rather, Horton continues, both science and religion begin with familiar models – those of common sense – and adapt them to account for a broader range of phenomena by changing or dropping certain features. The planetary model of the atom, for example, began with the model of our solar system, but changed the scale and dropped such features as colour. Similarly, such religious models as those of ancestors begin with persons and lineages, and modify or drop features such as embodiment. Gell (1998) similarly argues that magical thinkers using principles of contagion and sympathy do not so much contradict modern physics as simply do without it; and Saariluoma, this volume, also finds 'nothing unintuitive in inferring the properties God has in the human mind, culture and existing religious texts'.

A corollary of Horton's comparison of religious and scientific theories is that the more abstruse versions of both are the province of professional scientists and theologians. Most of us stick closer to home, where matter remains solid and gods are neither totally Other nor totally disembodied. (Barrett 1999 and 2000 also makes this point, distinguishing ordinary religious ideas from theological ideas. In this volume he writes similarly that, 'regardless of theological tradition, in non-reflective contexts, concepts of gods conform to intuitive expectations . . . about all intentional beings'. For most people, for example, God is not omnipresent but can be in only one place at a time.)

The third and last human capacity held to make religion unique to our species is that for language and associated symbolism. Scholars who assume that religion essentially *is* symbolism are a majority; just a few of the best-known include Durkheim (1915), Turner (1967), Geertz (1966) and Rappaport (1999). For most scholars, religious symbolism is a means indirectly to express, promote or control certain social relationships and our feelings about them (Anttonen (1996; 2000) offers persuasive versions of this view); and for most of these scholars, the uniqueness of humans is hardly in question. Rappaport (1999: 16) writes in his last book, 'religion emerged with language. As such, religion is as old as language, which is to say precisely as old as humanity.'

Against the view that symbols are uniquely human, one might counter that chimpanzees and other apes have rudimentary symbolism (e.g. branch-dragging to suggest a direction of travel and occasional false warnings, which Rappaport 1999: 55 calls 'proto-lies'). Moreover Rappaport, who sees ritual as the source of religion, makes plain that ritual is not only human but is shared also by 'the birds, the beasts and even the insects' (1999: 25). As an ethologist writes, 'attempts to place humans apart from and above nonhumans, have, in a sense, backfired. Comparative research in animal cognition has demonstrated evolutionary continuity in many cognitive abilities. It has also shown how connected humans are to other animals' (Bekoff 1998: 176). Nonetheless, religion as such – like most human institutions – typically does involve well-developed symbolism including language, and other animals do not have this. Language, of course, makes a big difference. Among other things (as Jensen, this volume, puts it), it 'permits us to imagine collectively'.

Animal animism, then, is not a system of symbols but rather a set of non-symbolic features of perception, cognition and action that appear basic to religion and that are present also in nonhuman animals. These features include, as noted, perceptual uncertainty (Kahneman and Tversky 1982), a need to discover hidden agents and an overestimation of agency. Although these features are unsystematized and non-symbolic in most nonhuman animals (the chimpanzee 'rain dance', which appears cultural and systematic, may be a borderline case), they are crucial both to humans and to nonhumans.

Religion in a biological matrix

A few scholars of religion have tried to bridge the gap between humans and nonhumans. One is A. F. C. Wallace (1966). For Wallace, religion is mainly ritual, and to understand it we must set it in the wider context of ritual in other animals. Wallace's evolutionary rationale is similar to mine: one can regard religion 'as a special case . . . of a more wide-spread pattern' (1966: 217). However, his (functionalist) view of religion as essentially ritual that promotes cooperation among humans encounters the problem found in all functionalist accounts: one cannot explain how something arises by the uses to which it may be put.

More recently, Walter Burkert (1996) also tries to place religions within a 'biological landscape' (1996: 65). Burkert sets this biological context partly by finding analogies for religion in nonhuman-animal behaviour. Many of his analogies are unpersuasive, such as that between religious sacrifice and the abandonment by zebras of one of their number to lions, or the abandonment by a lizard of its tail to an attacker. These analogies (as Saler 1999 notes) are distant or coincidental.

Nonetheless, Burkert produces a substantive, family-resemblance account of religion that is somewhat plausible. In his account, religion grows directly from innate dispositions that we share with other animals, especially with other primates. Most important are dispositions to deal with the world in general as though it were social and communicative. For all animals, Burkert (1996: 156) writes, the world is composed of signs and signals. Among humans, who attribute 'language . . . to nature' (p. 163), the abundant signs in nature turn 'into [voices everywhere] . . . as if every being, everywhere, were telling a message' (p. 160).

What is lacking both in Wallace and in Burkert is a unified account of what makes these (usually) unseen agents credible. Burkert (1996) does note – crucially, in my view – that we have inborn tendencies to think and act in social and linguistic ways vis-à-vis the world at large, and that the ambiguity of the natural environments against which these tendencies play out provides fertile ground for them (p. 118). Nonetheless, he concludes that the problem of explaining religion – 'serious communication with powers that cannot be seen' (p. 176) – has no single solution. Instead, he simply proposes that there are 'biological patterns of actions, reactions, and feelings' that stem from our ancestral contexts of evolution. Well and good. But what *were* those contexts, and how and why do the resulting patterns of perception include humanlike, but nonhuman, others?

Animism explained

The diverse biological patterns to which Burkert points may be unified under the more general heading of animism. Animism, of course, has meant many different things. Even within anthropology, the discipline that effectively created the term, it is ambiguous, sometimes meaning the belief (Evans-Pritchard 1965: 24–5) that 'not only creatures but also inanimate objects have life and personality' and sometimes the belief that 'in addition they have souls'. In Tylor's famous formulation, animism is the 'belief in spirit beings' – though exactly what spirit beings are remains unclear, as Saler points out (1993: 88–93). At present, owing largely to its widespread use by post-Tylorian comparative religionists, animism most commonly means a 'belief in living, personal powers behind all things' (Pals 1996: 24).

The varied meanings fit, I think, within animism as defined by Piaget and other developmental psychologists, namely as the attribution of characteristics of animacy to nonliving things and events. For the kinds of life that most concern humans, these characteristics may include form, such as eyes and bilateral symmetry. (As Dennett 1993 notes, through much of human evolution such symmetry may have represented the face of a predator gazing at us.) More important, however, is behaviour, including spontaneous motion, responsiveness and orientation to a goal. In cognitive ethology, for instance, a philosopher and an ethologist remark that it may be a mistake to assume that animals perceive predators mainly by 'morphology. Instead, predators may be conceptualised according to what they typically do' (Allen and Bekoff 1997: 121). Similarly, Uexküll, having described a tame jackdaw that chose a series of companions including Konrad Lorenz, a younger jackdaw and crows, notes that 'there is no uniform perceptual image for the companion in the jackdaw's world. Nor could there be one, since the role of the companion changes all the time' (1992: 371).

For such situations, Uexküll suggests, we should posit that animals employ not specific search images but instead 'search tones', which are more general. 'Now we do not always look for a definite object with a single receptor image, but far more often for one that corresponds to a specific *functional* image. Instead of a specific chair, we look around for something to sit on, that is, for a thing that may be connected with a certain performance tone. In this case we cannot speak of a search image, but only of a search tone' (1992: 375; emphasis added). This, together with the case of the starling and the imaginary fly, suggests once again that an emphasis on visibility and tangibility in agents, with its corollary of an expectation of specific form, may be misplaced.

Animism, in the sense of the attribution of agency to objects that do not have it, appears widespread among both humans and animals. I shall first address the question why this should be and then cite examples. Because I've offered a general theory both of animism and of the related phenomenon of anthropomorphism in other places (e.g. Guthrie 1993), the explanation here will be condensed. However, a preliminary note about what my explanation is *not* may be in order. This is the common notion that animism and anthropomorphism are 'projections', a notion popularized by Freud and adopted (and attributed to me) by Boyer in this volume. Projection has no place in my explanation. Indeed, the whole of Guthrie 2000 is an argument that, as a psychological concept, projection is without merit. (Its principal basis apparently is a folk psychology, dating back to the Greeks, of vision as a projection of beams from the eye.) Rather than projections, 'animism' and 'anthropomorphism' describe certain perceptions that we have decided, after the fact, were mistaken. The perceptual stance that produces these mistaken perceptions as occasional byproducts, however, is no mistake but a vital and unavoidable strategy.

In brief, we and other animals live in a perceptual world that always is ambiguous (as one writer on primate behaviour puts it, 'nature cloaks herself in many modes of unpredictability' (Miller 1997: 312)). In this world, we need to distinguish, among other things, what is animate from what is not. The world is ambiguous (though normally we're not aware of this) because even the simplest perception is an interpretation – or, as Gombrich (1973) puts it, a bet. (Quiatt and Reynolds 1993: 5, writing of primates, note similarly that 'perception, for all species, is the interpretation of sensations'.) Interpretation, in turn, aims at significance or meaning. The most meaning, finally, is in things that are alive, not inanimate. Hence we spontaneously interpret a tapping at our window as a visitor, not a branch, and a tickling on our neck as a bug, not a loose thread.

Figure 3.1 Ptarmigan on her nest: difficult to see although in plain view. The eye is toward the upper left.
Source: Gerald H. Thayer, *Concealing-coloration in the Animal Kingdom* (New York: The Macmillan Company, 1909)

Interpretation may be urgent, for example when what *is* alive is something we may want to capture (Figure 3.1), or something that may want to capture us (Figure 3.2).

Because ambiguity is chronic and time is short, we generally must interpret without enough evidence to be sure. In this situation, our strategy is, better safe than sorry (Guthrie 1993; 1997a; 1997b; 2001; forthcoming; Boyer, this volume, adopts the idea): when in doubt, we assume that it *is* alive. An S-shaped object on a woodland path might be either a stick or a snake, for example, but we tend automatically to see it first as a snake. As Ristau (1998: 139) puts it, a 'fail-safe mechanism for most species would be to interact with an unknown object as though it were animate, and probably predaceous'.

When we look at the world of animals, the ambiguity of perception is exacerbated by deception. This deception includes various means to

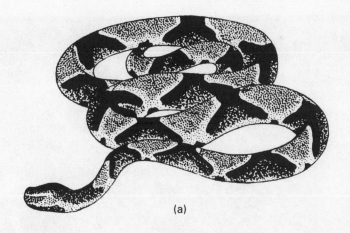

(a)

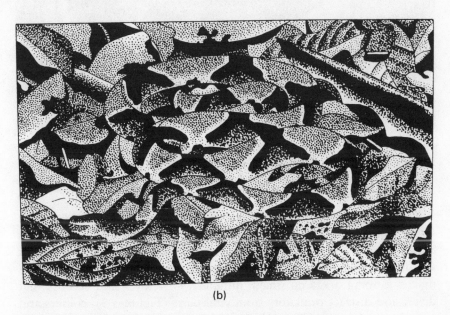

(b)

Figure 3.2   (a) Copperhead viper on a uniform background.
  (b) The same snake in its natural environment.
Source: Hugh Cott, *Adaptive Coloration in Animals* (London: Methuen, 1957)

invisibility and intangibility. These means are widely diverse and almost universal among wild animals, since 'if an animal is seen, heard or smelt it is potentially in danger [and hence] deception as a way of life occurs throughout the animal kingdom' (Owen 1980: 9, 17).

Figure 3.3 Eyespot display of South American frog *Physalaemus nattereri*.
Source: Denis Owen, *Camouflage and Mimicry* (London: Rainbird, 1980)

Visual deceptions alone include at least five distinct sorts (Owen 1980). These are camouflage (which makes the animal look like its background, often with countershading that destroys the appearance of solidity), colours that are diverse or changeable in individuals (this makes forming a search image difficult), structures and colours that divert and distract predators from vital parts (Figure 3.3), colours and patterns that startle (Figure 3.4), and imitation of noxious animals or material (Figure 3.5). Because of these deceptions, we and other animals often encounter others without knowing it. As a corollary, we often judge that others are there when they are not. The world is, in fact, full of invisible others, and we must always assume more than we see.

In addition to animals that are invisible, many animals are virtually intangible, for one of three reasons. One is a diffraction grating producing a shimmering opalescence that makes size and location difficult to judge (Hinton 1973). A second is swarming, flocking or schooling. This, too, presents predators with a target of indefinite location. A sea

Figure 3.4   Eyed hawk moth.
Source: Denis Owen, *Camouflage and Mimicry* (London: Rainbird, 1980)

lion trying to feed on a school of sardines, for example, may be baffled by the constantly shifting pattern confronting it. A third kind of intangibility – coupled with invisibility until microscopes appeared – is that of being very small, as in microorganisms. One result of the invisibility and intangibility of microorganisms is that until recently, most people saw contagious diseases, such as tuberculosis, smallpox, cholera and plague, as the work of intentional but invisible agents. As I have noted earlier (Guthrie 1993), people usually think they detect gods not by seeing them – though this also happens – but by seeing natural phenomena as the results of their actions. (Some see AIDS, for example, as divine punishment.) Moreover, recognizing invisible agents does not require sophisticated (or counter-intuitive) thought, as a study of preschoolers' understanding of germs suggests: 'three-year-olds recognized that the causes of illness may be invisible . . . children will focus on a specific invisible entity when judging a potential causal relationship within the domain of biology' (Kalish 1996: 99, 100).

Another kind of deception often occurs within groups of animals:

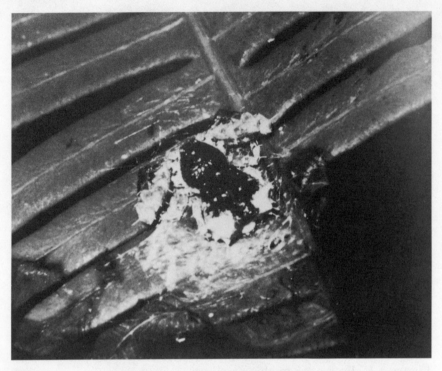

Figure 3.5 Tropical spider crab mimicking a bird dropping.
Source: Denis Owen, *Camouflage and Mimicry* (London: Rainbird, 1980)

misleading communication, such as warning calls when no danger is present. Such deceptions typically distract competitors. Shrikes living in mixed-species flocks, for instance, occasionally give false hawk warnings when a bird of another species is about to seize an insect, causing the other to flee for cover and leave the bug for the shrike (Gould and Gould 1994: 134).

Primates also deceive, often with apparent intent. Indeed, primate intelligence may be largely 'machiavellian', or devoted to deceiving, and avoiding being deceived by, their fellows (Byrne and Whiten 1988; Whiten and Byrne 1997). A vervet monkey on the losing side of a fight between troops may give a false leopard alarm, frightening off the combatants and resetting the contest at zero (Cheney and Seyfarth 1990). A baboon chased by another may stop and stare as though at a predator, halting the pursuer (Byrne 1995: 125).

Chimpanzees, bonobos and orangutans appear even more deceitful. Both wild and captive chimpanzees have been seen leading others away from hidden food that was known to the leaders but not to the led (Goodall 1972: 96; Byrne 1995: 132). A captive chimpanzee, subordinate to another that was afraid of the dark, went outside after dark, made banging noises and other strange sounds, and came back inside looking scared. His erstwhile oppressor, now frightened, approached him for reassurance (Savage-Rumbaugh and McDonald 1988: 228).

Capacities for deceiving others are related to capacities for self-deception and for play (Mitchell and Thompson 1986). Two captive chimpanzees developed a game in which they pretended to attack an imaginary opponent in a cage, and a captive bonobo has produced imaginary playmates (Savage-Rumbaugh and McDonald 1988). The sign-using orangutan Chantek signed 'cat and dog – animals which frightened and fascinated him – when he wished to prolong or start a walk, acting as though seeking out a hidden cat or dog' (Mitchell 1993: 81).

Burkert, invoking work on primate deception to help understand religion, writes:

The suspicion has been voiced repeatedly that religion is mainly trickery and make-believe produced by those who profit from it. Forms of deceit abound already at prehuman stages . . . *The unseen in particular can be the object of manipulation.* [*Monkeys, for example*] *may avoid confrontation by staring into a corner and voicing sounds of alarm, as if reporting 'there is a monster in the corner'.* (1996: 24–5; emphasis added)

Burkert also says religion assumes humanlike beings whom we normally do not see. He notes, with Lawson and McCauley (1990), that ritual 'refers through formulaic acts to nonpresent partners'. However, deceptions in themselves 'would be a grossly insufficient foundation for the origin of religion. Even among monkeys the trick cannot be repeated very often without being recognized . . . The point is that the common world of language characteristically produces contents beyond any immediate evidence' (Burkert 1996: 25).

In human communication, recent researchers have noted the 'ubiquity [and] sheer ordinariness' of deception (Lewis and Saarni 1993: v) and maintained that it is a normal consequence of communication and information (just as illusion is a natural outgrowth of perception). Communication, deception and play all appear interlinked. Creative abilities in this realm constitute abilities to envision a world and an alternative, what is present and what is not. These abilities are graded among animals and seem present among vervets and even among shrikes.

One consequence of ubiquitous deception, in addition to the inherent ambiguity of perception, is that it is perpetually difficult to tell what is living from what is not (Guthrie 1993: ch. 2). This prevents us from easily and reliably applying any domain-specific expectations we may have to any particular part of our environment. Carey (1995) levels this point against the notion, shared by Sperber (1994) and Atran (1994), that such domain specificity can characterize folk biology and indeed make such biology an innate 'core module' of the human mind. She notes, for example (1995: 275), that in 'one of the cultures that Atran has studied, the Itza Maya, fungi and lichens are not considered alive'. Raising the 'problem of perception', she asks (p. 278), 'On what basis does the [Sperber–Atran] input module categorize entities as animals? The folk-biology module will be useless unless the cognitive system can identify the animals in the world.'

Animism among animals

The attribution of characteristics of animacy to the nonliving and to plants appears widespread among complex organisms. Because illusion is an inevitable concomitant of perception, such attribution may be universal. Among invertebrates, known instances of susceptibility to such illusion range from echinoderms to insects. Regarding sea urchins, for instance, Uexküll remarks that 'a receptor image held in . . . general terms can always give rise to mistakes. This has already been shown in the sea urchin, in whose world cloud and ship are constantly confused with the enemy fish, because the sea urchin responds in the same way to any darkening of the horizon' (1992: 370). Various insects are fooled by insect-eating plants, such as the Venus fly-trap; and some flowers, by resembling bees or wasps, fool these insects into pollinating them as they attempt to mate.

Among vertebrates, evidence of hard wiring to detect signs of life, and evidence of corresponding illusions, are abundant from both experimental and natural settings. The possible signs of life include both form and motion. Regarding form, for example, 'we and many other creatures are built to be extremely capable of detecting eyes' (Ristau 1998: 141) and we respond readily to anything that resembles them. Ethologists have found sensitivities to eye-like displays in fishes (even larval ones; Miklosi et al. 1995), iguanas (Burger et al. 1991), garter snakes (Bern and Herzog 1994), wild birds (Scaife 1976), domestic chickens (Gallup 1971) and human infants (Morton and Johnson 1991). The eye displays need not be convincing to a human observer: even marbles on the ends of two sticks suffice to alarm chickens (Gould and Gould 1994: 135). This sensitivity also is exploited by many species, especially those of insects and fishes, that display false eye-spots as a means of defence. Similarly, sensitivity to bilateral symmetry, a feature of most mobile animals, has been shown in animals ranging from insects to birds to dolphins and other mammals.

Humans often exploit the animal tendency to animate. Fishermen can catch various fishes with nothing more than a bit of white rag on a hook. Hunters can lure waterfowl and other birds even with crude decoys. To frighten parrots from an orchard, I have set out a simple, weather-beaten plastic owl and found it mobbed within seconds by blue jays, blackbirds and a cardinal. Human-like scarecrows the world over are effective even with only a sketchy resemblance to people. Inuit, for example, are able to funnel caribou into ambush using scarecrows consisting of tall rockpiles.

In natural settings as well, birds and mammals may treat inert matter as though it were alive. Bekoff (personal communication) reports young coyotes mistaking sticks for grasshoppers, and a coyote stalking a blowing sage brush. Hinton (1973) reports birds mistaking twigs for caterpillars, and Marshall Thomas thinks 'many dogs treat cars as though they were animate' (1993: 12).

Primates animate at least as broadly. Menzel (1997: 231) writes, 'So-called "social" behaviour patterns can be directed toward inanimate objects. Rhesus macaque (monkey) infants form attachments to cloth-covered surrogate mothers; tamarins (a kind of monkey) will groom a fur-covered object; an infant chimpanzee will threaten an unfamiliar piece of food.' Vervet-monkey infants give the aerial-predator call on seeing falling leaves (Cheney and Seyfarth 1990), and, as noted, a young adult vervet's false terrestrial-predator call caused opponents to flee from a 'phantom leopard' (Gould and Gould 1994: 135). Macaques on Gibraltar have threatened an electric fence. When an observer there accidentally stepped on an electric cable in the grass, an infant macaque screamed at its motion, evidently taking it for a snake (Anne Zeller, personal communication). A baboon being chased may, as noted, stop and stare at nothing, apparently producing a phantom predator that deters the pursuer.

Chimpanzees, bonobos and orangutans show the most varied animism. In captivity, as noted, they all may produce phantom playmates or monsters (sometimes to fool a fellow ape or a caregiver). The orangutan Chantek 'engaged in chase games in which he would look over his shoulder as he darted about, although no one was chasing him. He also signed to his toys and offered them food and drink. Like children, Chantek showed evidence of animism, a tendency to endow objects and events with the attributes of living things' (Miles 1993: 49). A captive chimpanzee also has directed alarms calls toward its own shed teeth. Its caregiver (Sally Boysen, personal communication) thinks it saw the teeth as beings that had made its mouth hurt and bleed.

Finally and most tellingly, wild chimpanzees (Goodall 1975; 1992; personal communication; Whiten et al. 1999) often respond to thunderstorms, to rapid streams and to waterfalls with the kind of display (shaking and dragging branches and rushing about vigorously) that they use as a threat against predators and other chimpanzees. Observers have reported this behaviour in six communities of African chimpanzees, out of nine communities that have been closely studied (Whiten et al. 1999). Goodall and many other chimp-watchers think this behaviour is indeed a threat directed toward these inanimate targets as though they were alive. The response is both widespread and indiscriminable from those toward actual, natural agents, visible or not. Although no one knows whether chimpanzees think of storms and streams as 'supernatural', any hypothesis that they do so seems unnecessary. More likely, as Pyysiäinen (this volume) puts it, 'the thunderstorm triggers the same reaction as does a predator, without a representation of a . . . counter-intuitive agent being involved'.

Animism and anthropomorphism in humans

Most scholars (e.g. Piaget 1929) concerned with animism attribute it to children and to people in small-scale ('tribal' or 'primitive') societies, and most scholars see anthropomorphism – the attribution of human characteristics to nonhuman things and events – as unrelated to animism and as a minor though lamentable problem in human cognition (Mitchell et al. 1997 present a recent set of exceptions). In contrast, I see animism and anthropomorphism as pervasive in human thought and action, and as closely related, spontaneous over-attributions of organization to things and events (Guthrie 1993; 1997a; 1997b). Just as animism may be seen as one result of a better-safe-than-sorry strategy of perception in an ambiguous world, anthropomorphism may be understood the same way. The two often overlap.

Anthropomorphism has been the object of criticism for hundreds of years, yet it continues to flourish. It flourishes in the arts and even the sciences (Kennedy 1992; Guthrie 1993; forthcoming; Mitchell et al.

1997). It also flourishes in the spontaneous perceptions of daily life, as when we hear voices in the wind or the plumbing, or see some mechanism as resisting us. Animism is similarly widespread. Evidence of the pervasiveness of anthropomorphism and animism, even in complex, industrial societies, comes from many sources (Guthrie 1993). Here I'll only draw briefly on developmental, experimental and clinical psychology, and on commercial art.

Systematic work in psychology on animism and anthropomorphism began with Jean Piaget (1929), who called them both animism and found them universal among young children. Piaget's basic finding – that child animism and anthropomorphism are spontaneous and ubiquitous – has been disputed in some details, such as its relation to his scheme of cognitive stages. Generally, however, it has been broadly supported (e.g. Inagaki and Hatano 1987; Inagaki 1989; Ochiai 1989; Cherry 1992; Berry and Springer 1993; Harris 1994; Poulin-Dubois and Héroux 1994; Carey 1995). Harris (1994: 308) writes, for example, 'A long tradition of work on animism shows that children extend psychological explanations to . . . rivers, clouds, and so forth.'

Among the features that produce animistic and anthropomorphic responses, motion appears pre-eminent, as my epigraphs suggest. (Indeed, Aristotle made a capacity for self-movement the chief criterion of animacy.) Berry and Springer (1993: 275), for instance, write that 'very different methodologies have shown that certain movements by inanimate objects elicit attributions of animacy from preschoolers', and Poulin-Dubois and Héroux (1994: 329) similarly find that 'over-attribution of mental states' characterizes preschoolers' responses to moving objects. Such responses, of course, reflect the importance of motion. As Barry (1997: 46) writes, 'movement perception is so essential to our being . . . because the visual system has evolved to alert us to danger or to the presence of potential food'.

We not only animate the inanimate, but we also anthropomorphize the animate or the apparently animate (Guthrie 1980; 1993; 1997a; 1997b; 2001; forthcoming), whether moving or not. As Gigenrenzer (1997: 275) writes, 'human intelligence cannot resist [attributing] human social categories, intentions and morals [to] non-humans'. Carey (1995: 279) notes that 'infants attempt to interact socially with a mobile that moves in response to a leg kick'. Richards and Siegler (1986) write that children over a wide range of ages teleologically attribute anatomical and other features of organisms (plants, for example) to the 'purposes' of those organisms. More generally, Dennett (1987) posits an innate 'intentional' or design stance with which we interpret the world, Keil (1994: 251) sees both teleological and intentional 'modes of construal' as attitudes with which people are natively endowed, and Kelemen (1999: 280) proposes that an innate 'promiscuous teleology' makes humans 'prone to systematic biases in their reasoning about the natural world'. Most directly to my point, Kelemen also writes that 'one of the best indicators that people are compelled to reason in teleological terms is provided by the ubiquitous phenomenon of religion. Adults' propensity to view objects and events as purposefully caused by intentional agents or gods is . . . prevalent . . . [F]or all the profound differences between religions and their associated mythologies, a common moral tends to underlie most: objects and events have an intended purpose. Everything has a function to perform within a contrived natural order of which humanity is a significant part' (1999: 280). This closely parallels Piaget's classic description of teleology in young children. The phenomenon also supplies (as Guthrie 1993 notes) an answer to Hume's (1932: i. 157) quandary about the nature of our sense that the world shows design – a sense so strong as to underlie the Argument from Design for God's existence. As a Hume scholar writes, there is an apparently universal 'propensity of the mind to "see" design in natural order' and an 'insistent *feeling* in most of us that natural order springs from a designer' (Gaskin 1988: 127, 6; emphasis his). Kelemen dubs this phenomenon 'Promiscuous Teleology', noting that it 'is not inherently restricted to any category of objects' (1999: 290). Bacon (1960), of course, centuries ago began a scientific revolution by pointing out that humans, but not nature or even living things in general, have goals, and that the widespread human failure to understand this constitutes anthropomorphism.

Equally important for my purposes is one major correction of Piaget, made by various developmental and cognitive psychologists. The correction is that, contrary to his claim that animism disappears by the age of twelve, it appears to persist throughout life (Dennis 1953; Sheehan et al. 1980–1; Tamir and Zohar 1991; Cherry 1992; Kelemen 1999). Hauser and Carey (1998: 84) write that people generally are 'primed, perhaps innately so, to take an intentional stance . . . toward a wide array of moving objects'. Similarly, Barrett (this volume, *pace* Pyysiäinen, this volume) writes that 'given only enough evidence to believe an object can wilfully initiate its own action . . . children and adults automatically attribute a host of human-like psychological properties. To illustrate, when trying (with little success) to place small magnetized spheres in a particular configuration, college students described the marbles as having beliefs, desires and even personality traits, accusing some marbles of "attacking" others and being deliberately mischievous.'

The pervasive tendency to animate and anthropomorphize, moreover, is not limited to spontaneous interpretations such as those of young children and the college students cited but appears as well in more considered interpretations, including more-or-less scientific work. Of numerous examples (Guthrie 1993, esp. ch. 6), a particularly relevant one is Dawkins's (1978) genes, which notoriously are selfish, and his 'memes', which similarly are self-interested and which 'replicate'. Even more strikingly, Sperber (1996: 1) describes ideas as 'born in' and as 'invading' brains, as 'propagating', and as having 'descendants'. Whereas the Greeks saw the anima or life force as the central causal principle for the behaviour of human (and other) bodies, Sperber gives this role to ideas. 'The central theme of this book is quite simple,' he begins (p. 1). 'Our individual brains are each inhabited by a large number of ideas that determine our behavior.' These determinative ideas not only 'are born, live and die' but also constitute 'families' (pp. 81 and 83).

One might consider Sperber's terminology here as mere metaphor (on p. 2 he calls it 'barely metaphorical') except that his central notion, an epidemiology of culture, depends on it. Equally important, if, as Lakoff and Johnson argue (e.g. 1999, echoing Nietzsche 1966), most human thought is metaphoric, 'mere metaphor' is an oxymoron. What matters is not whether a given model is metaphoric or not, but whether it is useful or not. In the standard view – which I share – animistic and anthropomorphic models are not useful (though the strategy of perception that produces them as byproducts, i.e. scanning first for what matters most, certainly is). That animistic accounts such as Dawkins's and Sperber's nevertheless are appealing illustrates the continued vitality of animism among us all.

Other evidence of pervasive animism and anthropomorphism comes from clinical psychology, for example in Rorschach testing. Respondents see ink blots mostly as humans or parts of humans, and as certain animals such as bats and butterflies (Beck and Molish 1967). Other animals come next, followed distantly by plants and inanimate objects. A cross-cultural study (De Vos and Boyer 1989) suggests that this pattern is widespread. Still other sources of evidence include folklore (Thompson 1955), literature and graphic art, in which personification and other forms of anthropomorphism, as well as animism, are common worldwide (Guthrie 1993; Figure 3.6, p. 60). In sophisticated art, these phenomena are, to be sure, often self-conscious and sometimes

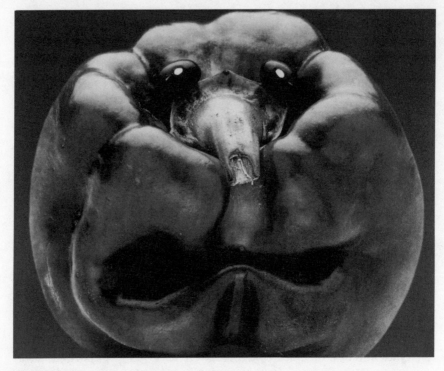

Figure 3.6   Green-pepper face with bean eyes.
Source: Photo © 1999 Joost Elffers and Saxton Freeman. Reprinted by permission.

manipulative, not spontaneous; but their pervasiveness and diversity there nonetheless reflect their power.

   Neither anthropomorphism nor animism in itself, of course, constitutes religion. Rather, religion is a form of them that is systematized, symbolically elaborated and taken seriously (Guthrie 1980; 1988; 1993; 1996c; 1997b; 2001). In this form, they are adapted to varied political, economic, military and other social purposes.

Conclusion: an evolutionary framework for explaining religion

Earlier writers on religion as anthropomorphism (most notably Spinoza 1955; Hume 1957; Feuerbach 1972; Freud 1964; and Horton 1993; and recently in a vein similar to my own, Wenegrat 1990), or as animism, have disagreed on the nature of these two phenomena and have produced no broadly convincing explanation of them. As a result they have produced no broadly convincing theory of religion. Part of what has been lacking, in my view, is a cognitive account of anthropomorphism and of animism that addresses them in general rather than only in religion. I have aimed much of my work at just such an account.

A related part of what has been lacking is an evolutionary framework for the issues in question. Such a framework, still very much in the making, potentially can link us to our animal relatives by joining cognitive science to ethology. Such a framework would encourage us to see that in chimpanzees, for example, both the ability to create an imaginary playmate or monster, and the ability to track other chimpanzees through the forest by visual signs such as litter and broken foliage, are the ability to imagine what is not present. It is no great leap to the ability, famous in hunter-gatherer peoples, to 'see' game from tracks and other traces. This ability means putting together a world from indirect evidence. This daily-life activity, of course, is the same in science as well (for example, in positing subatomic particles from their bubble tracks) and in religion (for example, in the Argument from Design).

In the search for an explanation of religion, I believe, we have been beguiled by symbolism and misled by a false sense of human uniqueness. As a result, we have forgotten a vital need that we share with other animals: to interpret an ambiguous world and to discover real agents hiding in it. In the course of discovering those real agents, all of us inevitably think we see agents where, in reality, none exist.

References

Allen, C. and M. Bekoff (1997) *Species of Mind: The Philosophy and Biology of Cognitive Ethology*. Cambridge, MA: MIT Press.

Anttonen, V. (1996) 'Rethinking the sacred: the notions of "human body" and "territory" in conceptualizing religion'. In *The Sacred and Its Scholars: Comparative Methodologies for the Study of Primary Religious Data*, 36–64, ed. T. A. Idinopulos and E. A. Yonan. Leiden: Brill.

Anttonen, V. (2000) 'Sacred'. In *Guide to the Study of Religion*, ed. W. Braun and R. T. McCutcheon, 271–82. London: Cassell.

Atran, S. (1994) 'Core domains versus scientific theories: evidence from systematics and Itza-Maya folk biology'. In *Mapping the Mind*, ed. L. A. Hirschfeld and S. A. Gelman, 316–40. New York: Cambridge University Press.

Atran, S. (1995) 'Causal constraints on categories and categorical constraints on biological reasoning across cultures'. In *Causal Cognition: A Multidisciplinary Debate*, ed. D. Sperber, D. Premack and A. J. Premack, 205–33. Oxford: Clarendon Press.

Bacon, F. (1960 (1620)). *The New Organon and Related Writings*, ed. Fulton H. Anderson. New York: Liberal Arts Press.

Barrett, J. (1999) 'Theological correctness: cognitive constraint and the study of religion'. *Method and Theory in the Study of Religion* 11: 325–39.

Barrett, J. (2000) 'Exploring the natural foundations of religion'. *Trends in Cognitive Sciences* 4: 29–24.

Barrett, J. and A. Hankes (Forthcoming) 'Losing our marbles? The attribution of intentional agency to inanimates'.

Barry, A. M. S. (1997) *Visual Intelligence: Perception, Image, and Manipulation in Visual Communication*. Albany: State University of New York Press.

Beck, S. and H. Molish (1967) *Rorschach's Test*, Vol. 2: *A Variety of Personality Pictures*, 2nd edn. New York: Grune & Stratton.

Bekoff, M. (1998) 'Playing with play: what can we learn about cognition, negotiation, and evolution?' In *The Evolution of Mind*, ed. D. Cummins and C. Allen, 162–82. New York and Oxford: Oxford University Press.

Bern, C. and H. A. Herzog, Jr (1994) 'Stimulus control of defensive behaviors of garter snakes (*Thamnophis sirtalis*): effects of eye spots and movement'. *Journal of Comparative Psychology* 108: 353–7.

Berry, D. S. and K. Springer (1993) 'Structure, motion, and preschoolers' perceptions of social causality'. *Ecological Psychology* 5(4): 273–83.

Boyer, P. (1994) *The Naturalness of Religious Ideas: A Cognitive Theory of Religion*. Berkeley: University of California Press.

Boyer, P. (1996) 'What makes anthropomorphism natural: intuitive ontology and cultural representations'. *Journal of the Royal Anthropological Institute* n.s. 2: 1–15.

Burger, J., M. Gochfeld and B. G. Murray, Jr (1991) 'Role of predator eye size in risk perception by basking black iguanas (*Ctenosuara similis*)'. *Animal Behavior* 42: 471–6.

Burkert, W. (1996) *Creation of the Sacred: Tracks of Biology in Early Religions*. Cambridge, MA: Harvard University Press.

Byrne, R. (1995) *The Thinking Ape: Evolutionary Origins of Intelligence*. Oxford: Oxford University Press.

Byrne, R. and A. Whiten (eds) (1988) *Machiavellian Intelligence: Social Expertise and the Evolution of Intellect in Monkeys, Apes, and Humans*. Oxford: Clarendon Press.

Carey, S. (1995) 'On the origin of causal understanding'. In *Causal Cognition: A Multidisciplinary Debate*, ed. D. Sperber, D. Premack and A. J. Premack, 268–302. Oxford: Clarendon Press.

Cheney, D. L. and R. M. Seyfarth (1990) *How Monkeys See the World*. Chicago: University of Chicago Press.

Cherry, J. L. (1992) 'Animism in thought and language'. Unpublished PhD dissertation, University of California.

Cosmides, L. and J. Tooby (1994) 'Origins of domain specificity: the evolution of functional organization'. In *Mapping the Mind*, ed. L. Hirschfeld and S. Gelman, 85–116. Cambridge: Cambridge University Press.

Darwin, C. (1871) *The Descent of Man, and Selection in Relation to Sex*. London: Murray.

Dawkins, R. (1978) *The Selfish Gene*. New York: Oxford University Press.

De Vos, G. A. and L. B. Boyer (1989) *Symbolic Analysis Cross-Culturally*. Berkeley: University of California Press.

Dennett, D. (1987) *The Intentional Stance*. Cambridge, MA: MIT Press.

Dennett, D. (1993 (1991)) *Consciousness Explained*. Harmondsworth: Penguin.

Dennis, W. (1953) 'Animistic thinking among college and university students'. *Scientific Monthly* 76: 247–9.

Durkheim, É. (1915 (1912)) *The Elementary Forms of the Religious Life*. New York: Macmillan.

Evans-Pritchard, E. E. (1965) *Theories of Primitive Religion*. London: Oxford University Press.

Feuerbach, L. (1972) *The Fiery Brook: Selected Writings of Ludwig Feuerbach*, translated with an introduction by Z. Hanfi. Garden City, NY: Anchor.

Freud, S. (1964 (1927)) *The Future of an Illusion*. Garden City, NY: Anchor.

Gallup, G. G., Jr (1971) 'Tonic immobility as a reaction to predation: artificial eyes as a fear stimulus for chickens'. *Bulletin of the Psychonomic Society* 8: 614–16.

Gaskin, J. C. A. (1988) *Hume's Philosophy of Religion*, 2nd edn. Atlantic Highlands, NJ: Humanities Press International.

Geertz, C. (1966) 'Religion as a cultural system'. In *Anthropological Approaches to the Study of Religion*, ed. Michael Banton, 1–46. London: Tavistock.

Gell, A. (1998) *Art and Agency: An Anthropological Theory*. Oxford: Oxford University Press.

Gigenrenzer, G. (1997) 'The modularity of social intelligence'. In *Machiavellian Intelligence*, Vol. 2: *Extensions and Evaluations*, ed. A. Whiten and R. Byrne, 264–88. Cambridge: Cambridge University Press.

Gombrich, E. H. (1973) 'Illusion and art'. In *Illusion in Nature and Art*, ed. Richard Gregory and Ernst Gombrich. London: Duckworth.

Goodall, J. (1972) 'A preliminary report on expressive movements and communication in the Gombe Stream chimpanzees'. In *Primate Patterns*, ed. P. Dolhinow, 25–84. New York: Holt, Rhinehart & Winston.

Goodall, J. (1975) 'The chimpanzee'. In *The Quest for Man*, ed. Vanne Goodall, 131–70. New York: Praeger.

Goodall, J. (1992) *In the Shadow of Man*. Boston: Houghton Mifflin.

Gould, J. L. and C. G. Gould (1994) *The Animal Mind*. New York: Scientific American Library.

Guthrie, S. E. (1980) 'A cognitive theory of religion'. *Current Anthropology* 21(2): 181–203, with *CA* treatment.

Guthrie, S. E. (1988) *A Japanese New Religion: Risshô Kôsei-kai in a Mountain Hamlet*. Ann Arbor: University of Michigan Center for Japanese Studies.

Guthrie, S. E. (1993) *Faces in the Clouds: A New Theory of Religion*. New York and Oxford: Oxford University Press.

Guthrie, S. E. (1996a) 'Theories of religion: review essay on *The Naturalness of Religious Ideas: A Cognitive Theory of Religion* (Pascal Boyer) and *"The Heathen in His Blindness . . ."*: *Asia, the West and the Dynamic of Religion* (S. N. Balagangadhara)'. *American Anthropologist* 98: 162–3.

Guthrie, S. E. (1996b) 'The sacred: a skeptical view'. In *The Sacred and Its Scholars*, ed. T. Idinopulos and E. Yonan, 124–38. Leiden: Brill.

Guthrie, S. E. (1996c) 'Religion: what is it?' *Journal for the Scientific Study of Religion* 35: 412–19.

Guthrie, S. E. (1997a) 'Anthropomorphism: a definition and a theory'. In *Anthropomorphism, Anecdotes, and Animals*, ed. R. W. Mitchell, N. S. Thompson and H. L. Miles, 50–8. Albany: State University of New York Press.

Guthrie, S. E. (1997b) 'The origin of an illusion'. In *Anthropology of Religion: A Handbook*, ed. S. D. Glazier, 489–504. Westport, CT: Greenwood.

Guthrie, S. E. (2000) 'Projection'. In *Guide to the Study of Religion*, ed. Willi Braun and Russell T. McCutcheon, 225–38. London and New York: Cassell.

Guthrie, S. E. (2001) 'Why gods? A cognitive theory'. In *Religion in Mind*, ed. Jensine Andresen, 94–111. Cambridge: Cambridge University Press.

Guthrie, S. E. (Forthcoming) 'Anthropomorphism'. In *Encyclopaedia Britannica*.

Hallowell, A. I. (1960) 'Ojibwa ontology, behavior, and world view'. In *Culture in History: Essays in Honor of Paul Radin*, ed. S. Diamond, 20–52. New York: Columbia University Press.

Harris, P. C. (1994) 'Thinking by children and scientists: false analogies and neglected similarities'. In *Mapping the Mind*, ed. L. A. Hirschfeld and S. Gelman, 294–315. Cambridge and New York: Cambridge University Press.

Hauser, M. and S. Carey (1998) 'Building a cognitive creature from a set of primitives: evolutionary and developmental insights'. In *The Evolution of Mind*, ed. D. D. Cummins and C. Allen, 512–106. New York: Oxford University Press.

Hinton, H. E. (1973) 'Natural deception'. In *Illusion in Art and Nature*, ed. R. Gregory and E. Gombrich. London: Gerald Duckworth.

Horton, R. (1960) 'A definition of religion, and its uses'. *Journal of the Royal Anthropological Institute* 90: 201–26.

Horton, R. (1993) *Patterns of Thought in Africa and the West: Essays on Magic, Science, and Religion*. Cambridge: Cambridge University Press.

Hume, D. (1957 (1757)) *The Natural History of Religion*, ed. H. E. Root. Stanford: Stanford University Press.

Hume, D. (1932) *The Letters of David Hume*, 2 vols, ed. J. Y. T. Greig. Oxford: Clarendon Press.

Inagaki, K. (1989) 'Developmental shift in biological inference processes: from similarity-based to category-based attribution'. *Human Development* 32: 79–87.

Inagaki, K. and G. Hatano (1987) 'Young children's spontaneous personification as analogy'. *Child Development* 58: 1013–20.

Kahneman, D. and A. Tversky (1982) 'Variants of uncertainty'. In *Judgment under Uncertainty: Heuristics and Biases*, ed. D. Kahneman, P. Slovic and A. Tversky. Cambridge: Cambridge University Press.

Kalish, C. W. (1996) 'Preschoolers' understanding of germs as invisible mechanisms'. *Cognitive Development* 11: 83–106.

Keil, F. C. (1994) 'The birth and nurturance of concepts by domains: the origins of concepts of living things'. In *Mapping the Mind*, ed. L. A. Hirschfeld and S. A. Gelman, 234–54. Cambridge: Cambridge University Press.

Kelemen, D. (1999) 'Beliefs about purpose: on the origins of teleological thought'. In *The Descent of Mind: Psychological Perspectives on Hominid Evolution*, ed. M. C. Corballis and S. E. G. Lea, 278–94. Oxford: Oxford University Press.

Kennedy, J. S. (1992) *The New Anthropomorphism*. Cambridge: Cambridge University Press.

Lakoff, G. and M. Johnson (1999) *Philosophy in the Flesh: The Embodied Mind and Its Challenge to Western Thought*. New York: Basic Books.

Lawson, E. T. and R. N. McCauley (1990) *Rethinking Religion*. Cambridge: Cambridge University Press.

Lessa, W. A. and E. Z. Vogt (eds) (1970) *Reader in Comparative Religion: An Anthropological Approach*. New York: Harper & Row.

Lewis, M. and C. Saarni (eds) (1993) *Lying and Deception in Everyday Life*. New York: Guilford Press.

Malinowski, B. (1948) *Magic, Science and Religion, and Other Essays*. Boston: Beacon.

McCutcheon, R. T. (1997) *Manufacturing Religion: The Discourse on Sui Generis Religion and the Politics of Nostalgia*. New York: Oxford University Press.

Menzel, C. R. (1997) 'Primates' knowledge of their natural habitat: as indicated in foraging'. In *Machiavellian Intelligence*, Vol. 2: *Extensions and Evaluations*, ed. A. Whiten and R. W. Byrne, 207–39. Cambridge: Cambridge University Press.

Miklosi, A., G. Berzsenyi, P. Pongracz, and V. Csanyi (1995) 'The ontogeny of antipredation behaviour in paradise fish larvae (*Macro porlus opercularis*): the recognition of eyespots'. *Ethology* 100: 284.

Miles, H. L. W. (1993) 'Language and the orangutan: the old "person" of the forest'. In *The Great Ape Project: Equality Beyond Humanity*, ed. P. Cavalieri and P. Singer, 42–57. New York: St Martin's Press.

Miller, G. F. (1997) 'Protean primates: the evolution of adaptive unpredictability in competition and courtship'. In *Machiavellian Intelligence*, vol. ii: *Extensions and Evaluations*, ed. A. Whiten and R. W. Byrne, 312–40. Cambridge: Cambridge University Press.

Mitchell, R. W. (1993) 'Animals as liars: the human face of nonhuman duplicity'. In *Lying and Deception in Everyday Life*, ed. M. Lewis and C. Saarni, 59–89. New York: Guilford Press.

Mitchell, R. W. and N. S. Thompson (1986) *Deception: Perspectives on Human and Nonhuman Deceit*. New York: SUNY Press.

Mitchell, R. W., N. S. Thompson and H. L. Miles (eds) (1997) *Anthropomorphism, Anecdotes, and Animals*. Albany: SUNY Press.

Mithen, S. (1999) 'Symbolism and the supernatural'. In *The Evolution of Culture: An Interdisciplinary View*, ed. R. Dunbar, C. Knight and C. Power, 147–69. New Brunswick, NJ: Rutgers University Press.

Morton, J. and M. Johnson (1991) 'The perception of facial structure in infancy'. In *The Perception of Structure: Essays in Honor of Wendell R. Garner*, ed. G. R. Lockhead and J. R. Pomerantz, 317–25. Washington, DC: American Psychological Association.

Nietzsche, F. (1966) *Werke in Drei Bänden*, Vol. 3, ed. von K. Schlecher. Munich: Carl Hanser.

Ochiai, M. (1989) 'The role of knowledge in the development of the life concept'. *Human Development* 32: 72–8.

Owen, D. (1980) *Camouflage and Mimicry*. Chicago: University of Chicago Press.

Pals, D. L. (1996) *Seven Theories of Religion*. Oxford: Oxford University Press.

Piaget, J. (1929) *The Child's Conception of the World*. London: Routledge and Kegan Paul.

Pinker, S. (1997) *How the Mind Works*. New York: Norton.

Poulin-Dubois, D. and G. Héroux (1994) 'Movement and children's attributions of life properties'. *International Journal of Behavioral Development* 17: 329–47.

Quiatt, D. and V. Reynolds (1993) *Primate Behavior: Information, Social Knowledge, and the Evolution of Culture*. New York: Cambridge University Press.

Rappaport, R. (1999) *Ritual and Religion in the Making of Humanity*. Cambridge: Cambridge University Press.

Richards, D. D. and R. S. Siegler (1986) 'Children's understandings of attributes of life'. *Journal of Experimental Child Psychology* 42: 1–22.

Ristau, C. A. (1998) 'Cognitive ethology: the minds of children and animals'. In *The Evolution of Mind*, ed. D. D. Cummins and C. Allen, 127–61. New York: Oxford University Press.

Saler, B. (1977) 'Supernatural as a Western category'. *Ethos* 5: 31–53.

Saler, B. (1993) *Conceptualizing Religion: Immanent Anthropologists, Transcendent Natives, and Unbounded Categories*. Leiden: Brill.

Saler, B. (1999) 'Biology and religion: on establishing a problematic'. *Method and Theory in the Study of Religion* 11: 386–94.

Savage-Rumbaugh, S. and K. McDonald (1988) 'Deception and social manipulation in symbol-using apes'. In *Machiavellian Intelligence: Social Expertise and the Evolution of Intellect in Monkeys, Apes, and Humans*, ed. R. W. Byrne and A. Whiten, 224–37. Oxford: Clarendon Press.

Scaife, M. (1976) 'The response to eye-like shapes by birds', parts I and II. *Animal Behavior* 24: 195–206.

Sheehan, N. W., D. E. Papalia-Finlay and F. H. Hooper (1980–1) 'The nature of the life concept across the life-span'. *International Journal of Aging and Human Development* 12: 1–13.

Sperber, D. (1994) 'The modularity of thought and the epidemiology of representations'. In *Mapping the Mind*, ed. L. A. Hirschfeld and S. A. Gelman, 39–67. New York: Cambridge University Press.

Sperber, D. (1996) *Explaining Culture: A Naturalistic Approach*. Oxford: Blackwell.

Spinoza, B. de (1955) *The Chief Works of Benedict de Spinoza: On the Improvement of the Understanding; The Ethics; Correspondence*, translated with an introduction by R. H. M. Elwes. New York: Dover.

Stark, R. and W. S. Bainbridge (1987) *A Theory of Religion*, Toronto Studies in Religion, 2. New York: Lang.

Talmy, L. (1995) 'Discussion'. In *Causal Cognition: A Multidisciplinary Debate*, ed. D. Sperber, D. Premack and A. J. Premack, 647–8. Oxford: Clarendon Press.

Tamir, P. and A. Zohar (1991) 'Anthropomorphism and teleology in reasoning about biological phenomena'. *Science Education* 75(1): 57–67.

Thomas, E. M. (1993) *The Hidden Life of Dogs*. Boston: Houghton Mifflin.

Thompson, S. (1955) *Motif-Index of Folk-Literature*, revised and enlarged edition. Bloomington, IN: Indiana University Press.

Turner, V. (1967) *The Forest of Symbols*. Ithaca: Cornell University Press.

Tylor, E. B. (1871) *Primitive Culture: Researches into the Development of Mythology, Philosophy, Religion, Language, Art, and Custom*. London: John Murray.

Uexküll, J. von (1992 (1934)) 'A stroll through the worlds of animals and men: a picture book of invisible worlds'. *Semiotica* 89: 319–91.

Wallace, A. F. C. (1966) *Religion: An Anthropological View*. New York: Random House.

Wenegrat, B. (1990) *The Divine Archetype: The Sociobiology and Psychology of Religion*. Lexington, MA: Lexington Books.

Whiten, A. and R. Byrne (eds) (1997) *Machiavellian Intelligence*, vol. 2: *Extensions and Evaluations*. Cambridge: Cambridge University Press.

Whiten, A., J. Goodall, W. C. McGrew, T. Nishida, V. Reynolds, Y. Sugiyama, C. E. G. Tutin, R. W. Wrangham and C. Boesch (1999) 'Cultures in chimpanzees'. *Nature* 399: 682–5.

4 Why Do Gods and Spirits Matter at All?

PASCAL BOYER

The world over, people's supernatural repertoire includes a variety of concepts of imagined artefacts, animals, persons and plants: concepts of floating islands, of mountains that digest food or have blood circulation, of trees that listen, of animals that change species or of people who can disappear at will. These are found in folktales, anecdotes, myths, dreams and religious ritual and correspond to a small 'catalogue' of templates for supernatural concepts (Boyer 1994a; 2000). We also find that a particular sub-set of these concepts is associated with more serious commitment, strong emotions, important rituals and/or moral understandings. An association between a supernatural concept and one or several of these social effects is our main intuitive criterion for what is 'religious' (Saler 1993; see also Pyysiäinen, Chapter 6 this volume).

Some supernatural concepts matter much more than others. Whether Puss-in-Boots did run faster than the wind or not is of no great moment, but whether the ancestors did find out that someone sacrificed to them certainly is. The question is, why do *some* concepts of imagined entities and agents rather than others matter to people?

There would seem to be a simple explanation. People *believe* in the real existence of their gods, spirits and ancestors, whereas Puss-in-Boots and the Bogeyman are all *fiction*. I do not think there is great merit in this argument, as it puts the conclusive cart before the explanatory horses. What we need to explain is why and how some concepts for supernatural agencies become sufficiently plausible to be construed as at least possibly real. There is nothing obvious about that. Anthropologists and historians know of many examples of themes and concepts migrating from religion to fiction or the other way around. Whether or not some theme is construed as fiction depends on people's assumptions about it, and these assumptions are precisely what we should explain, not take for granted.

The main strategy in the study of religion so far has been to just *ask* people why some concepts of imagined entities (agents in particular) matter to them. This is of course an indispensable first step, but we cannot stop there. It is not just that people's explanations may be vague and idiosyncratic (though they are). It is also because we have no good reason to assume that people have much access to the cognitive machinery that makes some concepts more salient than others. People after all have no access to the way their brains turn two-dimensional retinal images into three-dimensional visual representations. People can sense the difference between two sentences ('Who did you see me with?' and 'Who did you see me and?') without being able to explain why one of them is ungrammatical. The same point applies to concepts. Some notions are easier to acquire than others, some conceptual associations are better recalled, and some create stronger emotional effects. All this depends on processes largely beyond conscious access, in the same way as the workings of the visual cortex.

By the same token, we often assume that the reason why some religious concepts are important must be, precisely, a *reason*, that is, a set of facts that make sense of the concepts' import. When we say, 'People worry about the ancestors' reactions because [they believe] the ancestors are powerful,' we put these two facts together (a worry about ancestors, a belief in their power) because one seems to *make sense* in the context of the other. This again may be a good first step, but we must remember that many aspects of cognitive processing are explained by *causes* rather than *reasons*, that is, by functional processes that do not always make sense. We all have a very good memory for faces and a much poorer one for names. There is an explanation for that. But it is not that it makes more sense to recall faces than names. It is just the way human memory works.

Finally, we sometimes assume that there must be *one* main reason or cause for the salience and importance of religious concepts. The domain of religion is one where 'magic bullet' explanations are rife. People are said to have religious concepts because they want to explain the world, to escape the anguish of mortality, to explain the existence of evil, to account for misfortune, to keep society in order, or because they are superstitious, irrational or prone to cognitive illusions. (I only cite the more serious ones – there is no shortage of cranky explanations of religion.) It seems, however, rather less than plausible that the salience of religious notions (of gods, ancestors, witches, spirits and the like) can be explained by any one of these magic bullets (see discussion in Boyer 2001). It is not that such explanations are overly simple and reductionist, but that recurrent cultural phenomena are the outcome of a *selection* process. In the course of cultural transmission and individual rumination, a great many variants of religious concepts and associations with other concepts are constantly created. Not all survive in individual memory or communication, far from it. The mental representations we call 'religious concepts' happen to be the few survivors in this constant mutation and selection process. This suggests that they probably satisfy adaptive criteria on a *number* of different selective fronts. To take a distant analogy, there are not that many different body-plans in animals. One could say that the body-plans we find are efficient for locomotion, or for energy-exchanges with the environment, or for reproduction. It is quite likely that the only body-plans we find in nature are roughly satisfactory on all these fronts, otherwise they would have been selected out.

In the following pages I use various kinds of evidence to suggest how different *mental systems* are involved in the selection of religious concepts. The human mind is not a single system designed to produce an accurate representation of the world. Rather, it consists of multiple systems geared to representing and predicting various parts of the environment, or guiding action in different domains according to different principles. None of these evolved systems is about religion. But some of them may be activated, in the context of representing religious agents, in such a way that concepts of such agents have a high probability of transmission. So examining which systems are activated in this way, and how they fashion different aspects of viable cultural concepts, should explain not just why we have these religious notions but also why we do not have different ones, in other words it should explain the recurrent features of such concepts.

Here is a variety of ways in which religious concepts, by activating various mental systems, become easily acquired and transmitted, as well as salient and plausible:

1. They include minimal violations of domain-level conceptual expectations. (This is true of all supernatural concepts, not just religious ones.)
2. They activate intuitions about agency developed in the context of predation.
3. They activate social interaction systems (our 'social mind' systems) in a particular way.

4. They are parasitic upon moral intuitions that would be there, religion or not.
5. They are associated with a specific way of construing misfortune.

These are by no means the only factors involved in the acquisition and transmission of religion. But they constitute a first topography of the relevant mental activity. A set of concepts that satisfy constraints (1–5) would certainly gain great salience and a high probability of transmission. But only very few concepts are such that acquiring and representing them will have such effects.

Condition (1) need not detain us too long here, as it has been described extensively elsewhere (Barrett 2000; Boyer 1994b) and applies to a domain (supernatural imagination) that is wider than religion as commonly understood. It is, however, necessary to keep in mind that religious concepts are supernatural concepts, that they gain minimal salience by including a particular kind of expectation-violation. There are, to simplify matters a great deal, two major levels of conceptual information in semantic memory. One is that of *kind-concepts*, notions such as 'table' and 'tiger' and 'tarmac' and 'tree'. The other consists of *domain-concepts*, such as 'intentional agent', 'man-made object', 'living thing'. Most of the information associated with these broader concepts comes in the format, not of declared statements (e.g. 'living things grow with age') but of intuitive expectations and inferences. Without being aware of it, one expects living things to grow, intentional agents to have goals and their behaviour to be caused by those goals, the structure of artefacts to be explained by a function and the latter by a designer's intention.

Now supernatural concepts describe limited violations of such expectations: a tree is said to listen to people's conversations, a statue is said to bleed on particular occasions, a person is described as being in several places at once, another as going through walls, etc. Note that such concepts violate *domain-level* and not kind-level expectations. A listening tree goes against expectations not because trees in particular are usually silent but because plants are assumed to be non-intentional. Also, note that the violations are *limited*, keeping in place all the (non-violated) default assumptions that usually accompany a given domain-concept. A listening tree is still assumed to grow like all plants, ghosts that go through walls still perceive and represent their environment like other intentional agents. Indeed, these non-violated assumptions provide an indispensable grounding for people's inferences about supernatural entities and agents (Barrett and Keil 1996; Boyer 1994b).

71

This twofold condition – (a) include a violation of domain-level intuitions and (b) allow inferences from relevant non-violated assumptions – is sufficient to account for the recurrent features of supernatural concepts the world over. That is, the subject-matter of fantastic imagination, dreams, folk-tales and religion generally revolves around a small catalogue of concepts built in this way (Boyer 1994b). The *concepts* may be very different from one place to another, but the *templates* are few, consisting of a combination of one particular domain-concept and one particular violation (e.g. 'intentional agent' and 'physical solidity' for the 'ghost' concept). Also, experimental work in different cultures suggests that concepts built in this way are more likely to be recalled than either predictable conceptual associations, or oddities constructed by violating kind-level associations. A table made of sausages (violation of kind-level expectations) may be quite striking, but in the end is not quite as easily acquired and recalled as a table that understands conversations (violation of domain-level expectations). This effect seems to work in fairly similar ways in different cultural environments (Barrett 1998; Boyer and Ramble 2001).

Naturally, religious concepts are a sub-set of supernatural notions, with special additional features. But it is worth insisting on the fact that they belong to this broader domain, as this explains their mode of acquisition. In supernatural concepts, most of the relevant information associated with a particular notion is given by domain-level intuitions. In other words, it is spontaneously assumed to be true in the absence of contrary information. This is why no one in the world needs to be told that ghosts see what happens when it happens, or that gods who want some result will try to do what it takes to achieve it: such inferences are given for free by our specialized mental systems (intuitive psychology in this case). In religion as in other supernatural domains, the violations are made clear to people, but the rest is inferred. Concepts that are both salient (because of the violation) and cheaply transmitted (because of spontaneous inferences) are optimal from the viewpoint of cultural transmission.

Religious notions are special in that they satisfy, not just this minimal violation requirement, but also (some or all of) conditions (2–5), that is, they activate a variety of mental systems that are not usually activated by mere supernatural fantasy. In the following pages I will outline the ways in which this occurs, that is, how religious concepts are associated with intuitions about agency, about social interaction, about moral understandings and about dead bodies.

Agency: projection, predation and social interaction

Although there are many templates for supernatural concepts, the ones that really matter to people are invariably *person-like*. As Lawson and McCauley point out, a concept of agency is the foundation of religious concepts the world over, and many apparently specific features of religious behaviour result from activating cognitive resources for thinking about agents (Lawson and McCauley 1990). Now the fact that religious agents are, precisely, agents is not in itself a distinguishing mark, since most fiction is about persons too. The agents postulated in religious representations are somewhat different, and this accounts for the intuition that they are really around. To explain this, we must first understand in what particular way religious agents like gods and spirits are like persons.

There is certainly a tendency in the human imagination to project human-like and person-like features onto non-human or non-person-like aspects of the environment. Such representations are attention-grabbing or enjoyable; they are certainly found in many aspects of religious agency, as Stewart Guthrie has demonstrated (see Guthrie 1993; this volume). As Guthrie points out, such projections do not stem from an urge to make various situations or occurrences more familiar or more reassuring (which is seldom the result anyway) but to afford *richer inferences* about them. Projections of human-like features add complexity to the world, which is why they are easily created and transmitted by human minds (Guthrie 1993).

This constant search for relevant inferences may well be the reason why the 'anthropomorphism' of religious concepts is in fact rather selective. That is, the domain of intuitions and inferences that is projected is *intentional agency*, more frequently and more consistently than any other domain of human characteristics. Besides, intuitions concerning intentional agency are activated not just when interacting with humans, but also in our dealings with animals (Boyer 1996). This is why one can postulate that there is an intentional agent, and run various inferences about what it can perceive, what its next reactions might be, etc., without making it a human person in other respects (Barrett 2000).

This is consistent with developmental and other cognitive evidence concerning the complex intentional psychology or 'theory of mind' present in all normal human minds. This 'mind-reading' system is geared to interpreting other agents' (or one's own) behaviour, as well as figuring out what their goals, beliefs, intentions, memories and inferences are. Rudimentary forms of such mind-reading capacities appear very early in development (see for instance Meltzoff 1999), and develop in fairly similar forms in normal children. Their working is out of reach of conscious inspection; only the outcome of their computations is conscious.

There are two distinct 'origin scenarios' for our capacity to understand intentional agency, to create representations of other agents' behaviour, beliefs and intentions. They can be called the *social interaction* explanation and the *predation* explanation respectively.

A widely accepted evolutionary scenario is that we (higher primates) evolved more and more complex intentional psychology systems to deal with social interaction. Having larger groups, more stable interaction, and more efficient co-ordination with other agents all bring out significant adaptive benefits for the individual. But they all require finer and finer grained descriptions of others' mental states and behaviour. This is why we find, early developed in most humans, a hypertrophied 'theory of mind' that tracks the objects of other people's attention, computes their states of minds, and predicts their behaviour (Whiten 1991; Povinelli and Preuss 1995; Meltzoff 1999).

Another possible account is that at least some aspects of our Theory of Mind capacities evolved in the context of predator–prey interaction (Barrett 1999). A heightened capacity to remain undetected by either predator or prey, as well as a better sense of how these other animals detect us, are of obvious adaptive significance. They are present in primates and especially in humans, who made up for an unimpressive physique by simply being better at figuring out what other animals will do next; hence our record as efficient hunters. In particular, hunting and predator-avoidance become much better when they are more flexible, that is, informed by details about the situation at hand, so that one does not react to all predators or prey in the same way. Indeed, some primatologists have speculated that joint detection of predators may have been the primary context for the evolution of agency-concepts (Van Schaik et al. 1983). In the archaeological record, changes towards more flexible hunting patterns in modern humans suggest a richer, more intentional representation of the hunted animal's psychology (Mithen 1996).

These accounts are not necessarily incompatible, since they may be relevant to different sub-systems involved in the representation of agency. So far, I have followed the classical, slightly oversimplified description of intuitive psychology as a single system dedicated to the intentional description of behaviour. But it is very likely that several, relatively autonomous systems are engaged in such performance. That is, there may be a specialized system detecting goals from motion, while another one only deals with emotional cues on the faces of conspecifics, another is busy representing other agents' beliefs, another detects their presence on the basis of unexpected noises, etc. There is mounting experimental and clinical evidence for this fractionation of Theory of Mind. A disorder such as autism stems from an inability to represent other people's thoughts, but it does not seem to impair primitive animacy-detection (realizing that some objects in the environment are goal-directed) or gaze-following (Baron-Cohen 1995). Williams' syndrome children are very good at detecting, following and displaying emotional cues relevant to social interaction, although they often have a very poor understanding of the beliefs and intentions that motivate behaviour (Tager-Flusberg and Sullivan 2000). In a similar way, chimpanzees may pay attention to gaze-direction without associating it with specific intentions, showing that these two capacities are separable (Povinelli and Eddy 1996).

Now, if there are several distinct Theory of Mind components, there may be different ways in which human minds can postulate agents without much evidence. Indeed, I would argue that supernatural agents are made salient and relevant to human minds by two distinct routes, each of which contributes a particular aspect of these imagined agents. The first route is through those systems we developed in predator–prey interaction; the second is through those systems that are especially dedicated to social interaction.

As Guthrie has emphasized, detecting agents around, often on the basis of scant or unreliable evidence, is a hallmark of human minds. When we see branches moving in a tree or when we hear an unexpected sound behind us, we immediately infer that some *agent* (animal or human) is the cause of this perceptually salient event, and that some goal of that agent explains its behaviour. Note that the systems that detect agency do not need much solid evidence. On the contrary, they 'jump to conclusions', that is, give us the intuition that an agent is around, in many contexts where other interpretations (the wind pushed the foliage, a branch just fell off a tree) are equally plausible. There are many everyday situations where we detect agency and then abandon this interpretation, once we realize there was no agent around. But that is the important point: we spontaneously create these interpretations anyway. For Justin Barrett, there are important evolutionary reasons why we (as well as other animals) should have 'Hyper-Active Agent Detection'. In a species evolved to deal with both predators and prey, the expense of false positives (seeing agents where there are none) is minimal, if we can abandon these misguided intuitions quickly. By contrast, the cost of not detecting agents when they are actually around (either predator or prey) could be very high. So our cognitive systems work on a 'better safe than sorry' principle that leads to hyper-sensitive agent detection (Barrett 2000).

According to this evolutionary interpretation, predation-related capacities not only make it easy to detect agents when there is little or no evidence for their presence, but also inform some of their features. For one thing, our agent-detection systems trigger emotional arousal in a way that is quite automatic. That is, these systems lead us intuitively to assume not just that there are agents around, but that this presence may have rather dramatic consequences for us. This is a feature that directly translates into supernatural imagination. People may well imagine all sorts of supernatural agents that are irrelevant to their well-being (elves, goblins and suchlike); but the ones whose traces people think they have *seen* are generally of great emotional import. Second, agents are postulated, on the basis not of direct perception of their presence, but of indirect cues. As Barrett points out, what people claim to perceive are more often 'traces in the grass' than 'faces in the clouds'. A sudden noise, an unexplained shadow, a broken twig or someone's sudden death are explained as indices of the spirits' presence; this is far more frequent than a direct encounter with those agents. This feature too makes much more sense once we understand the contribution of predation-related mental systems, which after all are by design concerned with the interpretation of indirect cues and fragmentary signals as evidence for some agent's presence.

This evolutionary account makes good sense, although association with predation-related intuitions is probably only *part* of what makes religious concepts salient. In particular, we need additional factors to explain what makes people's notions of supernatural agents so stable and plausible, and why they are so strongly informed by what other people say. To take the first aspect, religious concepts are much less transient than experiences of 'hyper-active agent detection', that is, of interpreting some noise or movement as the presence of an agent. The latter are often discarded as mistakes. As I said above, it makes sense to 'over-detect' agents only if you can quickly discard false positives, otherwise you would spend all your time recoiling in fear, which is certainly not adaptive. But thoughts about gods and spirits are not like that. These are *stable* concepts, in the sense that people have them stored in memory, reactivate them periodically and assume that these agents are a permanent fixture in their environment. Now consider the sources of information that shape people's religious concepts. True, having experiences of elusive shadows and sounds probably strengthens the *general* notion that there may be unseen agents around. However, it is also striking that the details of such representations are generally derived, not from what one has experienced (hyper-active detection) but from what others have said. People take their information about the features of ghosts and spirits and gods, to an overwhelming extent, from socially transmitted information, not from direct experience. Conversely, intrinsically vague experiences are seen through the conceptual lenses provided by what others said about the gods and spirits. To sum up, people know vastly more about gods and spirits from listening to other people than from encountering these mysterious agents.

I insist on this seemingly obvious point because it introduces yet another way in which religious concepts activate mental systems. Information about gods and spirits mainly comes from other people. It is also connected in a crucial way to our representations of what other people believe and want. That is, the way people construe religious agents is informed by mental systems geared to describing and managing interaction with other human agents.

Supernatural agents and strategic information

In another paper (Boyer 2000) I emphasized the connections between representations of other people and representations of possible supernatural agents. A good part of the information concerning a situation of social interaction is processed by specialized *social mind systems*. An important part of our mental architecture consists of inference systems that deal with social interaction. For instance, human beings are very good at:

1. monitoring social exchange, that is, finding out who is co-operating with whom, under what circumstances, as well as punishing cheaters and avoiding people who fail to punish cheaters (Boyd and Richerson 1992; Cosmides and Tooby 1992);
2. representing other people's personalities, especially in terms of reliability, on the basis of indirect but emotionally charged cues (Bacharach and Gambetta 1999; Frank 1988);
3. building and maintaining social hierarchies, based either explicitly

on resources or on indirect, seemingly arbitrary criteria for dominance (Sidanius and Pratto 1999);
4. building coalitions, that is, stable co-operation networks where
benefits are shared, the cost of others defecting is high, and
measures are taken to pre-empt it (Tooby and Cosmides 1996);
5. gossiping, that is, taking pleasure at receiving or imparting information on adaptively significant domains (sex, resources, hierarchy) about and with other members of one's social network
(Gambetta 1994);

and many other such social interaction tasks. It is quite likely that such
capacities are supported by a variety of functional systems, so that one
does not so much have a 'social mind' as social mind capacities.

People engaged in a particular situation of social interaction have a
representation of that situation, associated with representations of all
sorts of background details. A subset of that information is such that it
activates social mind systems. That I drive a red car may be non-
strategic information (for most people in most contexts) but also
strategic (for instance in a social setting where that indexes wealth or
arrogance or hipness). That you saw a particular person yesterday may
be non-strategic for me, or may become strategic information if I
suspect that the two of you are in some conspiracy. So whether some
piece of information is strategic or not is in the eye of the beholder. To
say that information is strategic does not mean that it is important.
That two of my colleagues had an affair ten years ago is not really of
great importance to me, but it is strategic information in the precise
sense used here. To sum up, then, given a particular situation, there
will be in the minds of the participants some information that we call
strategic because it is handled by their social mind systems.

Now all standard social interaction, from a young age, is based on a
principle of *imperfect access*: that is, the assumption that other people
(and we ourselves) have only partial access to the strategic information
pertinent to a particular situation. By contrast, supernatural agents
seem to be implicitly construed as *perfect access* agents. A tacit assumption is that, given a situation x, and given some information about it
that is strategic, the supernatural agent has access to it. I must
emphasize a few points that may be ambiguous in the above
formulation:

1. This assumption often remains tacit. You do not need to represent an explicit principle, such as 'The ancestors have access to

what matters to our social mind systems,' any more than we need to represent a principle of the form 'Objects that are bounced against a wall will bounce at an angle equal to the angle of the collisions.

2. The assumption does not require that people represent what the strategic information in question amounts to. You can represent that 'if there is strategic information about this situation, the ancestors know it' without having any description of the strategic information in question. (In the same way, your inferences work on the assumption that there is something in giraffes that makes them grow differently from horses, and that it is innate in giraffes, without knowing or indeed having any representation of what this 'something' is.)

To illustrate this and some further arguments about concepts of gods and spirits, let me make use of Roger Keesing's vivid description of the spirit-ancestor (*adalo*) in Kwaio religion (Keesing 1982). The Kwaio live in the Solomon Islands; most of their religious activities, as described by the anthropologist Roger Keesing, involve interacting with ancestors, especially the spirits of deceased members of their own clans, as well as more dangerous wild spirits. Interaction with these *adalo* (the term denotes both wild spirits and ancestors) is a constant feature of Kwaio life. People frequently pray to the dead or offer them sacrifices of pigs or simply talk to them. Also, people 'meet' the ancestors in dreams. Most people are particularly familiar with and fond of one particular *adalo*, generally the spirit of a close relative, and maintain frequent contact with that spirit.

Now Kwaio people need not be told that the spirits can perceive what happens, or that they can make a difference between their wishes and reality. People are just told that for instance 'the spirits are unhappy because we failed to sacrifice a pig to them'. To make sense of that utterance one must activate one's intuitive-psychology inference systems. In the same way, no one is ever told that 'the gods (or spirits or ancestors) have access to whatever is strategic in any particular situation'. What is made explicit is most often a vague assumption that the spirits or the gods simply know more than we do. But it seems that people in fact assume something much more specific, namely that the gods and spirits have access to *strategic* information (as defined here) rather than information in general.

Kwaio people's statements about their ancestors highlight this. At first sight, what they say would seem to confirm that ancestors simply know everything: 'The *adalo* see the slightest small things. Nothing is hidden from the *adalo*. It would be hidden from us [living people, but not from them]' or again 'an *adalo* has unlimited vision'. But when people illustrate these statements, notice how they immediately move from 'agents who know more' to the much more specific 'agents who know more about what is strategic': 'An *adalo* has unlimited vision . . . something happens in secret and [the *adalo*] will see it; [if] someone urinates, someone menstruates [NB, in improper places: doing this is an insult to the ancestors] and tries to hide it, . . . the *adalo* will see it.'

In other words, although you can say that the *adalo* in general see what humans cannot see, what *first* comes to mind is that they can detect behaviours that would have consequences for social interaction: someone who has polluted a particular place puts others in danger and should perform the appropriate purification rites. Whether someone did violate these rules or not is clearly strategic information. When people represent possible violations, this activates their inference systems for social interaction. For them, it also goes without saying that it is *that* particular kind of information that the *adalo* have access to. It may be hidden from people (this is the 'imperfect access principle': people's access to strategic information is not guaranteed) but not from supernatural agents (they have full access). People are told that 'Someone urinates in a house; we humans cannot see it; but that makes the *adalo* very angry,' or some other statement of that kind. Interpreting such statements requires that the *adalo* (or whatever supernatural agent people in your group talk about) have access to strategic information.

The same remark would apply to agents (like the Christian God) described by theologians and other religious specialists as omniscient. Most believers would readily assent to statements such as 'God knows everything' or 'God sees everything.' This, however, does not mean that the religious agent is *literally* assumed to represent every aspect of every situation in the world. In people's conversations and trains of thought concerning God, it would seem that such statements as 'I bought broccoli *and God knows about it*' are somehow less frequent and salient than thoughts like 'He lied to her *and God knows it*' or 'I did my best *and God knows it*.' In other words, if something counts as strategic information, in the precise sense used here, it is more easily and naturally included in thoughts about God's thoughts.

In detailed experimental work, Justin Barrett has shown that people's explicit notions of an omniscient God are combined with an intuitive understanding of God as having a human-like mind (Barrett and Keil 1996). A person may (explicitly) declare that the gods see and hear everything, yet show them an offering or say a prayer out loud. The assumption of full access to strategic information is just another aspect of this discrepancy between official, and explicitly entertained, descriptions of supernatural agents, and the intuitive assumptions activated when thinking about them. Now why is the full-access expectation so important? I would claim that it changes the way one considers a situation, and this has effects in several domains. One of them is the construal of *moral understandings*, the other is the possible link between religious agents and *misfortune*.

Moral intuitions and full-access agents

A consideration of the cognitive process involved in representing religious agents can help us discard a widespread but misleading account of religious morality. In this account, people are for some reason convinced of the reality of some supernatural agents; these are described as particularly anxious that people should follow particular moral rules; so people follow these precepts, often against their inclination. Against this, it seems that moral intuitions and understandings develop in all human beings because of specialized, early-developed mental capacities connected with social interaction. This in turn creates all sorts of moral intuitions about possible courses of action. The intuitions do not require concepts of supernatural agents, but if there are such concepts around, moral intuitions will be associated with them. In other words, religious concepts are in part parasitic upon moral understandings.

To understand how this is the case, we must first examine the various ways in which people establish a link between their supernatural concepts and their moral understandings. I will call these three connections the *legislator, exemplar* and *interested party* models.

In the 'gods as legislators' model, there are moral principles because the gods or ancestors themselves have decided what these norms would be. Several world-religions include lists of prohibitions and prescriptions, of varying length, attributed to some direct communication from the supernatural legislature.

In the 'exemplar' model, some supernatural agents provide a model to follow. Saints or holy people are both different enough from common folk so that they approach an ideal, and close enough so their behaviour can serve as a model. This is the way people conceive of individuals with supernatural qualities, such as Gautama, Muhammad or the many Christian and Muslim saints, as also the miraculous rabbis of Judaism.

Supernatural agents are also represented as 'interested parties' in moral choices. This means that the gods or the ancestors are not indifferent to what people do, and this is why we must act in particular ways or refrain from certain courses of action. Interaction with the Kwaio ancestors is of this kind. But the 'interested parties' model is much more general than that. We find it in many 'world-religions', whether or not the theologians find it acceptable. Most Christians entertain this notion that every single one of their moral choices is relevant to their personal connection to God. That is, God not only gave laws and principles but also pays attention to what people do. For obvious reasons, the notion that supernatural agents are interested parties is generally associated with the idea that the gods or spirits are powerful and that it is within their capacities to inflict all sorts of calamities upon people – or help them prosper – depending on their behaviour.

In people's actual reasoning about particular situations, in the practical business of judging people's behaviour and choosing a course of action, the 'interested party' model is largely dominant. As far as anthropologists know, people in most places conceive of some supernatural agents as having some interest in their decisions. This can take all sorts of forms. Christians for instance consider that God expects some particular kinds of behaviour and will react to departures from the norm. People who interact with their ancestors, like the Kwaio, have a much less precise description of what the ancestors want, but it is part of their everyday concerns that the *adalo* are watching them. In either case, people do not really represent why the ancestors or gods would want to sanction people's behaviour. It is just assumed that they will.

When I say that this way of thinking about morality is 'dominant', I simply mean that it is constantly activated and generally implicit. It is the most natural way people think of the connection between powerful agents and their own behaviour. The 'legislator' and 'model' representations both have their limits. Explicit moral codes are often too abstract to provide definite judgements in particular cases (this is why scholars often augment them with a tradition of commentary and exegesis); conversely, moral paragons provide examples that are too specific to be easily applied to different circumstances.

More important, however, is the fact that there is something intuitive and natural in the notion of agents that are attentive and responsive to the way people behave. Indeed, this notion may be rooted in the way moral intuitions are developed from an early age. A conventional view would be that children acquire moral concepts by generalizing and gradually abstracting from social conventions. In this view, children start by noticing correlations between specific courses of action (e.g. beating up one's sibling or being noisy during class) and sanctions. They then abstract general principles of right and wrong from these specific cases. Also, children are described as building moral feelings by internalizing people's emotional reactions to their actions (Gibbs 1991). Both models may have underestimated the child's intuitive access to specifically *moral* dimensions of actions. Indeed, the psychologist Eliot Turiel has shown that even preschoolers have a good intuitive understanding of the difference between social conventions and moral prescriptions (so that beating up people is wrong even if no one has told you so, while being noisy is wrong only if there is an injunction to keep still) (Turiel 1983; 1998). Also, children seem to find it much easier to imagine a revision of *major* social conventions (e.g. a situation where boys wear skirts) than a revision of even *minor* moral principles (e.g. a situation where it is all right to steal an eraser). Finally, children make a difference between moral principles and prudential rules (do not leave your notebook near the fire-place!). They justify both in terms of their consequences, but assume that social consequences are specific to moral violations (Tisak and Turiel 1984).

Thus experimental studies show that there is an early-developed specific inference system, a specialized 'moral sense' underlying moral intuitions. Notions of morality are distinct from those used to evaluate other aspects of social interaction (this is why social conventions and moral imperatives are so easily distinguished). They provide an initial basis on which children can understand adult moral understandings. This capacity for entertaining abstract intuitions about the moral nature of courses of action (without, of course, being able to explicate them) has also been found in children with varying amounts of experience with other children (Siegal and Storey 1985), in different cultures (Song et al. 1987) and even in children with exceptional experience of abuse or neglect (Song et al. 1987; Sanderson and Siegal 1988).

The main conclusion to draw from this research is that moral understandings, far from being dependent upon socially transmitted (e.g. religious) explications, appear before such concepts are intelligible, and in the same way, regardless of what religious concepts are entertained by adults around the child; indeed, they develop regardless of whether there are *any* religious concepts in the child's cultural environment. But another aspect of these cognitive findings is also important. Early-developed moral understandings may well provide a context in which concepts of supernatural agents become more salient.

To the extent that people represent a situation in a way that triggers particular moral intuitions and feelings, they generally assume that these intuitions and feelings are true regardless of who is considering the situation. They also assume that the only way to disguise the true moral nature of an action is to mislead people about the action itself. If you want to exculpate yourself, you cannot argue that beating up one's sibling is right, but you can claim that what *seemed* to be a beating-up was something entirely different. You assume that, to the extent that people share your information (or information you hold true) about what happened, they probably share the same moral intuition about it, and therefore will be led to react to it in similar ways.

In other words, the way our moral intuitions operate allows for an empty place-holder, for the position of 'some agent who has access to my information about the situation at hand'. The moral system itself does not provide any description of that agent, although we try and make other people become such agents by explaining situations to them. Now, as I said above, *some* supernatural agents are represented *by default* as having full access to strategic information. That is, people represent a given situation, and represent some information about it that is relevant to social interaction, and they assume that the supernatural agent also has that information. (Again, all this consists of tacit assumptions.) This means that, in morally relevant situations, a concept of god or spirit or ancestor is very likely to be activated as the most relevant way to fill in the empty place-holder. After representing a particular behaviour as wrong, and feeling the wrongness of it, it seems quite natural to assume that some other agent with full access has similar feelings.

So in a sense concepts of gods and spirits are made more *relevant* by the organization of our moral thoughts, which themselves do not especially require any gods or spirits. What I mean by 'relevant' is that the concepts, once put in this moral context, are easy to represent, and also generate many new inferences. For instance, most people feel some guilt when acting in a way which they suspect is immoral. That is, whatever their self-serving justifications, they may have the intuition that an agent with a full description of the situation would still classify it as wrong. Now thinking of this intuition as 'what the ancestors think of what I did' or 'how God feels about what I did' provides an easy way of representing what is otherwise extremely vague. That is, most of our moral intuitions are clear but their origin escapes us, because it lies in mental processing that we cannot consciously access. Seeing these intuitions as someone's viewpoint is a simpler way of understanding why we have these intuitions. In this sense, moral intuitions and feelings contribute to the relevance of some supernatural concepts. The latter, again, can be seen as parasitic upon intuitions that would be there, spirits and gods or not.

Special powers, misfortune and social exchange

It may seem that gods and spirits matter to people mainly because these supernatural agents are described as having *special powers*. The ancestors can make you sick or ruin your plantations; God sends people various plagues. On the positive side, gods and spirits are also represented as protectors, guarantors of good crops, social harmony, etc. But why are supernatural agents construed as having such causal powers? Everything would be quite simple if these descriptions of supernatural agents were some kind of 'cultural postulates', from which people would then deduce that these agents do matter in particular circumstances. However, what seems to be a cultural 'postulate' is always the product of cultural transmission. There must be some processes that turn these propositions into plausible or indeed self-evident descriptions of what happens in the world. So even if people take the powers of gods and spirits as axiomatic, we still need to explain why they do that and do not adopt other 'postulates'.

The notion that gods and spirits matter because of their powers does not just beg the question of why they are represented as having such powers. It also creates difficult puzzles. For instance, in many places the most powerful supernatural agents are not the ones that matter most. The Fang of Cameroon and Gabon, among whom I have conducted anthropological fieldwork, have rituals and complex emotions associated with the possible presence of the ghosts-ancestors. Now the Fang also say that the world (meaning earth and sky and all living things) was created by a god called Mebeghe, vastly more powerful than either the living or the dead. His work was completed by another god, Nzame, who invented all cultural objects: tools, houses, etc., and taught people how to hunt, domesticate animals and raise crops. Neither of these gods seems to matter that much. That is, there are no cults or rituals specifically directed at Mebeghe or Nzame, and they are in fact very rarely mentioned. For a long time, this puzzled many travellers, anthropologists and of course missionaries. Many

African people seemed to recognize a Creator in the same sense as the biblical one, yet were remarkably indifferent to Him. We will see below the explanation for this apparent paradox.

For the time being, let us just keep in mind that what matters is not so much the 'powers' of supernatural beings considered in the abstract, as those powers that are relevant to *practical* concerns. In particular, ancestors, gods and spirits are readily mentioned when people represent or try to explain salient situations of misfortune. Indeed, this connection is so frequent that, for many non-specialists, it seems to provide an easy explanation for the origin and persistence of religious concepts. People are afflicted with various calamities, they cannot explain the amoral nature of their destiny, so they imagine gods and spirits that pull the strings. This, like many other popular 'origin of religion' scenarios, points to a real association, but in my view fails to appreciate the complexity of the mental operations involved.

Why would people want to understand their own misfortune? What drives their minds to seek an explanation? Again, this seems to have an obvious explanation. Minds are designed that way, because a mind that produces a richer understanding of what happens (especially bad things that happen) is certainly better equipped for survival.

Accepting this, it remains that some aspects of the association between religious agents and misfortune may seem paradoxical. To see this, let me return to the Kwaio example. The ancestors are generally responsible for whatever happens in a village: 'Spirits, a child learns early, are beings that help and punish: the source of success, gratification, and security, and the cause of illness, death, and misfortune; makers and enforcers of rules that must at first seem arbitrary' (Keesing 1982: 33). Good taro crops and prolific sows indicate that the ancestors are happy with the way the living behave. Illness and misfortune are generally an effect of the ancestors' anger. True, the Kwaio like most people in the world accept that some events 'just happen' and have no particular cause. Some illnesses may be interpreted as a straightforward weakening of the body, with no special implications; the fact that some ailments are cured by Western medicine shows that they are in this category of mere mishaps. But in general any salient event, particularly any remarkable misfortune, is seen as the action of the *adalo*. As a Kwaio diviner tells Keesing: 'If we see that a child is sick . . . we divine and then we sacrifice a pig [to the *adalo*].' Divination is required to understand which spirit is angry and why. A diviner will take a set of knotted leaves and pull them to see which side breaks first, indicating either a positive answer or no answer to a particular question. In most cases, ancestors are unhappy either because people have broken rules about what is proper and what is *abu* (forbidden or dangerous – from the Polynesian root *tapu* that gave us our 'taboo'). Ancestors, like humans, crave pork and demand frequent sacrifices of pigs (Keesing 1982: 115). Interaction with the ancestors can be quite complex, because it is not always clear which ancestor is causing trouble: 'If it is not really that *adalo* [discovered in divination] that asked for a pig, in order that our pigs or taro grow well, then even though we sacrifice it, nothing will happen.' So people may go through several cycles of divination followed by sacrifice to reach a satisfactory arrangement with the ancestors.

This case highlights some very common features of the association between misfortune and religious agents. Although people assume that the ancestors are involved in many occurrences (like bad crops, ill-nesses, death, etc.) they do not bother to represent *in what way* they bring about all these states of affairs. That is, people's reasoning, when thinking about such situations, is entirely centred on the *reasons* why an ancestor would want them to fall ill or have many children, certainly not on the *causal process* whereby they make it happen.

This is also true of other kinds of supernatural notions that people commonly associate with misfortune. One of the most widespread explanations of mishaps and disorders, the world over, is in terms of *witchcraft*, the suspicion that some people (generally in the community) perform magical tricks to 'steal' other people's health, good fortune or material goods. Concepts of witches are among the most widespread supernatural ones. In some places there are explicit accusations and the alleged witches must either prove their innocence or perform some special rituals to pay for their transgression. In most places the sus-picion is a matter of gossip and rarely comes out in the open. You do not really need to have actual witches around to have very firm beliefs about the existence and powers of witches. Witchcraft is important because it seems to provide an 'explanation' for all sorts of events: many cases of illness or other misfortune are spontaneously interpreted as evidence for the witches' actions. Witchcraft beliefs are just one manifestation of a phenomenon that is found in many human groups: the interpretation of misfortune as a consequence of envy. For another such situation, consider the widespread belief in an 'evil eye', a spell cast by envious people against whoever enjoys some good fortune or natural advantage (Pocock 1973). Witchcraft and evil eye notions do not really belong to the domain of religion, but they show that, religious agents or not, there is a tendency to focus on possible *reasons* for some agents to cause misfortune, rather than on the *processes* whereby they could do it.

Now that is not exactly what you would expect from a mind that is equipped to seek explanations for misfortune, as a way to avoid further bad occurrences. One would imagine that such a mind would consider *the ways* in which bad things happen, for they are at least as important to predicting and avoiding them as some agents' reasons for making them happen. Indeed, this is often the way we think of occurrences that are mostly within our control. We do not bother to represent reasons why people would want to steal our car, but we take precautions based on our notion of how people could manage to steal it. By contrast, for these occurrences that largely escape control, people rather focus on the *reasons* of an agent. The ancestors were angry, the gods demanded a sacrifice, or the god is just cruel and playful. But there is more to this. The way these reasons are expressed is, in a great majority of cases, supported by our *social exchange* intuitions.

To return to our examples. The Kwaio ancestors afflict people with some disease because they want some sacrifice. In some of these cases people admit that they should have performed the sacrifice to start with. They are guilty of 'neglecting' a particular ancestor. They failed to maintain proper relations with him. These are clearly construed as exchange relations. Ancestors provide some form of protection and people provide roasted pigs. In some cases people tend to think that the ancestors are 'pushing it' a little and feel justifiably resentful. This is the kind of emotion that we find in situations where one party in a social exchange seems to be deriving increased benefits without paying increased costs. In other words, relations with ancestors are framed by the understandings and associated emotions that are intuitively applied to social exchange. Witchcraft too seems to be clearly construed as an unfair exchange. The witches are trying to reap some benefit without paying any cost: witches are quite clearly 'cheaters' in the technical sense. Indeed, that is precisely what people like the Fang and many others who have witchcraft concepts say about witches: they are the ones who take but never give, who steal other people's health or happiness, who thrive only if others are deprived.

To sum up, then, people represent misfortune in terms of their social exchange templates. Evil spirits are enforcers of unfair deals, the angered ancestors are enforcers of fair ones, evil-eye people are over-reacting cheater-detectors and witches are genuine cheaters. These examples show that some *prior* mental process describes misfortune in such a way that it makes sense to include gods and spirits in an explanation of what caused it. That is, people's thoughts about such salient events are organized by the mental templates of social exchange. These do not necessarily require gods and spirits. But if you have concepts of gods and spirits, it is not too surprising that they should sometimes be included in explanations of salient events. If your representation of misfortune generally treats it as an effect of violations of social exchange, it will potentially include any agent with whom you interact. But spirits and gods are precisely represented as engaging in social interaction with people, especially in social exchange. So they are among the potential candidates for 'originators of misfortune', just like neighbours, relatives and envious partners.

Conclusion

Religious concepts are culturally successful: that is, they are acquired, stored and communicated in a way that roughly preserves most of their relevant features. This cannot be explained by the fact that people 'upload' concepts directly from cultural peers and elders. Cultural acquisition requires communication, an inferential process whereby people activate cognitive resources that make other people's utterances or gestures or their artefacts relevant in the sense of producing inferences (Sperber 1996). The fact that concepts of spirits or gods are found in similar form in so many different cultural environments does not mean that people have a special urge or need to have such notions. It only means that these concepts are such that, once they are entertained by somebody, they are very likely to be acquired by others and 'crowd out' less relevant forms of supernatural imagination.

Relevance should be understood here in a fairly technical sense, as the process whereby a given conceptual input produces inferences (Sperber and Wilson 1995). Input that produces comparatively *richer* inferences or produces them with *less* computational effort (or both) will, other things being equal, be better acquired, stored and communicated. Here I have tried to illustrate this process in a very specific domain, that of important, emotionally charged concepts of religious agents, to show how prior inferential systems fashion these concepts. Because we have an intuitive ontology with particular categories and inference systems, some concepts that go beyond experience are particularly easy to acquire and store (supernatural concepts). Because we have developed specific systems that deal with agency, those concepts that describe agents will be particularly salient (supernatural agents). Because we have social mind systems, some of these supernatural agents will become what we commonly recognize as religious agents. They will be tacitly construed as having access to whatever information activates our social mind systems. Also, this will allow people to include them in descriptions of their own moral intuitions, as well as in representations of misfortune.

All this would tend to show that religious concepts are *parasitic* upon intuitive understandings and inferences that would be there, religion or not. This point may not in itself be particularly new. What matters on the other hand is that cognitive science and other associated disciplines can now provide us with a much better description of the various mental systems that religious concepts activate. This in turn helps explain why religious concepts are the way they are, and why they are so easily acquired and communicated by human beings. This, obviously, is not quite as gratifying as having a 'magic bullet' that explains the whole of religion on the basis of one single factor (such as the fear of death, the need to explain the world, or the deification of society). But since magic bullets are largely illusory, it may be more promising to investigate the particular connections between religious notions and the common mental equipment of the species.

References

Bacharach, M. and D. Gambetta (1999) 'Trust in signs'. In *Trust and Social Structure*, ed. K. Cook. New York: Russell Sage Foundation.

Baron-Cohen, S. (1995) *Mindblindness: An Essay on Autism and Theory of Mind*. Cambridge, MA: MIT Press.

Barrett, H. C. (1999) 'Human cognitive adaptations to predators and prey'. Unpublished doctoral dissertation, University of California, Santa Barbara.

Barrett, J. L. (1998) 'Cognitive constraints on Hindu concepts of the divine'. *Journal for the Scientific Study of Religion* 37: 608–19.

Barrett, J. L. (2000) 'Exploring the natural foundations of religion'. *Trends in Cognitive Science* 4(1): 29–34.

Barrett, J. L. and F. C. Keil (1996) 'Conceptualizing a non-natural entity: anthropomorphism in God concepts'. *Cognitive Psychology* 31: 219–47.

Boyd, R. and P. J. Richerson (1992) 'Punishment allows the evolution of cooperation (or anything else) in sizable groups'. *Ethology and Sociobiology* 13(3): 171–95.

Boyer, P. (1994a) 'Cognitive constraints on cultural representations: natural ontologies and religious ideas'. In *Mapping the Mind: Domain-Specificity in Culture and Cognition*, ed. L. A. Hirschfeld and S. Gelman, 39–67. New York: Cambridge University Press.

Boyer, P. (1994b) *The Naturalness of Religious Ideas: A Cognitive Theory of Religion*. Berkeley, CA: University of California Press.

Boyer, P. (1996) 'What makes anthropomorphism natural: intuitive ontology and cultural representations'. *Journal of the Royal Anthropological Institute* n.s. 2: 1–15.

Boyer, P. (2000) 'Functional origins of religious concepts: conceptual and strategic selection in evolved minds' (Malinowski Lecture 1999). *Journal of the Royal Anthropological Institute* n.s. 6: 195–214.

Boyer, P. (2001) *Religion Explained: The Evolutionary Origins of Religious Thought*. New York: Basic Books.

Boyer, P. and C. Ramble (2001) 'Cognitive templates for religious concepts: cross-cultural evidence for recall of counter-intuitive representations'. *Cognitive Science* 25: 535–64.

Cosmides, L. and J. Tooby (1992) 'Cognitive adaptations for social exchange'. In *The Adapted Mind: Evolutionary Psychology and the Generation of Culture*, ed. J. H. Barkow, L. Cosmides and J. Tooby, 163–228. New York: Oxford University Press.

Frank, R. (1988) *Passions within Reason: The Strategic Role of the Emotions*. New York: Norton.

Gambetta, D. (1994) 'Godfather's gossip'. *Archives Européennes de Sociologie* 35: 199–223.

Gibbs, J. C. (1991) 'Toward an integration of Kohlberg's and Hoffman's moral development theories. Special section: Intersecting conceptions of morality and moral development'. *Human Development* 34(2): 88–104.

Guthrie, S. E. (1993) *Faces in the Clouds: A New Theory of Religion*. New York: Oxford University Press.

Keesing, R. (1982) *Kwaio Religion: The Living and the Dead in a Solomon Island Society*. New York: Columbia University Press.

Lawson, E. T. and R. N. McCauley (1990) *Rethinking Religion: Connecting Cognition and Culture*. Cambridge: Cambridge University Press.

Meltzoff, A. N. (1999) 'Origins of theory of mind, cognition and communication'. *Journal of Communication Disorders* 32(4): 251–69.

Mithen, S. (1996) *The Prehistory of the Mind*. London: Thames & Hudson.

Pocock, D. F. (1973) *Mind, Body and Wealth*. Oxford: Blackwell.

Povinelli, D. J. and T. J. Eddy (1996) *What Young Chimpanzees Know about Seeing*, Monographs of the Society for Research in Child Development, 61(3), v–vi, 1–152.

Povinelli, D. J. and T. M. Preuss (1995) 'Theory of mind: evolutionary history of a cognitive specialization'. *Trends in Neurosciences* 18(9): 418–24.

Saler, B. (1993) *Conceptualizing Religion: Immanent Anthropologists, Transcendent Natives and Unbounded Categories*. Leiden: Brill.

Sanderson, J. A. and M. Siegal (1988) 'Conceptions of moral and social rules in rejected and nonrejected preschoolers'. *Journal of Clinical Child Psychology* 17(1): 66–72.

Sidanius, J. F. Pratto (1999) *Social Dominance: An Intergroup Theory of Social Oppression and Hierarchy.* Cambridge: Cambridge University Press.

Siegal, M. and R. M. Storey (1985) 'Day care and children's conceptions of moral and social rules'. *Child Development* 56(4): 1001–8

Smetana, J. G., M. Kelly and C. T. Twentyman (1984) 'Abused, neglected, and nonmaltreated children's conceptions of moral and social-conventional transgressions'. *Child Development* 55(1): 277–87.

Song, M.-J., J. G. Smetana and S. Y. Kim (1987) 'Korean children's conceptions of moral and conventional transgressions'. *Developmental Psychology* 23(4): 577–82.

Sperber, D. (1996) *Explaining Culture: A Naturalistic Approach.* Oxford: Blackwell.

Sperber, D. and D. Wilson (1995 (1986)) *Relevance: Communication and Cognition.* Oxford: Blackwell.

Tager-Flusberg, H. and K. Sullivan (2000) 'A componential view of theory of mind: evidence from Williams' syndrome'. *Cognition* 76(1): 59–89.

Tisak, M. S. and E. Turiel (1984) 'Children's conceptions of moral and prudential rules'. *Child Development* 55(3): 1030–9.

Tooby, J. and L. Cosmides (1996) 'Friendship and the banker's paradox: other pathways to the evolution of adaptations for altruism'. In *Evolution of Social Behaviour Patterns in Primates and Man*, ed. W. G. Runciman, J. M. Smith et al., 119–43. Oxford: Oxford University Press.

Turiel, E. (1983) *The Development of Social Knowledge: Morality and Convention.* Cambridge: Cambridge University Press.

Turiel, E. (1998) 'The development of morality'. In *Handbook of Child Psychology*, 5th edn, ed. W. Damon, vol. iii, 863–932. New York: Wiley.

Van Schaik, C. P., M. A. Van Noordwijk, B. Warsono and E. Sutriono (1983) 'Party size and early detection of predators in Sumatran forest primates'. *Primates* 24(2): 211–21.

Whiten, A. (ed.) (1991) *Natural Theories of Mind: The Evolution, Development and Simulation of Everyday Mind-Reading.* Oxford: Blackwell.

5 Dumb Gods, Petitionary Prayer and the Cognitive Science of Religion

JUSTIN L. BARRETT

Often when laypeople think about the theory of gravity, they only consider its usefulness in accounting for why objects fall to earth, perhaps recalling a school-days' tale of Newton getting bumped on the head with an inspirational apple. Certainly part of the draw of the theory is in explaining *regularities* in the movement of physical objects that we all observe. But a great theory does more than explain regularities; it also helps discover and make understandable *variability* in phenomena. The theory of gravity is attractive because it also enables scientists to predict the non-obvious behaviour of objects at various distances from the surface of the earth, even nearer the surface of the moon or Mars, thus facilitating space travel. Similarly, the potential gravity of the cognitive science of religion will rise and fall with its ability to account for both the regularities and the variability of religious phenomena.

As many of the chapters in this volume illustrate, the cognitive science of religion holds great potential for explaining the cross-cultural regularities of a number of human phenomena sometimes deemed 'religious'. Guthrie's anthropomorphism hypothesis may account for why people generate and find salient concepts of superhuman agents across groups (1980; 1993; this volume). Boyer's theory of cultural transmission specifies mnemonic and conceptual structures that facilitate the spread of just those sorts of concepts that populate religious systems generally (1993; 1994; 1995; 1996a; 1996b; 2000; this volume). According to Whitehouse (1992; 1996; 2000; this volume), quite aside from cultural considerations, memory dynamics relating to emotions may account for the relative frequency in performing religious events and their characteristic exegetical reflections. Similarly, Lawson and McCauley's work on cognitive representations of religious ritual form helps to account for why rituals from various religious systems have common intuitions governing their practice apart from the rituals' meaning (1990; this volume). Finally, in my own work with colleagues, I have presented evidence that conceptual structures inform and restrict the way people understand superhuman agents of various religions, in both children (Barrett 2001a; Barrett and Newman 1999; Barrett et al. 2001) and adults (Barrett 1998; 1999; Barrett and Keil 1996; Barrett and VanOrman 1996).

To sum up, evidence continues to mount that the cognitive science of religion provides powerful tools for explaining regularities. But can a cognitive perspective contribute to predicting and understanding variability as well? In this chapter, I continue to develop the thesis that regularities of the human mind importantly inform and constrain religious thought and practice, by examining two types of religious practice: rituals and petitionary prayer. I will present data that illustrate predictable covariation between how religious agents are represented in the minds of believers and the sorts of resulting intuitions that constrain religious practices. The particular characteristics attributed to the god being petitioned during petitionary prayer provide believers with intuitions about what to ask the god for, even in the absence of explicit instruction. In rituals, depending on the sort of god appealed to in the ritual system, different aspects of the rituals' performance may vary in relative importance. The variability in performance and performance-related intuitions in both cases can be predicted and explained in terms of culturally non-specific cognitive structures.

The argument for the ability of the cognitive scientific perspective to predict and explain some variability in religious phenomena across traditions proceeds in three sections. In the first section, I make some observations regarding the representations of superhuman agents and consequential cognitive assumptions these representations generate. Second, I discuss some recent psychological research on petitionary prayer among North American Protestants and its implication for the cognitive programme. Finally, I review two experiments, inspired by Lawson and McCauley's theory of ritual competence (1990), that both demonstrate support for the theory and hold non-obvious implications for the character of rituals in different religious systems.

Conceptual resources and religious agents

Both petitionary prayer and the class of religious ritual considered below appeal to some special agent (directly in prayer, indirectly in ritual) for the accomplishing of change in natural states of affairs. A prayer might ask a god to assist in improving someone's health. A ritual might be conducted to ensure a successful hunt, using the power of a god or gods. Gods occupy a central role in both circumstances. Therefore, how practitioners cognitively represent these special agents might bear directly on the character of these behaviours.

In experiments conducted on adults of various faiths in the United States (Barrett and Keil 1996; Barrett and VanOrman 1996), and on Hindus in Northern India (Barrett 1998), colleagues and I have demonstrated that while engaged in real-time problem-solving, prediction or inference generation, Christians (Roman Catholic and Protestant), Jews, Hindus, atheists and agnostics use strikingly similar concepts of gods. Regardless of theological tradition, in non-reflective contexts, concepts of gods conform to intuitive expectations people hold about all intentional beings: that they have fallible beliefs, desires that motivate purposeful action, limited attention, limited sensory-perceptual systems for gathering information about the world, a particular physical location in space and time, and so forth. In short, when rapidly generating inferences about religious agents, people automatically attribute to them many human properties – even when they are inconsistent with explicitly endorsed theology.

As Boyer and I have both argued (Boyer 1994; Barrett 1999), the reason god concepts show fairly rigid adherence to human-like property assumptions is that people represent both humans and gods with the same cognitive resources. Unless deliberately representing them otherwise, people implicitly understand humans and gods by elaborating tacit assumptions about intentional agents. Psychological research suggests that given only enough evidence to believe that an object can wilfully initiate its own action, not requiring physical contact to move or act, children and adults automatically attribute a host of human-like psychological properties. To illustrate, when trying (with little success) to place small magnetized spheres in a particular configuration, college students described the marbles as having beliefs, desires and even personality traits, accusing some marbles of 'attacking' others and being deliberately mischievous (Barrett and Hankes forthcoming). Psychologists have obtained similar results from adults observing geometric shapes 'chase' each other on a video display (Heider and Simmel 1944; Michotte 1963). Apparently, the bias to attribute these properties to objects classified as agents is so strong that even approximating a human-like form is unnecessary. Consequently, that people readily attribute to gods many human-like properties is not surprising.

At least two general implications of these observations bear on religious practices such as prayer and ritual. Importantly, if a practice performed is either cognitively demanding or in a cognitively demanding context, or performed in a fairly spontaneous manner, the god concept used will include few conceptually difficult, theological properties. Rather, as in the studies cited above, the god concept would include such assumptions as having fallible knowledge, a limited focus of attention, a single physical location, but being able to act on other agents at a distance as through communication. Second, as a human-like intentional agent, schemata for interacting with human-like agents will be activated when performing many types of religious actions. For example, when requesting that someone of a higher status do something, typically people show appropriate respect and deference. Such socially informed behavioural patterns and assumptions might operate automatically when interacting with nonhuman agents as well. These implications applied to petitionary prayer lead to specific predictions, detailed in the following two sections.

How ordinary cognition informs petitionary prayer

In Christianity, and other faiths as well, believers may ask God to act in the natural world in any number of ways. Biblical precedent includes the faithful asking God to work in physically impressive ways, as in Elijah asking God to burn the altar on Mount Carmel; asking God to make biological interventions, as in the numerous healings Jesus performed; and asking God to act psychologically, for example, to 'soften' Pharaoh's 'heart'. As long as the petition is offered in faith and in accordance with the will of God, any mode of divine action is acceptable. As long as God is understood as an omnipotent and omnipresent being, God can potentially act through any causal mechanisms. Theologically, then, it seems that no domain of petitionary prayer (psychological, biological or physical) should necessarily hold an advantage over any other when it comes to the real prayer practices of individuals. That most Christian traditions do not explicitly advocate one domain of activity for God over others leaves just the theological vacuum that cognitive biases may fill.

As sketched above, data suggest that in many real-time situations, people represent even highly abstract concepts of gods as human-like beings with psychological and physical limits, including a single location in space. Given that during many instances of prayer God is represented as a psychosocial being with a particular location (in heaven, perhaps), petitioners might be biased to favour requests that ask God to act in ways at which agents acting at a distance are best.

Human-like agents are generally poor at acting mechanistically or physically at a distance. Even infants know it takes physical contact to move a physical object (Spelke et al. 1995); one must touch a chair to be able to move it. Similarly, human-like agents are not skilled at performing biological interventions at a distance. What humans and similar agents do well at a distance is influencing psychological states: beliefs, opinions, desires and emotions. A growing body of developmental research demonstrates that from infancy people know that people can act on each other at a distance, altering behaviours (Legerstee 1994; Lempers et al. 1977; Masur 1983; Poulin-Dubois and Shultz 1988). If God is implicitly conceptualized as a human-like agent far away, then perhaps, in the absence of pertinent theology, petitionary prayer will tend toward requests for God to act psychologically.

I have begun testing this hypothesis in a series of four studies of American (mostly Protestant) college students (Barrett 2001b): a prayer journalling study, a questionnaire and two experiments.

In the first study, twelve college students (mean age 19.4 years) from introductory psychology classes at a Protestant liberal arts college in the Dutch Calvinist tradition recorded all of their petitionary prayers over a two-week period. All twelve students identified themselves as Protestant Christians: seven Reformed (Dutch Calvinist), two Baptist and three from other traditions. The number of petitionary prayers reported over the two weeks ranged from 9 to 183. The vast majority of classifiable petitionary prayers were psychological in nature. For example, students asked for God to help them to remember things, to help people to reach an understanding, and to emotionally adjust to difficult situations. On average, 37 per cent of the total number of requests were psychological in nature. By comparison, 16 per cent were biological (as in asking God to heal someone), 3 per cent were mechanistic or physical (as in asking God to fix a car) and 44 per cent were not classifiable in one of these three classes (e.g. asking for forgiveness or for God to 'be with me'). On the whole, students in this sample appeared to pray for psychological intervention more often than other domains.

In a second study, a new sample of 70 students (mean age 18.7 years) completed a questionnaire regarding their prayer practices. Students answered questions asking whether they would pray for God to work through physical mechanisms, through biological mechanisms, or through the psychological mechanisms governing volitional activities. A number of filler items were included to distract participants from the issue of central interest. As in the prayer journal study, participants

97

most often reported they would pray for God to interfere with psychological regularities, significantly more often than any other type of request. Fifty-seven agreed they would pray for this sort of action. Forty-nine said they would pray for biological intervention, whereas only two said they would pray for God to act mechanistically.

Although these first two studies produced data affirming the hypothesis, alternative explanations could challenge any confident conclusions. One weakness of simply observing praying behaviours or analysing self-reported behavioural generalities is the possibility of confounding variables. Might psychological intervention be needed in situations of greater urgency or importance? Possibly, psychological causation is more mysterious than biological and mechanistic and thus is viewed as a more appropriate domain for God's activity. College students might be answering based on the salience of mental activities associated with learning and formal education. To help neutralize the impact of any such factors, two additional experiments asked participants to reason about more tightly controlled hypothetical situations.

In these experiments, I asked students to read eight scenarios that all presented some kind of dilemma. For example:

You live in the South Pacific. One day you boat out in the ocean by yourself. After you get a ways from any inhabited islands, you notice that a seal in the bottom of your boat is beginning to leak. At the rate it is leaking, you will not make it back to any inhabited islands, so you decide to rest on a small island nearby. Once you land, you discover that the island has no fresh water of any kind. Big problem! You can last the rest of the day, but if you don't get water in the next 36 hours, you will dehydrate. A ferry goes by this island regularly, but the next time the ferry goes by isn't until about 48 hours from now. Fortunately, you do have your two-way radio to call for help. Unfortunately, the only island within range of your radio is inhabited by helpful people who do not understand your language well. It wouldn't be a problem if the seal in your boat stopped leaking. It wouldn't be a problem if you could last until the ferry came by. All of this wouldn't be a problem if the people could understand your radio message.

Participants were then asked to 'Please rate the likelihood you would pray for the following solutions to your dilemma (1 = not at all likely, 7 = extremely likely)', and were presented with three solutions for each scenario. For example:

Pray the people understand your radio message.   1 2 3 4 5 6 7
Pray the seal stops leaking.   1 2 3 4 5 6 7
Pray you are able to last until the ferry comes by.   1 2 3 4 5 6 7

Each scenario presented a problem that was said to be solvable if any one of three things happened: one a physical change, one a biological change and one a psychological change. In the example above, the first solution is psychological (understanding a language), the second is physical and the third is biological (surviving without water). The order for each scenario was random, as was the order of mention of the possible solutions in the body of the scenario description.

For each of 43 Protestant college students (mean age 19.0 years) who participated, a total psychology score, biology score and physical score were calculated by averaging across the eight relevant items for each score. Once again, participants significantly favoured psychological scores (mean = 5.77) over biological (mean = 4.93) and physical (mean = 4.23) solutions. A separate group of participants drawn from the same population rated each of the solutions for how likely they would come about by chance, how 'good' a solution to the dilemma they were and how theologically appropriate each suggested prayer would be. Statistical tests demonstrated that these factors did significantly predict the 'likelihood of praying' ratings but still did not compromise the preference for psychological solutions.

The second prayer experiment replicated the first, but instead of using covariate ratings, I used two additional comparison conditions. College students recruited from a college psychology department subject pool were randomly assigned to one of three conditions. The first group of 14 performed the same task as described above. The second group of 15 completed a task that was identical except that God was replaced by a futuristic supercomputer called Uncomp. A description preceding the scenarios detailed Uncomp as having all of the requisite properties and appropriate programmed disposition to perform any of the suggested petitions. In many ways Uncomp was described as god-like. However, the description specified that Uncomp had components physically located all over the earth. That is, Uncomp would not be acting at a distance. Similarly, the 17 participants in the third condition completed the rating task with God replaced by Superman (the super-hero) who was said to have been nearby lately. The term 'pray' was removed from the task and replaced by 'ask for' in both the Uncomp and Superman conditions.

Once again, in the prayer condition, participants rated the psychological solutions as significantly more likely prayers (mean = 5.31) than either the biological (mean = 4.70) or physical (mean = 3.66) options. However, participants in neither the Superman nor the Uncomp conditions significantly preferred psychological solutions over physical ones; and only participants in the Superman condition significantly favoured psychological (mean = 5.21) over biological solutions (mean = 4.37). This preference could be because Superman simply does not have the ability to act biologically as well as physically or psychologically. Physical item ratings from the Uncomp group (mean = 4.87) were significantly greater than in the prayer condition (mean = 3.66), and the difference was even greater with the Superman condition (mean = 4.99).

These data support the claim that psychological intervention in the prayer scenarios was not just because of the particular options offered but a consequence of the requests being directed at God. Participants were less inclined to ask God to act using physical causation than Uncomp or Superman. Why might that be? One real possibility is that, in the absence of theological reasons for favouring one sort of causation over another, intuitive assumptions about God being a person far away bias against God acting through physical mechanisms. Agents do not act on physical objects at a distance. However, Uncomp and Superman were both physically present and able to act.

The control ratings of the first experiment with hypothetical scenarios and the Uncomp and Superman comparisons of the second experiment successfully rule out many alternative explanations for the preference of psychological causation over biological and mechanistic. Relative helplessness was neutralized in the hypothetical scenarios. In all cases, the person was utterly helpless and the gravity of the situation across the three prayer options was constant. While the results of the prayer journal and questionnaire studies could have been due to psychological problems being more common than biological ones or mechanistic ones, the experimental results cannot be explained in this way. Another possibly confounding factor is the likelihood an event will come about by chance. That is, perhaps Christians pray for things that are more likely to happen even if they don't pray. Though the control ratings of the first experiment support this conjecture, the advantage for psychological prayers persisted even when statistically factoring out chance likelihood. Also note that the idea of something coming about by 'chance' is difficult to negotiate within some theistic world-views in which everything is ultimately controlled by a god. A final confound could be that psychological causation is harder to observe and verify than biological or mechanistic causation, and this accounts for its favoured status. One can see a rock being moved (mechanistic causation) but cannot see an opinion being changed (psychological causation). Note, however, that in the case of biological causation, mechanisms can be just as invisible as in psychological causation. Likewise, in the hypothetical scenarios, the mechanistic changes were all due to causation that a casual observer would not be able to observe, as in keeping a fence from breaking under stress, and the viscosity of mud changing.

What implications might these data have for comparative studies of religion? Given a system in which (1) the god has no specified nearby location and (2) salient theological instruction regarding what is appropriate to pray for is absent, a simple prediction can be made. The research suggests that prayers for the god to act in ways that do not violate the 'no action at a distance' rule will be favoured. That is, psychological and ambiguous forms of causation will be favoured over mechanistic ones: controlling the weather (ambiguous) and helping people with emotional, cognitive or relational issues would be more natural domains of intervention than in moving rocks or strengthening walls.

Certainly these data represent only a starting point in exploring how ordinary cognition informs petitionary prayer. No doubt other cognitive variables may be identified and examined. However, these data do illustrate the potential of the cognitive scientific approach for making theoretically motivated and non-obvious testable predictions regarding variable religious phenomena.

Smart gods, dumb gods and religious rituals

The second line of research concerning religious rituals also supports the general claim that cognitive scientific approaches to the study of religion can explain variability as well as regularity across cultural groups. I turn now to my own variation of Lawson and McCauley's theory of ritual competence (Lawson and McCauley 1990; Lawson 2001; Lawson and McCauley, this volume), particularly the basic claim that inferences and judgements regarding the structure of rituals and their efficacy are parasitic on ordinary human cognition.

Lawson and McCauley argue that a particular group of religious rituals can be distinguished from other religious actions by a characteristic form. These rituals are those in which someone does something to someone or something in order to bring about some non-natural consequence (i.e. consequences that would not otherwise result from the particular actions), by virtue of appeal to superhuman agency. For example, a holy person striking a special pot in order to bring rain, through the power of a god, would be such a ritual. I argue that since rituals such as these consist of an action that evokes superhuman power to justify non-natural consequences, the sort of cognition in play is social cognition. Specifically, ritual intuitions prey upon ordinary expectations governing how intended agents act in ways to motivate the action of others. In these religious rituals, the action performed (someone doing something to something in order to get a god to do something) is a social act involving players that observers and participants implicitly presume to know a lot about, no matter their culture. Very little information about the relationships between the agents is necessary to generate relevant inferences about the potential success of the action. As suggested above, intuitive knowledge structures used to represent the interactions of psychosocial intentional agents are used to process the interactions of agents in religious contexts as well.

The first predicted inference is that (unlike in mechanistic causation) participants or observers of a ritual will judge having the right kind of agent as being more important than doing exactly the right kind of action. For example, when breaking a stick, it is not important who does it – an animal could step on it as well as a human. The result is the same. If, however, the stick to be broken is an arrow, and the act is a social act of declaring an end to a war, a horse stepping on the arrow will not do. If indeed observers of a ritual will generate inferences based on ordinary cognition and not knowledge of a particular religious system, then observers with no special knowledge of the system would produce converging intuitions about the relative importance of having a proper agent versus performing the proper action. This prediction runs counter to the folk understanding of rituals as highly specialized series of actions that must be completed precisely.

To test this prediction, a group of ritually naive adults offered judgements of the likelihood of success of a number of fictitious rituals (Barrett and Lawson 2001: Experiment 2). Sixty Protestant Christian college students from introductory psychology courses participated. The experimenter presented each participant with a set of eight fictitious rituals. Each of the eight successful ritual descriptions was followed by seven variations of the ritual that participants rated for likelihood of success. Of the seven variations, two changed just the agent in the original ritual, two changed just the action in the original ritual, two changed just the instrument used in the original ritual, and one was a restatement of the original. For example, one item read:

Given that: A special person cleans a trumpet with a special cloth and the village is protected from an epidemic. How likely is each of the following actions to protect the village from an epidemic? Please rate each action: 1 = extremely likely the action will work, 7 = extremely unlikely.

(a) A special person cleans a trumpet with a special plant. 1 2 3 4 5 6 7
(b) A special beetle cleans a trumpet with a special cloth. 1 2 3 4 5 6 7
(c) A special person cleans a trumpet with a special paper. 1 2 3 4 5 6 7
(d) A special dog cleans a trumpet with a special cloth. 1 2 3 4 5 6 7
(e) A special person covers a trumpet with a special cloth. 1 2 3 4 5 6 7
(f) A special person stuffs a trumpet with a special cloth. 1 2 3 4 5 6 7
(g) A special person cleans a trumpet with a special cloth. 1 2 3 4 5 6 7

The presentation order of each type of variation was randomized for each item. In one condition, the 'religious' condition, the set of ritual ratings included an explanation of the term 'special': 'For the following ratings, "special" means someone or something that has been given special properties or authority by the gods. All of the following are proposed religious actions. Try to use as much of the rating scales as is reasonable.' To be sure any results from the religious condition were due to understanding the actions as appealing to superhuman agency and not merely a consequence of the particular actions, a second condition was conducted. In the 'other-world' condition, the word 'special' was dropped from the descriptions, and the packet included a different explanation: 'All of the following are proposed actions on a world very much like ours. Try to use as much of the rating scales as is reasonable.'

In the religious condition, participants rated the rituals with changed agents as significantly less likely to be successful than rituals in which the action was changed, supporting the prediction that having a proper agent is more important than the particular action. Participants gave agent-changed rituals an average rating of 5.0 compared with an average of 3.99 for the action-changed rituals. In contrast, when participants rated the same 'rituals' in the other-world condition, the agent was no longer considered important for the success of the ritual. Indeed, agent-changed rituals were rated as significantly more likely to succeed (mean = 2.96) than action-changed rituals (mean = 3.93).

That relative judgements reversed as predicted between the two conditions strongly supports the interpretation that participants used different intuitive theories of causation to generate inferences about the efficacy of the actions. In the other-world condition, participants used ordinary mechanistic causal expectations – the action is more important to bring about a particular state of affairs than the agent. When the same actions were performed as appeals to superhuman agency, intuitions changed as they would in situations of social causation with agency acquiring a more substantive role in determining the outcome.

If, as I have argued, social causal cognition underlies naive observers' judgements of religious ritual efficacy, an additional prediction can be made. The reason having an appropriate agent is important in social exchanges is because of the need for appropriate intentions to motivate the action. Breaking an arrow can end a war if the person who breaks the arrow intends to end the war through the action. Accidentally breaking the arrow might not produce the same result. Similarly, a woman who receives flowers to which she is allergic is likely to respond quite differently if they were sent by a bitter ex-lover who knows of her allergies than by an innocent and adoring new suitor. What hangs in the balance in social causation is not merely performing an action but also having the correct intentions. If social cognition undergirds ritual intuitions, then even ritually naive observers should rate having the correct intentions as more important than a particular action, *provided* that the other person in the social exchange is aware of the 'good intentions'. The woman who receives the allergy-provoking flowers will only respond positively to the sender if she knows of the sender's good intentions. But aren't intentions usually discerned by examining actions?

These observations motivate a specific prediction regarding how rituals will be understood given the sort of god appealed to through the ritual. In the case of all-knowing gods who can read minds and thus tap intentions directly, having the proper intentions when performing a ritual will be judged as more important for the ritual's success than performing the proper action. However, when the god being appealed to is fallible and can only discern intentions based on a person's actions, then the particular action will have relatively greater importance.

This prediction was tested much like the previous one. The experimenter presented a group of 64 Protestant American college students with six fictitious rituals each followed by five permutations (Barrett and Lawson forthcoming). For example:

Given that: Intending to cause a drought, a special person knocks two special stones together and a drought occurs, how likely is each of the following actions to *cause a drought*? Please rate each action: 1 = extremely likely the action will work, 7 = extremely unlikely.

(a) Intending to cause a drought, a special person rubs two
     special stones together.   1 2 3 4 5 6 7
(b) Intending to cause an earthquake, a special person
     knocks two special stones together.   1 2 3 4 5 6 7
(c) Intending to cause a drought, a special person knocks
     two special shoes together.   1 2 3 4 5 6 7
(d) Not intending to cause a drought, a special person
     knocks two special stones together.   1 2 3 4 5 6 7
(e) Intending to cause a drought, a special person knocks
     two special stones together.   1 2 3 4 5 6 7

One variation of the original differed in intended consequence for the ritual, one differed by negating the original intention, one differed in action, one differed in instrument used, and one was a reiteration of the original. These variations appeared in random order. The negated intention variation and the changed action variation were the two measures of central interest.

The experimenter randomly divided the participants into two conditions. In the 'Smart god' condition, the participants received information defining the term 'special': 'For each situation, "special" means someone or something given unusual properties or authority by a superhuman being who can read minds, knows all, has amazing powers, and is immortal.' In the 'Dumb god' condition, the description was changed to emphasize a god with fallible knowledge: 'For each situation, "special" means someone or something given unusual properties or authority by a superhuman being who *cannot* read minds, *doesn't* know everything, has amazing powers, and is immortal.' The pivotal difference between the two conditions was the knowledge of the gods referenced by the ritual actions.

The Smart god condition replicated the findings of the previous experiment. Participants rated the versions with negated intentions (e.g. Not intending to cause a drought) as significantly less likely to bring about the original consequence (mean = 4.31) than versions with a changed action (mean = 3.36). Apparently, when intentions are known, participants judge them as more important for ritual efficacy than the particular action. However, in the Dumb god condition, participants judged performing the correct action as significantly more important for the success of the ritual (mean = 4.24) than in the Smart god condition. Just as when reasoning about people performing a social action when the intentions are known, religious rituals performed for gods with infallible knowledge need not follow the action precisely. But fallible gods must read intentions through the actions.

Together, these two experiments support the claim that ordinary cognition, ordering understandings of social causation, informs thought about religious ritual. If these patterns of social reasoning hold in other cultural settings, independent of the particular theology, religious ritual practices will be similarly predictable. In religious systems in which the gods have fallible knowledge, performing actions just right will take priority over having appropriate intentions in the minds of performers and observers. This neglect of intentions leaves open the possibility of individuals accidentally performing religious rituals and getting unintended results. On the other hand, in systems with 'smart gods', less care might be taken in performing the actions, but more care taken in having appropriate states of mind. Accidental ritual success will be less widely regarded as possible.

Conclusions

At the start of this chapter I posed the question, can a cognitive scientific perspective contribute to predicting and understanding variability in religious phenomena as well as accounting for regularities? Research to date provides reason to be optimistic.

Given that the cognitive structures of individual minds shape distributed religious concepts (Boyer 1994; Lawson and McCauley 1990), variability is explainable as far as we understand the ordinary cognition that is operative for a particular phenomenon. In the illustrative cases of petitionary prayer and religious rituals, depending on how the god or gods in a system are represented, predictable behaviours follow. If a god is represented as a distant psychosocial being, mechanistic causation is more counter-intuitive than psychological causation. Thus believers are biased toward praying for the god to act through psychological intervention as opposed to mechanistic intervention. Since religious rituals get represented using the same conceptual architecture as ordinary social causation, on average, the intentions of the person performing a ritual are more important than the particular action performed. However, when the god has fallible knowledge, the particular action increases in importance, probably as a reasonable index of the actor's intentions. These predictions follow from cognitive observations about how minds function, not from specifics of a given culture. Similarly, a cognitive approach eliminates the need to look for evidence that members of a culture are explicitly taught or explicitly model these intuitions. Rather, religious cognition is spontaneously generated from ordinary natural and social cognition. Comparable explanations no doubt wait to be discovered in other domains of religious thought and action.

As with other great scientific theories, the cognitive science of religion provides weighty tools for explaining regularities. Further, a cognitive perspective may impact predicting and understanding variability as well. It follows, then, that the cognitive science of religion has enough gravity to merit the number of scholars attracted to it and the growing attention it is receiving as a promising new approach to the study of religion (Andresen 2001; Barrett 2000).

References

Andresen, J. (ed.) (2001) *Religion in Mind: Cognitive Perspectives on Religious Belief, Ritual and Experience.* Cambridge: Cambridge University Press.

Barrett, J. L. (1998) 'Cognitive constraints on Hindu concepts of the divine'. *Journal for the Scientific Study of Religion* 37: 608–19.

Barrett, J. L. (1999) 'Theological correctness: cognitive constraint and the study of religion'. *Method and Theory in the Study of Religion* 11: 325–39.

Barrett, J. L. (2000) 'Exploring the natural foundations of religion'. *Trends in Cognitive Sciences* 4: 29–34.

Barrett, J. L. (2001a) 'Do children experience God like adults? retracing the development of god concepts'. In J. Andresen (ed.), *Religion in Mind: Cognitive Perspectives on Religious Belief, Ritual and Experience.* Cambridge: Cambridge University Press.

Barrett, J. L. (2001b) 'How ordinary cognition informs petitionary prayer'. *Journal of Cognition and Culture* 1(3): 259–69.

Barrett, J. L. and A. Hankes (forthcoming) 'Losing our marbles? the attribution of intentional agency to inanimates'.

Barrett, J. L. and F. C. Keil (1996) 'Conceptualizing a nonnatural entity: anthropomorphism in God concepts'. *Cognitive Psychology* 3: 219–47.

Barrett, J. L. and E. T. Lawson (2001) 'Ritual intuitions: cognitive contributions to judgements of ritual efficacy'. *Journal of Cognition and Culture* 1(2): 183–201.

Barrett, J. L. and E. T. Lawson (forthcoming) 'Dumb gods versus smart gods: the role of social cognition in structuring ritual intuitions'.

Barrett, J. L. and R. M. Newman (1999) 'Knowing what God knows: understanding the importance of background knowledge for interpreting static and active visual displays'. Poster presented at Cognitive Development Society Meeting, UNC-Chapel Hill, October.

Barrett, J. L. and M. Nyhof (2001) 'Spreading non-natural concepts: the role of intuitive conceptual structures in memory and transmission of cultural materials'. *Journal of Cognition and Culture* 1(1): 69–100.

Barrett, J. L., R. A. Richert and A. Driesenga (2001) 'God's beliefs versus mom's: the development of natural and non-natural agent concepts'. *Child Development* 72(1): 50–65.

Barrett, J. L. and B. VanOrman (1996) 'The effects of image use in worship on God concepts.' *Journal of Psychology and Christianity* 15: 38–45.

Boyer, P. (1993) 'Pseudo-natural kinds'. In *Cognitive Aspects of Religious Symbolism*, ed. P. Boyer, 121–41. Cambridge: Cambridge University Press.

Boyer, P. (1994) *The Naturalness of Religious Ideas: A Cognitive Theory of Religion*. Berkeley: University of California Press.

Boyer, P. (1995) 'Causal understandings in cultural representations: cognitive constraints on inferences from cultural input'. In *Causal Cognition: A Multidisciplinary Debate*, ed. D. Sperber, D. Premack and A. J. Premack, 615–49. Oxford: Oxford University Press.

Boyer, P. (1996a) 'Cognitive limits to conceptual relativity: the limiting-case of religious categories'. In *Rethinking Linguistic Relativity*, ed. J. Gumperz and S. Levinson, 203–31. Cambridge: Cambridge University Press.

Boyer, P. (1996b) 'What makes anthropomorphism natural: intuitive ontology and cultural representations'. *Journal of the Royal Anthropological Institute* n.s. 2: 1–15.

Boyer, P. (1999) 'Cognitive aspects of religious ontologies: how brain processes constrain religious concepts'. In *Approaching Religion*, part I, ed. T. Ahlbäck, 53–72, Scripta Instituti Donneriani, 17:1. Åbo: Donner Institute.

Boyer, P. (2000) 'Evolution of a modern mind and the origins of culture: religious concepts as a limiting case'. In *Evolution and the Human Mind: Modularity, Language and Meta-Cognition*, ed. P. Carruthers and A. Chamberlain, 93–112. Cambridge: Cambridge University Press.

Guthrie, S. (1980) 'A cognitive theory of religion'. *Current Anthropology* 21: 181–203.

Guthrie, S. (1993) *Faces in the Clouds: A New Theory of Religion*. Oxford: Oxford University Press.

Heider, F. and M. Simmel (1944) 'An experimental study of apparent behaviour'. *American Journal of Psychology* 57: 243–59.

Lawson, E. T. (2001) 'Psychological perspectives on agency'. In J. Andresen (ed.), *Religion in Mind: Cognitive Perspectives on Religious Belief, Ritual and Experience*. Cambridge: Cambridge University Press.

Lawson, E. T. and R. N. McCauley (1990) *Rethinking Religion: Connecting Cognition and Culture*. Cambridge: Cambridge University Press.

Legerstee, M. (1994) 'Patterns of 4-month-old infant responses to hidden, silent, and sounding people and objects'. *Early Development and Parenting* 3: 71–80.

Lempers, J. D., E. R. Flavell and J. H. Flavell (1977) 'The development in very young children of tacit knowledge concerning visual perception'. *Genetic Psychology Monographs* 95: 3–53.

Masur, E. F. (1983) 'Gestural development, dual-directional signaling, and the transition to words'. *Journal of Psycholinguistic Research* 12: 93–109.

Michotte, A. E. (1963) *The Perception of Causality*. New York: Basic Books.

Poulin-Dubois, D. and T. R. Shultz (1988) 'The development of the understanding of human behaviour: from agency to intentionality'. In *Developing Theories of Mind*, ed. J. W. Astington, P. L. Harris and D. R. Olson, 104–25. Cambridge: Cambridge University Press.

Spelke, E. S., A. Phillips and A. L. Woodward (1995) 'Infants' knowledge of object motion and human action'. In *Causal Cognition: A Multidisciplinary Debate*, ed. D. Sperber, D. Premack and A. J. Premack. New York: Oxford University Press.

Whitehouse, H. (1992) 'Memorable religions: transmission, codification, and change in divergent Melanesian contexts'. *Man* 27: 777–97.

Whitehouse, H. (1996) 'Rites of terror: emotion, metaphor, and memory in Melanesian initiation cults'. *Journal of the Royal Anthropological Institute* n.s. 2: 703–15.

Whitehouse, H. (2000) *Arguments and Icons: The Cognitive, Social, and Historical Implications of Divergent Modes of Religiosity*. Oxford: Oxford University Press.

6 Religion and the Counter-Intuitive

ILKKA PYYSIÄINEN

I want to put forward the hypothesis that we can form an analytically powerful concept of religion by taking counter-intuitiveness, as defined by Pascal Boyer, as a necessary but not sufficient criterion for religion. Counter-intuitiveness is at once the lowest common denominator of all religion and a phenomenon wider than just its religious form. In other words, religion is much more than just counter-intuitive representations, and not all counter-intuitiveness is religious. Religion is also a graded category; as Benson Saler has argued, it does not have any clear boundaries.

I think, however, that Saler's pessimism about our possibilities of singling out religion as a specific category relates to his way of making use of prototype theory without a proper theory of what to compare in 'religion' and in what sense (cf. also Saariluoma, Chapter 11 this volume). I try to show that the 'theory theory' of categorization may help us carry out comparisons at the more abstract level of cognitive processes. We can thus postulate some general criteria which will help us to identify religion as a phenomenon. This does not entail any closed definition of 'religion', however; there always remains a certain ambiguity as to what actual phenomena in any particular instance can be considered religious.

In the following pages, I first discuss the inherent problems of trying to define 'religion', and then introduce the concepts of 'counter-intuitiveness' and 'intuitive ontology'. I then briefly review the results of empirical studies of religion and counter-intuitiveness carried out by myself, Marjaana Lindeman and Timo Honkela. I also discuss the questions of why and how only some counter-intuitive representations become selected for religious use and what makes the category of 'religion' coherent. I pay special attention to religion and the social, since the social use of counter-intuitive ideas is an important characteristic of religion, although religion cannot be defined as merely a symbolic expression of the social. Finally, I try briefly to relate my theory to those of Stewart Guthrie and Saler.

'Religion' as a problematic concept

Defining 'religion' is a notorious problem (see Wilson 1998; Platvoet and Molendijk 1999). I tend to agree with Boyer (1994b: 29–34), who argues that many of the definitions hitherto suggested are not actually definitions, and that in any case theories of religion are much more important than definitions (also Lawson 1998: 43–4). Definitions are important only insofar as they are theories in a nutshell. Definitions based only on a scholar's untheoretical intuition and common sense cannot form a basis for scientific analysis. Boyer (1994b: 5, 14) also remarks that we should not worry too much about whether religion really is a universal category and whether there are features that are common to all religions; what is important is that there obviously are cross-culturally recurrent (though not necessarily universal) patterns that can be termed 'religious'. Among the conceptions that seem to be most widely diffused in the world's religious traditions are the ideas of non-observable, extra-natural agencies; the belief in a non-physical component of persons surviving death; and the notion of special categories of persons receiving some kind of 'divine' inspiration (Boyer 1994b: 33–4).

Thus Boyer seems to think that religion is a real phenomenon, although it is not a clearly defined category (see Boyer and Walker 2000). It is not merely an academic construct, as some scholars argue (e.g. Smith 1982: xi; Saler 2000: 212–13, 225; McCutcheon 1997: viii). Donald Wiebe (1994: 838; 1999: 295 n. 6) has criticized such scholars as Russell McCutcheon and Jonathan Smith for claiming that religion does not exist as an autonomous phenomenon, but is only a product of the scholar's attention. For him, religion exists as a real phenomenon. Ivan Strenski (1998) goes so far as to claim that behind the works of Timothy Fitzgerald, McCutcheon and the 'NAASR gang' there is a hidden (or even explicit) agenda to play down the whole study of religion as a separate field and to reduce religion to culture without residue.

Whether or not such an agenda exists, I want to emphasize strongly that the term 'religion' can be shown to refer to a real although somewhat vague phenomenon, despite the fact that there is some variation in what counts as religious at different times and in different cultural contexts. In other words, although religion does not have clear boundaries, it yet is not merely a theoretical term which we can apply indiscriminately to any cultural phenomena whatsoever (see Pyysiäinen 2000). Were that the case, the study of religion, or comparative religion, would indeed be in danger of diffusing into cultural anthropology, sociology, etc. (see also McCauley and Lawson 1996). A discipline without an object of its own, defined merely by a specific point of view, approach, or theory, which can be applied to any phenomena whatsoever, is in danger of turning into empty speculation. In such case it is difficult to say what the study in question is really about, what its primary data are and what would in principle falsify hypotheses put forward within its domain. If one cannot even in principle falsify a hypothesis, then the hypothesis is religious rather than scientific. Against such arbitrariness, I argue that there exist real phenomena that can be taken to form the basis of what is generally known as 'religion'.

Notwithstanding Boyer's and Saler's pessimism about universal characteristics of religion, I argue that there is one condition which can be taken as a universal characteristic of *all* religion, although it is not a *sufficient* criterion for religion: counter-intuitiveness. In counter-intuitiveness, the boundaries separating domains of intuitive ontology are violated, for example by transferring psychological properties to solid objects, or denying physical and biological properties to a person. Such phenomena violate people's intuitive, tacit expectations of how entities normally behave. Boyer too agrees that such counter-intuitive representations constitute the category of religious ideas, and that a concept that only confirms intuitive ontologies is *ipso facto* nonreligious, although counter-intuitiveness as such is not a sufficient criterion for religion. (Boyer 1994a: 408; 1994b: 122, 124; 1996a. See also Atran 1996: 234.) Yet Boyer considers all evidence to point to the conclusion that there is no domain-specialization in 'religious thinking', i.e. that there is no distinct domain of 'religious cognition'. (Boyer 1999: 68; 1996b; Boyer and Walker 2000: 151–3.)

It should, however, be emphasized that, although counter-intuitive representations actually exist in people's minds, taking counter-intuitiveness as a necessary part of the *concept* of 'religion' is a scholar's choice. We cannot show, or prove, that all religion is characterized by counter-intuitiveness; we can only decide to understand 'religion' in this way. The question is conceptual, not empirical. Whether this is a good choice or not depends on whether it allows us to put forward testable hypotheses about an observed cross-cultural pattern (see Boyer 1994b: 32).

Naturally the phenomenon of religion thus defined must be somehow compatible with the common-sense understanding of religion (see Spiro 1968: 91; Saler 2000: 77, 212). There is never an absolute gap between folk theories and scientific theories, because scientific theories ultimately rest on common-sense assumptions and conceptual postulates that cannot be proven (Churchland 1998: 149; Saariluoma 1997; this volume). The common-sense understanding of 'religion' provides the starting point from which the scientific study of religion proceeds, turning folk categories into analytic, scientific categories (Saler 2000: 1).

Identifying the object of the study of religion has hitherto been guided by the prototype effect of the Judaeo-Christian tradition (see Saler 2000: xii–xiv, 208–26), or by the habit of choosing certain salient features of traditions that are generally regarded as religious and claiming that they are necessary or even sufficient criteria for religiousness. In other words, judging what is religion and what is not has been based on intuitive folk theories without much theoretical reflection. Even taking the concept of counter-intuitiveness as a marker of religion has so far been based only on the scholarly intuition according to which all religions seem to involve counter-intuitiveness.

Experimental evidence for counter-intuitiveness as a characteristic of religion

There is now empirical evidence that counter-intuitiveness is an important element in folk theories of religion. Pyysiäinen, Lindeman and Honkela have conducted three empirical studies to test the hypothesis that – *ceteris paribus* – people are more likely to consider counter-intuitive representations to be religious than purely intuitive ones. In the first study, the subjects (N = 85) were presented with 39 brief sentences expressing various kinds of intuitive and counter-intuitive beliefs and descriptions of events. They were then asked to rate on a scale from 1 to 5 how likely they considered each sentence to be religious. The sentences were presented in the form of 13 sets of 3 sentences each, of which one was always counter-intuitive and two were intuitive. The result was that the counter-intuitive representations were considered significantly (p < .001) more likely to be religious than the intuitive ones. Typical examples of intuitive representations were 'Old man Cluang wept while listening to John's sad story', 'The Vezzi believe that the sceptre of the king is made of fine gold' and 'Boming is present on the hills.' Counter-intuitive representations are exemplified by 'The wooden statue of Bonong wept while listening to John's sad story', 'The Vezzi believe that the sceptre of the king can read people's thoughts' and 'Boming is present everywhere at once.' There were altogether 26 intuitive and 13 counter-intuitive representations, i.e. each counter-intuitive sentence had two intuitive alternatives. The subjects consisted of three groups of university students from Finland, the Republic of Ireland and midwestern USA (Pyysiäinen et al., forthcoming).

In the second study, the participants – 22 linguistics undergraduates from Lyon, France – were asked to rate the same sentences. This time the sentences were presented in mixed order. Again the counter-intuitive representations were judged more likely to be religious; the differences were significant (p < .001). (Pyysiäinen et al. forthcoming.)

In the third study, we wanted to see whether such counter-intuitiveness as includes an agent, and especially an agent that has knowledge about and interest in the affairs of humans, is regarded as more likely to be religious (along the lines suggested by Boyer, this volume). The subjects were recruited from among philosophy and anthropology undergraduates in Atlanta and in New York, USA (N = 71). In this study too counter-intuitive representations scored higher than intuitive ones. Those involving an agent scored higher (mean 3.39) than those without an agent (mean 2.47). Those involving an agent aware of and interested in the affairs of humans scored higher (mean 3.57) than those involving an agent without such interest and capacity (mean 3.12), but the reliability of the ignorant agent sentences was very low (4 items, Cronbach's α = .63) (p < .001). (Pyysiäinen et al., forthcoming.)

Thus counter-intuitiveness seems to be a statistically relevant phenomenon with regard to religiousness, in the sense that, when explicitly asked, people tend to connect the idea of counter-intuitiveness with religion. More precisely, when people have to evaluate different kinds of representations in terms of their probable religiousness, they tend to regard representations involving counter-intuitiveness as more probably religious than purely intuitive representations. Mere counter-intuitiveness as such, however, is not enough; representations of agency are important.

Counter-intuitiveness and the bounds of religion

The idea of counter-intuitiveness as a marker of religion involves the problem that not all counter-intuitiveness can be regarded as religious. Counter-intuitive representations also typify for example fiction and mental disturbance. Moreover, even scientific representations are usually in some sense counter-intuitive. Science is based on similar analogies and ontological violations as religious symbolism, although it aims at developing exact theoretical formulations about its subject matter, and at finding empirical evidence in support of theoretical claims. (See Atran 1996: 250–2; Sperber 1996: 91; McCauley 2000: 69–73; Pyysiäinen 2001b: ch. 7.) This problem has also been noted by Scott Atran (1998: 602; also Pyysiäinen 2001a; 2001b): symbolism, as explained by Atran, Dan Sperber and Boyer, cannot be distinguished from mere fiction, such as Mickey Mouse cartoons, without some additional criteria.

For Sperber (1996: 69–71) both religious/symbolic and scientific representations are 'reflective beliefs' in the sense of not being based on mere perception or on specific innate schemata. They are based almost exclusively on communication, and their formation takes a good deal of time. Both symbolism and science contrast with everyday empirical knowledge that consists of 'spontaneous' representations based on perception and communication, and which are stored in the encyclopaedic memory as true descriptions of the world.

Thus a mere distinction between spontaneous and reflective beliefs à la Sperber is not enough to single out religion as something distinctive: although both religion and science are about reflective beliefs, religion is natural and science unnatural in the sense that religious representations are acquired without explicit tuition, whereas scientific representations need to be explicitly taught (Wolpert 1992; McCauley 2000). Theological representations thus more closely resemble scientific than religious representations (Wiebe 1991; McCauley 2000; Pyysiäinen 2001b). I shall here not discuss the issue of whether ordinary and scientific thinking are endpoints on a continuum or whether they are two qualitatively different phenomena. Lawson and McCauley (1990: 26–7), as well as Deanna Kuhn (1996), for example, favour the first option, while Atran (1994; 1996; 1998) prefers the latter. In both cases, however, scientific thinking is so understood that it is possible to differentiate between symbolic and scientific thinking.

The domain of the counter-intuitive thus includes not only religious but also scientific, disturbed and fictional representations, and counter-intuitiveness is not a sufficient criterion for religion. It is important to realize that atheists too can form the kind of counter-intuitive representations that typify religion; they merely do not consider that they convey any information about external reality, and do not organize their lives employing such ideas. In this sense, intuitive ontologies and their counter-intuitive violations form the necessary basis of religion, but are not sufficient to explain what is at stake in religious belief and behaviour. We also have to explain why religious beliefs are held to be unquestionably true in the absence of evidence, or even when the empirical evidence is exactly contrary (cf. Boyer, this volume).

It thus seems natural to take 'religious belief' to distinguish religious counter-intuitive representations from mere fiction (Pyysiäinen 2001a). Religious counter-intuitive representations are considered to be true, i.e. to have reference to some mysterious counter-intuitive dimension of reality, whereas fictional counter-intuitive representations convey truth only in so far as they metaphorically describe the ordinary reality of intuitive ontologies. Thus, even if all *descriptions* of God, for example, were regarded as metaphorical, these metaphors would still be believed to *refer* to an objective God (Soskice 1985: 109, 137–48). This is not to deny the obvious fact that believers may have doubts about the truth of their beliefs; doubt and belief go together. Such balancing of doubt and belief is not found in our attitudes towards fiction, however: no sane person is unsure whether for example Mickey Mouse really exists or not. The religiosity of a representation thus is not an intrinsic property, but is based on the way someone uses it. As Saler (2001: 66) says, people do not just 'have' beliefs; they use them. This use is also marked by a strong emotional attitude towards these beliefs ('religious experience'). (See Pyysiäinen 2001a; 2001b. Cf. Boyer, Chapter 4 this volume.)

There is also the problem that it is easy to imagine a schizophrenic who seriously believes some counter-intuitive representation to be literally true, even though its truth cannot be established (or it obviously is not true). Such a belief would only be distinguished from religious beliefs by the fact that it is strictly idiosyncratic and therefore hinders communication between the person in question and other people. Such strange beliefs separate the person from others as a schizophrenic, and may be a symptom of an underlying neurobiological disorder.

Consequently, the difference between religious and disturbed representations can also be approached on the one hand on the levels of thought and behaviour, on the other on the level of neurophysiology. On the level of thought and behaviour, two types of relevant differences between religion and mental disturbance can in principle be found. The first is the difference between individual, idiosyncratic representations and cultural representations: religious representations are always part of some tradition and thus shared by a group of people. Disturbed representations do not form such traditions even within a group of schizophrenics (although there might be certain widely distributed motifs). Thus, whereas religious representations can be effectively used in communication and in life management (they often do a good job in that), disturbed representations only mean trouble. The second difference might be that while such widely distributed representations as religious ones must conform to Boyer's cognitive optimum, disturbed ones may not be so constrained. This, however, has not been empirically studied. (See Pyysiäinen 2001b.)

According to Boyer's cognitive optimum, a representation must be at once learnable and nonnatural in order to become widely distributed in a population. Were a representation completely counter-intuitive, we could not say anything about it. Such an idea would be difficult to acquire and represent and therefore would be unlikely to become widely distributed. Optimal nonnaturalness, for its part, is attention-demanding, salient, easy to recall and also easy to distribute. Thus a widely distributed representation must contain some counter-intuitiveness but not too much. It must either violate some intuitive expectations or have some counter-intuitive properties transferred to it, but not both at once. (Boyer 1994b: 114, 118–24; 1999; 2000; Atran 1996: 234, 239–41; see Barrett and Nyhof 2001 and Boyer and Ramble 2001.)

As to science, whereas religion tends to favour explanations that refer to counter-intuitive agents, scientific explanations are exactly the opposite: they tend to reduce personalistic explanations to mechanistic ones (see Lawson 2001; McCauley 2000: 70). Here they may also violate Boyer's optimum, in the sense that no intuitive elements are retained if evidence and logical coherence require that they be abandoned. Scientific reasoning is also more disciplined than common sense, which often leans on abduction. (See Boyer 1994b: 146–51; Oatley 1996.)

Towards a new understanding of 'religion'

Religion and the social

In this perspective, religion consists of such thought and behaviour in which counter-intuitive representations are employed by a group of people to express, organize, interpret and abductively explain life, the world and the nature of the self. Here counter-intuitive representations are not used as mere metaphors. They are taken as testimony to the fact that there are important forces and beings whose nature cannot be understood by natural intuition, but which nevertheless are believed to exist (cf. Guthrie 1993; Chapter 3 this volume). As the structure and vocabulary of human language reflect the categories of the natural world (intuitive ontologies), it can be used to describe the counter-intuitive reality only negatively or figuratively (see Pyysiäinen 1999: 118). But this does not mean that the existence of counter-intuitive beings and forces is also understood as only metaphorical. For believers they are real, although their exact nature is considered to be beyond the reach of our perceptual and imaginative abilities.

Thus religion as a specific category cannot be reduced to any one domain of knowledge. It is not *only* an expression of the social (e.g. Durkheim 1937; Douglas 1984), or of psychodynamic conflicts (e.g. Freud 1950); not *only* derived from folk biology gone wild (nature mythology, see Dorson 1955); and not *only* an attempt to find a foundation for naive physics (e.g. God as the unmoved mover; Capra 1975). Not all serious belief, not everything that is socially shared, not all counter-intuitiveness and not everything that is used in interpretations of life is necessarily an instance of religion. A concept of religion that is to have analytic value and explanatory power must be based on all these three criteria together. Yet many scholars have considered each of these criteria in turn as *the* foundation of religion.

Granted that purely idiosyncratic ideas are not religious, religion as a phenomenon in fact seems to have an intrinsic relationship with the social, although this does not mean that we can define religion as an expression of social categories only. Even Mary Douglas (1984: 101, 112) admits that, although she considers beliefs about spiritual powers always to have a relation to social order, such a relation naturally is not possible when there is no such order among a group of people. As I see it, the view of religion as just a way of giving expression to social order makes the concept of 'religion' too general and vague and also ignores one salient recurrent pattern: counter-intuitiveness. (See Pyysiäinen 2001b: ch. 4.) It does not tell us why people express social order by representations of gods, etc., and not by something else (see Hempel 1965: 297–330), and why believers themselves are not conscious of the real nature of their religion.

How, then, do some counter-intuitive beliefs acquire a religious status, becoming selected for social use in the 'life management' of a community? Jared Diamond (1999: 277–8) claims that in what he calls 'bands', as distinguished from tribes, chiefdoms and states, supernatural beliefs did not serve to justify central authority or the distribution of wealth, or to maintain peace between individuals. In short, counter-intuitive beliefs did not form institutionalized religious systems.

Diamond, who has attempted to construct a comprehensive theory of the evolution of human societies, argues that it is the size of the regional population that determines the development of societal complexity. Chiefdoms and states arise following four developments: (1) population growth leads to an increase in conflict between unrelated strangers; (2) communal decisions become increasingly difficult or impossible; (3) a need arises for a means of transferring goods between members of society; and (4) there is a need for some arrangement to determine the rights and obligations of individuals sharing the same territory. The first humans lived in bands, as our closest relatives, the gorillas, chimpanzees and bonobos still do. Tribal organizations consisting of more than one formally recognized kinship group began to emerge around 13,000 years ago in the Fertile Crescent, in south-west Asia, and later in some other areas. Chiefdoms arose by around 5500 BC in the Fertile Crescent and by around 1000 BC in Mesoamerica and the Andes. According to Diamond, it was only now, for the first time in history, that people had to learn to encounter strangers regularly without attempting to kill them, the monopoly on the right to use violence having been vested in the chief. The new elite had four types of solutions to the problem of how to gain popular support while yet maintaining a more comfortable lifestyle: (1) arming the elite and disarming the populace; (2) making the masses happy by redistributing in popular ways much of the tribute received; (3) using the monopoly of force to promote happiness by maintaining public order; and (4) constructing an ideology or religion justifying the existing order. States, for their part, arose around 3700 in Mesopotamia, around 300 BC in Mesoamerica, over 2000 years ago in the Andes, China and South-east Asia, and over 1000 years ago in West Africa. It was the emergence of food production, the domestication of plants and animals, and the agricultural way of life that ultimately made this development possible. (Diamond 1999: 88–90, 265–92; also Mithen 1999. Cf. Sahlins 1968: 5, 15. See Ehrenberg 1995: 85–90; Pyysiäinen 2001b: ch. 6.)

Diamond's analysis thus suggests – correctly in my opinion – that counter-intuitive representations are primary, and their social use secondary (also Boyer 1996a). Counter-intuitive representations have arisen as a by-product of the intuitive ontologies, possibly some 50,000 to 100,000 years ago when humans became capable of transcending the boundaries between ontological domains in their thinking, at least if Steven Mithen's (1998) theorizing is correct (cf. Boyer 2000). Whether we should regard them as a rudimentary form of religion depends on what kind of concept of religion we want to use. According to the view adopted here, the important question is how and when more or less organized bodies of counter-intuitive representations started to emerge and be used in legitimating social order and laying a foundation for ethics (cf. Douglas 1984: 133–6; see Whitehouse 2000).

From this perspective, it is remarkable that Durkheim (1937) developed his theory of religion on the basis of materials concerning Australian totemism only, yet intending it as a general theory of religion. Durkheim (1926: 148) claimed that while primitive societies were based on mechanical solidarity and the 'common conscience' expressed in religion, in complex societies division of labour had assumed the role that was formerly played by the common conscience (and thus by religion). But if it is the division of labour on which organic solidarity and thus the social structure is based, what, then, is the role of religion in complex societies? It clearly cannot be the same as in a primitive society. Division of labour implies a functional differentiation of society (see Luhmann 1982), and religion is no longer the sole source of social cohesion. (See also Lukes 1977: 519; Giddens 1978: 99–104.)

Religious institutions thus have to adapt themselves to the society, although religious ideas cannot be taken as simply a reflection of the society. Conceptions of counter-intuitive agents do not form a code language for talking about the society (see Sperber 1995). They are beliefs about counter-intuitive agents and realities that are really believed to exist, although their form and use are affected by the form of the society.

An interesting perspective on the question of how religion may be differentiated from non-religion is provided by Boyer (Chapter 4 this volume), who argues that especially such counter-intuitive agents as have what he calls 'strategic knowledge' (see Morton 2000) are important in religion. This view, as we have seen, also received support from an empirical study by Pyysiäinen, Lindeman and Honkela (forthcoming). The notion of strategic knowledge, however, clearly brings us back to the question of the social, as it concerns specifically the interactions of a group of humans. Counter-intuitive agents which are really believed to exist are also believed to be capable of interfering in the lives of humans. This naturally opens up a perspective on the questions of why and how religious ideas are used in organizing society. For the time being, however, there are no empirical studies directed towards solving clearly formulated problems related to the use of counter-intuitive representations in legitimating specific social practices. My intention here has merely been to direct attention on the one hand to the importance of counter-intuitive representations as a necessary characteristic of religion, on the other to the fact that the scholar of religion cannot ignore their social use.

It seems to me, for example, that the spread of religious ideas cannot be explained merely by the mechanisms of memory, since religion is not the same as culture. A given type of representation may have cultural success, yet not religious success. The nature of human memory may well prove to be one crucial determinant in the process whereby certain representations become widespread in a culture, but it cannot explain why some counter-intuitive representations are believed to be true (Pyysiäinen 2001a; cf. Boyer, Chapter 4 this volume). If we really can identify religion as a phenomenon along the lines here presented, then we need some new tools for explaining how religious belief arises (see Pyysiäinen 2001b: ch. 5) and affects social processes. I have presented counter-intuitiveness as a necessary element in religion, but in fact it is only the bedrock of religion. Upon it is built a very complex phenomenon, the boundaries of which are fuzzy.

The bounds of religion

My account of religion is similar to Guthrie's (1980; 1993; 1996; this volume) in the sense that I have identified a phenomenon which on the one hand is wider than religion, on the other forms the lowest common denominator of all religion. Moreover, I share with Guthrie the idea that this common denominator is the human tendency to postulate special kinds of beings that are believed to be responsible for various things and events. I differ from Guthrie, however, in that I think that these beings should be conceptualized as counter-intuitive agents. As also Boyer (1996a) and Justin Barrett (1998: 617) observe, it is not general humanlikeness that is important, but agency, especially belief-and-desire psychology; only humans are prototypical agents (also Lawson 2001). An agent is typified by cognitive processes, by intentional behaviour and by the fact that it can move around as though it had an internal source of energy (Leslie 1994; 1996).

For Guthrie (1996: 414–15), religious agents are humanlike and yet nonhuman. They are in no way counter-intuitive. Guthrie claims that it is an 'ethnographic and ethological fact' that invisibility and intangibility are natural, not counter-intuitive. After all, animals can be invisible and intangible through camouflage, travelling in complex and deceptive flocks, etc. This seems like a misunderstanding of Boyer and a misrepresentation of religious beliefs. Boyer never says that invisibility *as such* is counter-intuitive, or that 'invisible', i.e. camouflaged, animals are counter-intuitive. It is perfectly natural that I for example cannot see Guthrie when he is in another room (or is cleverly camouflaged). There is nothing mysterious about that. But from this it does not follow that the invisibility of gods is natural. It has to be borne in mind that the counter-intuitiveness of gods derives from an unnatural *combination* of characteristics, such as for example belief-and-desire psychology and lack of a physical body. It runs counter to human intuitive expectations for a person not to have a body, although many believe that such strange persons do exist (Boyer 1994b: 117–24; 1996a; Atran 1996: 234, 241–2; Sperber 1994: 62). Gods are not invisible in the same sense as camouflaged animals. The former are invisible even in principle, while the latter only sometimes in practice. Counter-intuitive agents are not just 'something-out-there', but beings about whose nature believers have more or less detailed descriptions, but which yet are never perceived in any ordinary way. We therefore use different kinds of scientific explanations in explaining on the one hand the perception of physical objects, animals and human beings, on the other counter-intuitive agents (i.e. visions, hallucinations, etc.).

There is no unambiguous evidence that animism and anthropomorphism arise because our perceptions are always ambiguous and we have to scan the environment trying to detect camouflaged beings, as Guthrie holds (see Boyer 1996a: 87–92). Ideas about agents without biology and physics, as well as ideas about physical objects with psychological properties, might also arise merely as a by-product in our cognitive system. Once we have such counter-intuitive ideas, we are also forced to consider the possibility that counter-intuitive agents (and not just something-out-there) might actually exist in objective reality. It is thus not only that perception and its ambiguities force us to postulate counter-intuitive beings. The nature of human cognition, i.e. the ability to form counter-intuitive ideas, makes us suspect that reality is not faithfully reflected in our perception; this then makes it seem possible, or even likely, that counter-intuitive agents might exist. In other words, I am arguing that mere ambiguity of perception is not enough for the idea of counter-intuitive agents to arise. What is also needed is a cognitive fluidity (Mithen 1998: 171–222) that allows for the mixing of knowledge from different ontological domains.

Now, Guthrie's favourite example of chimpanzees in a thunderstorm (1996: 415; Chapter 3 this volume) might be raised as a counter-example to this: the chimps react to the storm aggressively, as though they were thinking that an invisible agent is acting against them. They clearly display a behaviour that is typical of them when they want to threaten their conspecifics and predators. So are they not postulating an invisible agent behind the thunderstorm? Here we must distinguish between an ordinary, natural being which is for some reason invisible in some particular situation, and counter-intuitive beings which are invisible even in principle: they are *never* perceived. For the moment, there seems to be no unequivocal evidence that the chimpanzees have an idea of a special kind of invisible being responsible for thunderstorms. A more economic solution would be that, *if* the chimps' reaction is expressive of aggression towards an agent, it is a reaction towards another aggressive chimpanzee or a predator which is only invisible at that specific moment. In other words, the thunderstorm triggers the same reaction as does a predator, without a representation of a special kind of counter-intuitive agent being involved. In religion, however, people not only react for example to various misfortunes and calamities as though they were caused by an agent, but also put forward conscious explanations as to the special, counter-intuitive nature of this agent. This is not to say that there is no continuity between animals and humans; even though we humans have some novel cognitive capacities compared to other animals, we yet are part of the very same evolutionary process.

Guthrie (1980; 1993; 1996; Chapter 3 this volume), however, thinks that religion arises as a by-product of a perceptual and cognitive strategy (i.e. animism and anthropomorphism) which is not distinctively human. His analyses focus heavily on these strategies, while the question of what makes some instances of animism/anthropomorphism specifically *religious* receives almost no attention. According to Guthrie (1996: 418) the concept of 'religion' stems from the Western culture and thus requires adjustments along the lines of prototype theory. Yet he holds that we cannot really distinguish between religion and non-religion (see also Saler 2000: 131–7), and, in the end, leaves the concept of 'religion' unexplained.

I have above suggested some ways of distinguishing religion from non-religion: among the things that typify religion are counter-intuitiveness and agency, serious belief, social use and emotional reactions. These are not meant as the characteristics of everything that 'really' is religion, but only as characteristics on the basis of which we can form a useful concept of 'religion'. Counter-intuitive representations form the solid basis on which religion rests, although religion itself is an 'impure subject' (Boyer 1996b) in which many kinds of things combine, and the precise boundaries of which are fuzzy. Saler's (2000) way of conceptualizing religion on the basis of the idea of family resemblance and prototype theory has much to offer in explaining the coherence of such a category of religion. Although we can, in principle, list various things that are required for a phenomenon to fall into the category of the 'religious', it may not always be clear whether a particular phenomenon fulfils the criteria. What counts as serious belief? How many people are needed to form a social group? There are only graded answers to these questions (see Saler 2000: xiii–xiv).

Saler (2000: 25) thus argues that there are no necessary character-istics of religion, and that also no set of characteristics can be regarded *a priori* as sufficient. I have argued that counter-intuitiveness is a *necessary* characteristic of religion, although it is not limited to religion alone. However, I do not think that there is an exhaustive list of *sufficient* characteristics. In this sense, there is room for 'family resem-blance' and prototypicality effects. I also think that the distinction between *a priori* and *a posteriori* is itself a fuzzy one, because even *a priori* ideas are entertained in human minds and thus are already shaped by experience (see Quine 1980). The fact that I have suggested counter-intuitiveness as a necessary characteristic of religion may thus have been in some sense *a priori*, but it is based on experience as well: counter-intuitiveness seems to be a pervasive phenomenon in religion in the light both of the experience of a historian of religions and of empirical evidence concerning the folk theory of religion. Religious counter-intuitiveness is 'a graded category the instantiations of which are linked by family resemblances' (to quote Saler (2000: xiv)).

Saler, however, has remarked (private communication) that taking counter-intuitiveness as a necessary characteristic of religion creates the dilemma that there may well be traditions that lack counter-intuitiveness but yet have all or nearly all the other characteristics of religion (e.g. communism). Would it not be a very artificial judgement to exclude them from the family of religion? I agree that this *may* be a problem, but for the moment it is just an unexplored assumption that such cases actually exist. In fact, it would be rather strange if counter-intuitiveness really were only one characteristic of religion among others, having no special consequences of its own. It is more likely that if counter-intuitiveness is lacking, then certain other characteristics that typify religion will also be missing. (See Lawson and McCauley, this volume.) Nor is it necessary for a scientific concept of 'religion' to include everything that to common sense appears as religious, as far as the scientific concept is not completely at odds with the commonsensical one. It would not be a catastrophe if for example the official doctrines of Confucianism turned out to be lacking counter-intuitiveness and therefore not to be instances of religion. On the contrary, this would only clarify the concept of religion. Mere vague analogies are not a good reason to accept something, such as communism, as an instance of religion; to the best of my knowledge nothing more substantive has hitherto been suggested.

Saler (2000: xiv, 25, 208–12, 227) says that although Judaism, Christianity and Islam are the clearest examples, or most prototypical exemplars, of the category of religion, this is only so because these are the ones with which most scholars so far have been most familiar. We should, however, not restrict the study of religion to these traditions, but explore the whole world of religion. We have to go beyond the folk category and turn it into an analytical category. According to Saler, this can be done employing the prototype theory developed within cognitive science.

The prototype approach to categorization holds that there are no sufficient and necessary features by which we can decide whether an object belongs to a given category. People do not recognize different kinds of objects merely by classifying them under some particular concept, but by comparing them to prototypes serving as exemplars for things of the relevant category. These prototypes are not anything concrete, but rather some kind of ideal types. Such prototypicality means three things: first, a prototypical member of a class is recognized as belonging to that particular class more quickly than others; second, when asked to name members of a given class, people mention the most prototypical member first; and third, children learn first to recognize the most prototypical member of a class. (Rosch 1975; 1978; Rosch and Mervis 1975. See Boyer 1994b: 61–3. Cf. Saariluoma, Chapter 11 this volume.)

Saler's (2000: 212–20, 225) argument, then, is that 'religion' is an abstraction, and that for analytical purposes we may conceptualize it in terms of a pool of elements that more or less tend to occur together in the best exemplars of the category (i.e. the 'Western monotheisms'). There is no hard and fast line separating religion from non-religion, no universal criteria for inclusion and exclusion, only diminishing (or increasing) degrees of typicality. Scholars of religion are free to conceptualize their subject matter with reference to, but not in terms of, their understanding of Judaism, Christianity and Islam.

However, prototype theory only tells us how people recognize something as being an instance of a category, not what makes categories coherent (see also Saariluoma, this volume). The category of odd numbers, for example, is made coherent by the sufficient and necessary requirement that it consists of numbers that are not multiples of 2. People tend to judge certain numbers, such as 7, as more prototypically odd than others, as shown by Sharon Armstrong and her colleagues, but this can be said to be a misrepresentation of the category. (See Osherson and Smith 1981; Armstrong et al. 1983.) Saler (2000: 202) admits this, and acknowledges that there may be also essentialist categories, but he does not consider 'religion' to be such a category. All coherence there is in religion as an analytical category is based on mere family resemblances.

My problem with this kind of prototype approach is that the scholar seems to be forced to operate purely on the level of folk theories and *emic* terminology: religion is whatever resembles Judaism, Christianity and/or Islam, understood in a simple, non-theoretical way. Religion is not sought in the light of scientific theories, but only on the basis of an everyday understanding of surface-level phenomena. The folk theory is not after all successfully transformed into a scientific one.

There is, however, an alternative to the prototype theory, the so-called 'theory theory'. It has emerged from research on children's theory of mind as well as on their thinking about natural kinds (see Perner 1993: 240–1; Gopnik and Wellman 1996; Atran 1998: 599). Gregory Murphy and Douglas Medin (1985), as well as Lance Rips (1995), for example hold that conceptual coherence is based on so-called naive theories about the world. People categorize things on the basis of 'minitheories' or 'microtheories' that consist of three elements: (1) an idea of what makes an instance a member of the category; (2) some specification of the default properties that such an instance possesses; and (3) some account of the relation between (1) and (2). Categories thus are not based on a simple similarity between their members, but on an intuitive and implicit theory according to which observed regularities are systematized. (See also Boyer 1994b: 62–8.)

The theory theory thus shifts the emphasis from concrete exemplars to the cognitive processes responsible for categorizing something as an instance of a given category. We cannot make meaningful comparisons without a theory which says which similarities are relevant and why (Lawson 1996). By the same token the theory theory also provides better possibilities for the scholar to develop scientific explanations of the processes involved, and to transform the folk theory of religion into a scientific one. (I do not mean a theory of religion *tout court*, but a theory that accounts for why certain types of phenomena are grouped together as somehow special, i.e. religious in terms of Western terminology.) Thus, although there might be both cultural and temporal variation in what counts as religion, the criteria of reasoning according to which something is judged to be religious are the same, i.e. counter-intuitiveness plus the additional criteria I have mentioned (see also Pyysiäinen 2000).

Thus the emphasis is shifted from prototypical exemplars to actual cognitive processes. To characterize religion, we no longer have to list the constituent phenomena that form the 'pool of elements that more or less tend to occur together' (Saler 2000: 170–2). The 'religion-ness' of religion does not derive from any particular content described in the language of religions, but rather from the way something is cognitively and emotionally appreciated. Ritual behaviour for example does not as such make an event religious. Only when a ritual involves counter-intuitive representations and fulfils some additional criteria should we regard it as religious. In particular counter-intuitiveness as a necessary marker of religion serves to replace the Western monotheisms as the most prototypical religions in the light of which other forms of religion are recognized. Beliefs that involve a counter-intuitive agent are easiest to recognize as religious, i.e. they are the most prototypically religious beliefs. More precisely, the most unequivocal presence of representations of counter-intuitive agents which are seriously believed to exist, which tend to provoke emotional reactions, and which are used to organize life, characterize the most prototypical instances of religion, be it within the confines of Christianity, Buddhism, the UFO cult or whatever. Rather than a similarity to any particular religion, it is counter-intuitiveness that draws the scholar's attention to a phenomenon as possibly religious.

Yet there is also room for family resemblance and prototypicality, in the sense that the theoretical criteria presented may not always allow for a clear decision on whether something is an instance of religion or not. They are not sufficient criteria. In thus arguing I am not trying to reveal what religion 'really' is, but only attempting to construct a useful analytical concept of 'religion', which can serve to identify a real recurrent phenomenon.

Acknowledgements

In addition to the participants of the Seili workshop, I want to thank Benson Saler for comments on an earlier draft of this paper.

References

Armstrong, S. L., L. G. Gleitman and H. Gleitman (1983) 'What some concepts might not be'. *Cognition* 12: 263–308.

Atran, S. (1994) 'Core domains versus scientific theories: evidence from systematics and Itza-Maya folkbiology'. In *Mapping the Mind*, ed. L. Hirschfeld and S. Gelman, 316–40. Cambridge: Cambridge University Press.

Atran, S. (1996) 'Modes of thinking about living kinds'. In *Modes of Thought*, ed. D. R. Olson and N. Torrance, 216–60. New York: Cambridge University Press.

Atran, S. (1998) 'Folk biology and the anthropology of science: cognitive universals and cultural particulars'. *Behavioral and Brain Sciences* 21: 547–609.

Barrett, J. L. (1998) 'Cognitive constraints on Hindu concepts of the divine'. *Journal for the Scientific Study of Religion* 37: 608–19.

Barrett, J. L. and M. A. Nyhof (2001) 'Spreading non-natural concepts: the role of intuitive conceptual structures in memory and transmission of cultural materials'. *Journal of Cognition and Culture* 1: 69–100.

Boyer, P. (1994a) 'Cognitive constraints on cultural representations: natural ontologies and religious ideas'. In *Mapping the Mind*, ed. L. Hirschfeld and S. Gelman, 39–67. Cambridge: Cambridge University Press.

Boyer, P. (1994b) *The Naturalness of Religious Ideas: A Cognitive Theory of Religion*. Berkeley: University of California Press.

Boyer, P. (1996a) 'What makes anthropomorphism natural: intuitive ontology and cultural representations'. *Journal of the Royal Anthropological Institute* n.s. 2: 1–15.

Boyer, P. (1996b) 'Religion as impure subject: a note on cognitive order in religious representation in response to Brian Malley'. *Method and Theory in the Study of Religion* 8: 201–13.

Boyer, P. (1999) 'Cognitive aspects of religious ontologies: how brain processes constrain religious concepts'. In *Approaching Religion*, part I, ed. T. Ahlbäck, 53–72, Scripta Instituti Donneriani, 17:1. Åbo: Donner Institute.

Boyer, P. (2000) 'Evolution of a modern mind and the origins of culture: religious concepts as a limiting case'. In *Evolution and the Human Mind: Modularity, Language and Meta-Cognition*, ed. Peter Carruthers and Andrew Chamberlain, 93–112. Cambridge: Cambridge University Press.

Boyer, P. and C. Ramble (2001) 'Cognitive templates for religious concepts: cross-cultural evidence for recall of counter-intuitive representations'. *Cognitive Science* 25: 535–64.

Boyer, P. and S. Walker (2000) 'Intuitive ontology and cultural input in the acquisition of religious concepts'. In *Imagining the Impossible: Magical, Scientific, and Religious Thinking in Children*, ed. K. S. Rosengren, C. N. Johnson and P. L. Harris, 130–56. Cambridge: Cambridge University Press.

Capra, F. (1975) *The Tao of Physics*. Boston: Shambhala.

Churchland, P. S. (1998 (1986)) *Neurophilosophy: Toward a Unified Science of the Mind/Brain*. Cambridge, MA: MIT Press.

Diamond, J. (1999 (1997)) *Guns, Germs, and Steel*. New York: Norton.

Dorson, R. (1955) 'The eclipse of solar mythology'. *Journal of American Folklore* 68: 393–416.

Douglas, M. (1984 (1966)) *Purity and Danger*. London etc.: Ark Paper Backs.

Durkheim, É. (1926 (1893)) *De la division du travail social*. Paris: Alcan.

Durkheim, É. (1937 (1912)) *Les Formes élémentaires de la vie religieuse*. Paris: Alcan.

Ehrenberg, M. (1995 (1989)) *Women in Prehistory*. London: British Museum Press.

Freud, S. (1950 (1913)) *Totem and Taboo*, trans. J. Strachey. New York: Norton.

Giddens, A. (1978) *Durkheim*. Glasgow: Fontana/Collins.

Gopnik, A. and H. M. Wellman (1996) 'The theory theory'. In *Modes of Thought*, ed. D. R. Olson and N. Torrance, 257–93. New York: Cambridge University Press.

Guthrie, S. (1980) 'A cognitive theory of religion'. *Current Anthropology* 21: 181–203.

Guthrie, S. (1993) *Faces in the Clouds*. New York: Oxford University Press.

Guthrie, S. (1996) 'Religion: what is it?' *Journal for the Scientific Study of Religion* 35: 412–19.

Hempel, C. G. (1965) *Aspects of Scientific Explanation and Other Essays in the Philosophy of Science*. New York: Free Press.

Kuhn, D. (1996) 'Is good thinking scientific thinking?' In *Modes of Thought*, ed. D. R. Olson and N. Torrance, 261–81. New York: Cambridge University Press.

Lawson, E. T. (1996) 'Theory and the new comparativism, old and new'. *Method and Theory in the Study of Religion* 8: 31–5.

Lawson, E. T. (1998) 'Defining religion . . . going the theoretical way'. In *What Is Religion?*, ed. T. A. Idinopulos and B. Wilson, 43–9, Studies in the History of Religions (Numen Book Series), 81. Leiden: Brill.

Lawson, E. T. (2001) 'Psychological perspectives on agency'. In *Religion in Mind: Cognitive Perspectives on Religious Belief, Ritual and Experience*, ed. J. Andresen, 141–72. Cambridge: Cambridge University Press.

Lawson, E. T. and R. N. McCauley (1990) *Rethinking Religion: Connecting Cognition and Culture*. Cambridge: Cambridge University Press.

Leslie, A. (1994) 'ToMM, ToBy, and Agency: core architecture and domain specificity'. In *Mapping the Mind*, ed. L. Hirschfeld and S. Gelman, 119–48. Cambridge: Cambridge University Press.

Leslie, A. (1996 (1995)) 'A theory of agency'. In *Causal Cognition*, ed. D. Sperber, D. Premack and A. J. Premack, 121–41. Oxford: Clarendon Press.

Luhmann, N. (1982) 'The differentiation of society'. In N. Luhmann, *The*

Differentiation of Society, 229–54, trans. S. Holmes and C. Larmore. New York: Columbia University Press.

Lukes, S. (1977 (1973)) *Émile Durkheim*. Harmondsworth: Penguin.

McCauley, R. N. (2000) 'The naturalness of religion and the unnaturalness of science'. In *Explanation and Cognition*, ed. F. C. Keil and R. A. Wilson, 61–85. Cambridge, MA: MIT Press.

McCauley, R. N. and E. T. Lawson (1996) 'Who owns "culture"?' *Method and Theory in the Study of Religion* 8: 171–90.

McCutcheon, R. T. (1997) *Manufacturing Religion: The Discourse on Sui Generis Religion and the Politics of Nostalgia*. Oxford: Oxford University Press.

Mithen, S. (1998 (1996)) *The Prehistory of the Mind*. London: Phoenix.

Mithen, S. (1999) *Problem-Solving and the Evolution of Human Culture*, Monograph Series, 33. London: Institute for Cultural Research.

Morton, A. (2000) 'The evolution of strategic thinking'. In *Evolution and the Human Mind: Modularity, Language and Meta-Cognition*, ed. P. Carruthers and A. Chamberlain, 218–37. Cambridge: Cambridge University Press.

Murphy, G. and D. Medin (1985) 'The role of theories in conceptual coherence'. *Psychological Review* 92: 289–316.

Oatley, K. (1996) 'Inference in narrative and science'. In *Modes of Thought*, ed. D. R. Olson and N. Torrance, 123–40. New York: Cambridge University Press.

Osherson, D. N. and E. E. Smith (1981) 'On the adequacy of prototype theory as a theory of concepts'. *Cognition* 9: 35–58.

Perner, J. (1993 (1991)) *Understanding the Representational Mind*. Cambridge, MA: MIT Press.

Platvoet, J. C. and A. L. Molendijk (eds) (1999) *The Pragmatics of Defining Religion: Contexts, Concepts, and Contests*, Studies in the History of Religions (Numen Book Series), 84. Leiden: Brill.

Pyysiäinen, I. (1999) 'God as ultimate reality in religion and in science'. *Ultimate Reality and Meaning* 22(2): 106–23.

Pyysiäinen, I. (2000) 'No limits? Defining the field of comparative religion'. In *Ethnography Is a Heavy Rite: Studies of Comparative Religion in Honor of Juha Pentikäinen*, ed. N. G. Holm et al., 31–40, Religionsvetenskapliga skrifter, 47. Åbo: Åbo Akademi.

Pyysiäinen, I. (2001a) 'Cognition, emotion, and religious experience'. In *Religion in Mind: Cognitive Perspectives on Religious Belief, Ritual and Experience*, ed. J. Andresen, 70–93. Cambridge: Cambridge University Press.

Pyysiäinen, I. (2001b) *How Religion Works: Towards a New Cognitive Science of Religion*, Cognition and Culture Bookseries, 1. Leiden: Brill.

Pyysiäinen, I., M. Lindeman and T. Honkela (Forthcoming) 'Religion and counter-intuitive representations'. Work in progress.

Quine, W. van O. (1980 (1951)) 'Two dogmas of empiricism'. In Quine, *From a Logical Point of View*, 20–46. Cambridge, MA: Harvard University Press.

Rips, L. J. (1995) 'The current status of research on concept combination'. *Mind and Language* 10: 72–104.

Rosch, E. (1975) 'Cognitive representations of semantic categories'. *Journal of Experimental Psychology* 104: 192–233.

Rosch, E. (1978) 'Principles of categorization'. In *Cognition and Categorization*, ed. E. Rosch and B. B. Lloyd, 27–48. Hillsdale, NJ: Erlbaum.

Rosch, E. and C. B. Mervis (1975) 'Family resemblances: studies in the internal structure of categories'. *Cognitive Psychology* 7: 573–605.

Saarilouma, P. (1997) *Foundational Analysis: Presuppositions in Experimental Psychology*. London: Routledge.

Sahlins, M. (1968) *Tribesmen*, Prentice-Hall Foundations of Modern Anthropology Series. Englewood Cliffs, NJ: Prentice-Hall.

Saler, B. (2000 (1993)) *Conceptualizing Religion: Immanent Anthropologists, Transcendent Natives, and Unbound Categories*, with a new preface. New York: Berghahn Books.

Saler, B. (2001) 'On what we may believe about beliefs'. In *Religion in Mind: Cognitive Perspectives on Religious Belief, Ritual and Experience*, ed. J. Andresen, 47–69. Cambridge: Cambridge University Press.

Smith, J. Z. (1982) *Imagining Religion*. Chicago: University of Chicago Press.

Soskice, J. M. (1985) *Metaphor and Religious Language*. Oxford: Clarendon Press.

Sperber, D. (1995 (1974)) *Rethinking Symbolism*. Cambridge: Cambridge University Press.

Sperber, D. (1994) 'The modularity of thought and the epidemiology of representations'. In *Mapping the Mind*, ed. L. Hirschfeld and S. Gelman, 39–67. Cambridge: Cambridge University Press.

Sperber, D. (1996) *Explaining Culture: A Naturalistic Approach*. Oxford: Blackwell.

Spiro, M. E. (1968 (1966)) 'Religion: problems of definition and explanation'. In *Anthropological Approaches to the Study of Religion*, ed. M. Banton, 85–126. London: Tavistock.

Strenski, I. (1998) 'On "religion" and its despisers'. In *What Is Religion?*, ed. T. A. Idinopulos and B. Wilson, 113–32, Studies in the History of Religions (Numen Book Series), 81. Leiden: Brill.

Whitehouse, H. (2000) *Arguments and Icons: Divergent Modes of Religiosity*. Oxford: Oxford University Press.

Wiebe, D. (1991) *The Irony of Theology and the Nature of Religious Thought*, McGill-Queen's Studies in the History of Ideas, 15. Montreal: McGill-Queen's University Press.

Wiebe, D. (1994) 'From religious to social reality: the transformation of "religion" in the academy'. In *The Notion of 'Religion' in Comparative Research*, Selected Proceedings of the 16th IAHR Congress, ed. U. Bianchi, 837–45. Rome: 'L'erma' di Bretschneider.

Wiebe, D. (1999) *The Politics of Religious Studies*. New York: St Martin's Press.

Wilson, B. C. (1998) 'From the lexical to the polythetic: a brief history of the definition of religion'. In *What Is Religion?*, ed. T. A. Idinopulos and B. Wilson, 141–62, Studies in the History of Religions (Numen Book Series), 81. Leiden: Brill.

Wolpert, L. (1992) *The Unnatural Nature of Science*. London: Faber & Faber.

7 Implicit and Explicit Knowledge in the Domain of Ritual

HARVEY WHITEHOUSE

Social and cultural theorists have long struggled with the problem of how to characterize the types of knowledge involved in the performance of rituals. Eighteenth- and nineteenth-century scholars of religion mostly envisaged ritual as an enactment of consciously formulated rules, transmitted verbally. As Robertson-Smith (1907: 16) astutely observed, with respect to this scholarship: 'the study of religion has meant mainly the study of Christian beliefs, and instruction in religion has habitually begun with the creed, religious duties being presented to the learner as flowing from the dogmatic truths he is taught to accept. All this seems to us so much a matter of course that, when we approach some new or antique religion, we naturally assume that here also our first business is to search for a creed, and find in it the key to ritual and practice.' But Robertson-Smith argued, with regard to the earliest religions, that procedural knowledge preceded declarative, exegetical knowledge, rather than the other way around. As he put it: 'in ancient religion . . . practice preceded doctrinal theory. Men form general rules of conduct before they begin to express general principles in words' (Robertson-Smith 1907: 20).

Despite Robertson-Smith's suggestions, the development of religious anthropology in the early to mid-twentieth century continued to envisage ritual procedures as an application of declarative knowledge. As Leach noted towards the end of this period: 'the classic doctrine in English social anthropology is that the rite is a dramatisation of the myth, the myth is the sanction or charter for the rite' (1954: 13). In the 1960s and 1970s, however, the eclipse of functionalism by structuralist, symbolic and interpretive approaches in religious anthropology generated a wealth of new models, suggesting that rituals are governed by implicit rules, unavailable for verbal report. Not all of these approaches, however, were psychologically plausible.

For instance, Lévi-Strauss's argument that cognitive processing of concepts is unconsciously guided by the principle of binary opposition finds little support from experimental studies of implicit concept-formation and categorization (Boyer 1993: 16–17). Similarly, those pulling against the tide of structuralism seldom did so with reference to precise and well-supported cognitive assumptions. Theories of 'multivocality' (Turner 1967; Munn 1973) and 'analogic codification' (Bateson 1972; Barth 1975) challenged the notion of arbitrary structures of signification by focusing instead on the iconic and connotative qualities of ritual symbols. The resulting analyses sometimes invoked psychoanalytic principles of unconscious processing (e.g. condensation, displacement, primary association, symbolization, etc.), which were neither testable experimentally nor verifiable via standard procedures of ethnographic research.

Contemporary religious anthropology has done less than it might to advance our understanding of unconscious knowledge in the domain of ritual. Often inspired more by obscure philosophical writing than by clearly formulated and well-supported assumptions, many recent theoretical trends have entertained notions of procedural memory that are crude and, in some cases, demonstrably false. For instance, Bourdieu's (1977; 1990) notion of *habitus* as unconscious knowledge that is widely shared and automatically learned is substantially transcended by the precision, subtlety and empirical productivity of schema theory and connectionist models in psychology and neuroscience (see Strauss and Quinn 1997: ch. 2). Nevertheless, anthropologists writing about ritual are much more inclined to invoke the concept of *habitus*, with all its associated limitations, than the sort of cognitive architecture painstakingly constructed through rigorous experimental research. Or, to take another example, Connerton's discussion of the role of 'habit memory' in ritual performance, often cited by anthropologists, is founded upon a host of dubious claims about sensorimotor intelligence, such as the insistence that manual dexterity consists, not in conditioned reflexes, but in 'knowledge and remembering in the hands and the body' (Connerton 1989: 95), despite a wealth of neuropsychological evidence to the contrary (see Luria 1973 and Edelman 1992).

Anthropology has produced many superb ethnographic descriptions of religious rituals, but it has so far been unable to specify and demonstrate in detail the types of knowledge entailed by ritual performances, and the ways in which these forms of knowledge are transmitted and learned.

The questions posed in this chapter derive from my own experience of ethnographic research, but they are also based on models and findings in cognitive science. Specifically, I will be asking why some ritual practices are associated with an abundance of widely recognized and stateable meanings, whereas others are not publicly accorded exegesis and their meanings (if they have any) appear to be restricted to elders and ritual experts. My answers to these questions may seem counter-intuitive or, at any rate, paradoxical.

In the case of frequently repeated rituals, much of the procedural knowledge available to participants is implicit, taking the form of automatized or 'embodied' habits. Habituated ritual actions are capable of being reproduced on 'autopilot', in the absence of exegetical reflection. Paradoxically, these are precisely the sorts of rituals that tend to be accorded elaborate and widely disseminated exegesis. The explanation is that routinized rituals provide cognitively optimal conditions for the attribution of meanings from outside, for instance by religious authorities (the guardians of orthodoxy). On the one hand, because long-term participation in highly repetitive rituals does not automatically result in exegetical reflexivity, authoritative interpretations are not at great risk of distortion or corruption by internally generated, speculative exegesis. On the other hand, routinization provides ideal conditions for the rote-learning and stable reproduction of a standard, centrally formulated exegetical tradition.

In the case of rare and climactic rituals, the situation is very different. Procedural knowledge does not take the form of automatized habits but constitutes a form of explicit knowledge, largely organized in episodic memory. The reproduction of such rituals cannot be achieved on the basis of implicit knowledge. It requires explicit, off-line processing which, in turn, makes a reflexive stance on questions of symbolic motivation and exegesis virtually inevitable. And yet, traditions founded upon infrequent, climactic rituals also furnish the main examples, in the ethnographic record, of rites that seem to lack extensive exegesis. Here is a second paradox. The solution advanced in this chapter is that exegetical knowledge, in such cases, is internally generated only very gradually, due to the infrequency of ritual performances. The reason why exegesis is commonly restricted to elders and ritual experts is that it takes a long time for the clustering and sequencing of metonymical features, and thus the 'inner' meanings of rituals, to be inductively generated. Exegetical knowledge, in such traditions, is not simply secret or unspoken; in a very real sense, it can only be acquired through a lifetime's experience.

Implicit and explicit memory

Within cognitive psychology, studies of unconscious knowledge and learning attach considerable importance to a distinction between 'knowing how' to do something and 'knowing that' something is the case. Cohen and Squire (1980) suggest that 'knowing how' and 'knowing that' are functions of 'procedural' and 'declarative' memory respectively. In the case of procedural memory, recollection is unconscious – that is, we may know 'how to do' a particular thing, such as riding a bicycle, without being aware of what it is we are remembering. By contrast, declarative memory entails conscious acts of recollection (see Figure 7.1). Semantic memory, consisting of general, encyclopaedic knowledge (e.g. that Penny Farthings are an old-fashioned type of bicycle), and episodic memory, consisting of knowledge of specific episodes in one's experience (e.g. a particular occasion when one's bicycle toppled over), are both forms of declarative memory. In such cases, we are conscious of the act of remembering, and capable of stating what it is we remember. The distinctiveness of these memory systems is supported by evidence from amnesic patients, many of whom display massive deficits with regard to declarative memory but whose procedural memory systems may be unimpaired.

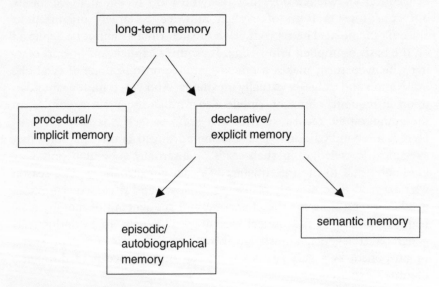

Figure 7.1 A standard classification of long-term memory systems in cognitive psychology.

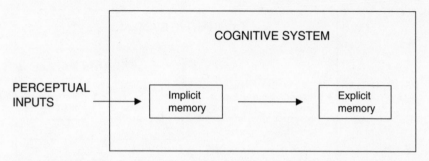

Figure 7.2   The relationship between implicit and explicit memory in processing theory.

Graf and Schacter (1985) and Schacter (1987) propose a distinction between implicit and explicit memory, along lines closely resembling the procedural/declarative distinction. A problem with Cohen and Squire's model is that it merely describes, but does not explain, certain patterns of cognitive impairment associated with amnesia. One possibility is that amnesics suffer from encoding or 'activation' problems. Activation theory (e.g. Graf et al. 1984) suggests that implicit memory (but not explicit/declarative memory) is handled by dedicated neural structures that operate automatically and are relatively independent of other brain functions. Processing theory (e.g. Roediger and Blaxton 1987) meanwhile suggests that implicit and explicit memory systems, whether or not they also correspond to discrete neural architecture, have different proprietory inputs. In this view, implicit/procedural memory processes data presented by perceptual systems, whereas explicit/declarative memory is geared up to process the outputs of internal cognitive mechanisms (see Figure 7.2).

The general relationship between implicit and explicit memory presented by processing theory seems intuitively plausible, up to a point; but, clearly, the construction of implicit knowledge is not always empirically driven (i.e. driven by the outputs of input/perceptual systems). Some forms of implicit knowledge seem to result from the repeated application of explicit rules. For instance, learning to drive a car may begin by encoding a set of verbal instructions, such as 'press down on the clutch pedal before engaging the gear stick; then apply pressure to the accelerator while slowly releasing the clutch'. Anderson (1983) develops a detailed model, known as ACT*, to account for the processes by which declarative knowledge, of the above sort, is transformed through repeated rehearsal (i.e. by practising) into automatic,

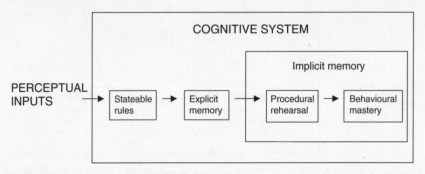

Figure 7.3 The relationship between implicit and explicit memory in the ACT* model.

habitual, and thus implicit skills. In its general outline, the ACT* model (Figure 7.3) contrasts starkly with the picture presented by processing theory (as depicted in Figure 7.2). Nevertheless, this contrast does not necessarily amount to a contradiction. The relationship between implicit and explicit memory is most profitably envisaged as a two-way street. Karmiloff-Smith's recent theory of 'representational redescription' (or 'RR') may help to explain why.

According to Karmiloff-Smith (1992), learning is a recursive process in which input systems dynamically interact with internal cognitive processes, producing progressively more explicit, consciously accessible understandings. Karmiloff-Smith envisages learning as a four-phase process. In the first phase, procedural competence may develop through empirically driven experimentation or through the application of explicit instructions. Once a set of automatized skills and habits has been established, it takes the form of unconscious or implicit knowledge. As such, it is informationally encapsulated – it cannot be modified by information from other parts of the cognitive apparatus. A nice illustration of this feature of implicit knowledge is provided by Roy D'Andrade (1995: 144–5), who points out that Americans driving in England may be able to combine implicit driving skills with explicit knowledge of the 'drive on the left' rule but when suddenly presented with a risk of head-on collision will feel compelled to swerve to the right (with potentially disastrous consequences). Implicit knowledge is 'informationally encapsulated' in the sense that it cannot take into account explicit knowledge, even when this is a matter of life and death.

Thus, Karmiloff-Smith argues that implicit knowledge is bracketed off from knowledge in other domains, even (as in the car-driving example) within the domain to which it becomes attached. Such knowledge constitutes a set of 'representational adjunctions' which 'neither alter existing stable representations nor are brought into relationship with them' (1992: 18). Encodings at this level are 'procedure-like' and 'sequentially specified' (1992: 20), giving rise to increasingly fluent behavioural repertoires and correspondingly rapid and automatic perceptual and sensorimotor adjustments. Phase one, in Karmiloff-Smith's model, thus culminates in 'behavioural mastery', which she refers to as 'level I' (i.e. Implicit).

The second phase consists of the formation of more explicit representations – the progressive reformulation of implicit knowledge as a set of inductively derived principles ('level E1'). This is a process by which the internal processing apparatus reformulates information encoded in the input systems as a set of essential elements or metonymical features. Nevertheless, this sort of internally processed, inductive knowledge is initially inaccessible to consciousness. As such, it cannot be brought into accordance with implicit representations contained in the input systems. Internally generated, explicit knowledge, however, exercises greater control over inferential processes than the implicit representations from which it was constructed. Expressed somewhat differently, theoretical considerations override purely empirical ones. In some domains, this can result in a marked, albeit temporary, deterioration of behavioural mastery.

The third phase in Karmiloff-Smith's model involves a sort of reconciliation of knowledge encoded in the input systems, on the one hand, and generated by internal, inter-domain computations, on the other. This is a process in which our representations become available to consciousness but, initially, cannot be verbalized ('level E2'). Further processing of such intuitive knowledge across domains can lead to its recodification as a 'cross-system code' (Karmiloff-Smith 1992: 23) capable of being verbally described ('level E3').

Karmiloff-Smith develops her argument through a series of fine-grained studies of learning in a wide range of domains (including language, number, physics and notation). For present purposes, it is not necessary to set out the details of her model, or the experimental data available to substantiate (and to challenge) it. Of interest here are the general features of Karmiloff-Smith's model and these can be illustrated by her favourite anecdotal example – how people learn to play the piano.

A novice pianist has to laboriously practice sequences of individual notes before being able to remember them as discrete strings, capable of being reproduced automatically and fluently. Such fluency amounts to behavioural mastery and, as such, constitutes learning only at an implicit level, engaging on-line cognitive functions. Processing of such knowledge is fast, mandatory, informationally encapsulated, and so on (see above). Anyone, like myself, who has failed to advance much beyond this level in learning to play an instrument, will recognize the difficulty of remembering a piece that one has not played for a long time. Strings of notes and chords, internally fluent, are often hard to combine into an integrated piece. The cues that allow sudden recollection of the links between one musical string and another, or the reactivation of whole strings that were temporarily forgotten, elicit irreducible and automatic units of knowledge. Starting again within a string is extremely difficult, and changing the sequential, procedural features of a string in accordance with a conscious plan proves virtually impossible during the on-line experience of playing. More advanced musicianship requires representational redescription, such that:

the knowledge of the different notes and chords (rather than simply their run-off sequence) becomes available as manipulable data . . . The end result is representational flexibility and control, which allows for creativity. Also important is the fact that the earlier proceduralized capacity is not lost: for certain goals, the pianist can call on the automated skill; for others, he or she calls on the more explicit representations that allow for flexibility and creativity. (Karmiloff-Smith 1992: 16)

The development of explicit theoretical musical knowledge, unlike the achievement of behavioural mastery at the piano, allows the transfer of knowledge within the domain of music (encompassing many instruments), but also between domains (such as mathematics and musical notation). At the most explicit level (E3), such knowledge can be verbalized as advanced musical theory, capable of informing and being informed by similarly explicit knowledge in any domain. It follows, of course, that learning in a given domain does not have to proceed unilineally. The development of new forms of behavioural mastery are driven by explicit knowledge. But the reverse is also true: continually developing forms of performative competence are the motor driving new forms of explicit knowledge. Nevertheless, intra-domain learning cannot proceed downwards (i.e. E3–E2–E1 . . . etc.). As with any two-way street, traffic on each side must proceed in one direction only (see Figure 7.4).

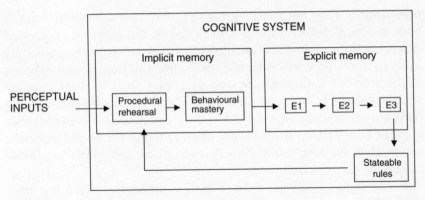

Figure 7.4 The relationship between implicit and explicit memory in the RR model.

Memory and frequently repeated rituals

Psychological accounts of the relationship between implicit and explicit memory, outlined in the last section, concern themselves with forms of learning that involve procedural rehearsal and the repetitive application of skills. Explicit knowledge with respect to such skills is organized in semantic memory, for instance in the form of a musician's stateable knowledge about melodic sequences, chords, rhythms and so on. These psychological principles ought to be applicable, not only to automatized skills applied in secular life, but also to frequently repeated religious rituals.

A particularly simple example of a frequently repeated ritual action is the Catholic practice of crossing oneself. This behaviour may be initiated in childhood by spontaneous imitation, by explicit instruction, by being guided/manipulated through the motions, or by a combination of the above. It requires a certain amount of procedural rehearsal to achieve fluency with respect to this body practice. Achievement of 'behavioural mastery', however, does not necessarily imply explicit knowledge of the wider procedural context for acts of crossing oneself. An experienced churchgoer in Spain, for instance, may know that a salient trigger for the act of crossing oneself is the sight of the receptacle containing the Eucharistic Host, which in turn may be attributed certain agentive characteristics (e.g. sight and hearing) possessed by God. Thus, the act of crossing oneself is felt to be observed directly by God and directed towards Him. From the viewpoint of a young child, by contrast, the act of crossing oneself and any attendant behavioural proscriptions (e.g. not speaking loudly), may be mastered as a set of body practices before explicit knowledge of the religious procedural context has become fully established. Level E1 representations are likely to develop rapidly with the achievement of behavioural mastery, in the form of inductively derived principles such as: 'cross oneself when solemnity is required'. Principles of this sort are applied with the same automaticity as ones that are widespread in secular contexts, such as 'wipe your feet on the doormat when entering the house' or 'shake hands when greeting a stranger'. As such, these behaviours are highly susceptible to overgeneralization.

For instance, Catholics may cross themselves in solemn but non-religious contexts without being aware of doing so. Similarly, people sometimes go through the motions of wiping their feet in the absence of doormats or initiate handshaking with persons who are incapable of participating. A higher level of conscious access to procedural schemas is necessary in order to avoid such overgeneralization (although the need for avoidance varies greatly with the cultural setting). Only by representing automatic actions at a stateable (E2/3) level can a balance be struck between habitual impulses and inductively derived principles, such that one can discriminate readily between situations in which particular body practices are obligatory, optional or simply inappropriate.

Loyalist gangs of youths in Belfast are accustomed to stopping strangers on the street to enquire about their religious identities. I once heard a joke about a Catholic who, having almost succeeded in bluffing his way past, crossed himself in relief, with consequences no less disastrous than for the American driver (above) who swerved to the right. The joke worked (up to a point) because crossing oneself is obviously an automatized habit. Other examples of crossing oneself are clearly optional, rather than inappropriate. But, for most Catholics, crossing oneself with holy water is obligatory when entering or leaving the church, and procedural schemas may incorporate a supernatural agent (God) towards whom the self-crossing is directed. Such knowledge is potentially stateable and helps to distinguish the act of crossing oneself in church from the same action performed in most other settings. Note, however, that the stateable knowledge available in semantic memory, with regard to the act of crossing oneself in church, does not have to be verbally transmitted. According to the RR model, it is perfectly possible in theory (and probably common in practice) for such knowledge to be acquired, without ever receiving rule-like instructions, simply through regular participation in rituals.

Participants in highly repetitive, liturgical rituals are normally capable of venturing exegetical commentaries on their activities, usually deriving from a body of publicly transmitted, official dogma (see Whitehouse 1992; 1994; 1995; 1996a; 1996b; 1998; 2000; 2001). But are these forms of stateable knowledge also capable of being internally generated, rather than verbally or textually transmitted, via processes of 'representational redescription'? I think not. The RR model may help to explain the development of procedural ('how-type') knowledge in relation to repetitive rituals, but it is hard-pressed to explain the development of elaborate ('why-type') doctrinal discourse. Indeed, what the RR model shows is that the distinction between 'knowing how' and 'knowing that' does not, after all, adequately distinguish implicit and explicit forms of knowing. The RR model suggests that procedural memory ('knowing how') can take both implicit and explicit forms, the latter developing out of the former. Exegesis, on the other hand, is always entertained at an explicit level and is not reducible to procedural schemas.

The practice of crossing oneself with holy water is a good example of a repetitive ritual action that lacks official exegesis (or for which official exegesis is generally unknown). The process of representational redescription may generate simple procedural schemas such as 'cross oneself when entering and leaving the church', but the deeper 'why-type' question, concerning possible exegetical meanings of the act, can only be generated through conscious, off-line reflection. For instance, one could argue that the mimed inscription of a crucifix is to be understood as a way of commemorating Christ's suffering. But this exegetical possibility is not widely entertained, and there is no obvious reason why most Catholics should engage in this sort of speculative theologizing.

Frequently repeated rituals, exhibiting a high degree of automaticity, are eminently capable of being reproduced in the absence of exegetical reflection. Unless pressured to do so, people tend not to ask themselves the symbolic motivations or origins of their embodied habits, and this provides ecclesiastical authorities with a golden opportunity for the dissemination of orthodox exegesis. True, the case of self-crossing has been somewhat overlooked in the Roman Catholic Church, but the Vatican provides notably comprehensive and widely disseminated exegetical commentaries on most of its rituals. Thus, the fact that participation in frequently performed rituals does not, in itself, encourage exegetical theorizing opens a vacuum to be filled by the pronouncements of religious authorities. What motivates such pronouncements has been the subject of much of my previous work on the topic (see especially Whitehouse 1995; 2000). But, from a cognitive viewpoint, it is crucial to note that the transmissive conditions of routinized rituals are ideally suited to verbal transmission of a stable and authoritative exegetical tradition. Repetition acts as a powerful mnemonic device. The exegetical richness we generally find in routinized traditions could not be reproduced in conditions of rare or sporadic transmission (Whitehouse 1992). What we have are congregations of people whose minds are relatively uncluttered by personal (internally generated) exegesis and, at the same time, highly susceptible to authoritative (externally generated and reiterated) pronouncements. It is quite a different matter where religious rituals are rarely enacted.

Memory and infrequently performed rituals

The RR model, as set out by Karmiloff-Smith, focuses exclusively on forms of learning that result from behavioural rehearsal/repetition. Not only is this the means to behavioural mastery, but further repetition is what drives the redescription of this knowledge at progressively more explicit levels. Whereas behavioural mastery is the incorporation of automatized habits, its more explicit redescription appears to consist of the development of schemas or scripts, culminating in 'semantic memory' – a body of encyclopaedic knowledge about the world, manipulable via higher-level, explicit, inter-domain principles of logical motivation, thematic association, and so on. But where, in all of this, do we locate enduring memory for distinctive, rare (or unique) events? Episodic or autobiographical memory seems to be left out of the RR model, even though its role in various forms of learning is manifestly important.

I have previously used the term 'imagistic practices' to refer to a complex set of interconnected features in Melanesian religions, which include rare, climactic rituals, the establishment of enduring episodic memories for ritual performances, and highly localized group cohesion (Whitehouse 1995). More recently, I have explored the implications of this model for debates and evidence from a range of disciplines (Whitehouse 2000). Although the latter research attempted to provide a richer description of the cognitive underpinnings of imagistic practices, it proved difficult to account precisely for characteristic features of codification with regard to such imagery. The RR model, somewhat modified to accommodate the phenomenon of long-term, vivid episodic memory, allows a more precise explanation, at a cognitive level, for the ethnographic findings.

Religious systems indigenous to Melanesia, in common with many other 'tribal' religions around the world, are often founded around highly emotive 'life crisis' rituals, especially initiations, in contrast with the highly repetitive, liturgical, doctrinal religions originating in complex societies (Whitehouse 2000). The former, imagistic mode of religiosity is often incorporated into the world religions as a set of locally variable practices, focused around shrines, saints, minor deities and so on. Such practices tend to be found mainly in cohesive, rural, face-to-face communities, although they are also expressed in minor (albeit sometimes notorious) urban cults, usually of a millenarian and/or apocalyptic nature. Be that as it may, the pre-Christian religions of Melanesia were never of the doctrinal (large-scale, routinized) sort, and most tended towards the imagistic end of the spectrum. Such religions are notable for their lack of elaborate doctrine, or for the restriction of doctrine-like knowledge to small groups of ritual experts. Thus, for the majority of people engaged in imagistic practices, exegetical knowledge appears (on the whole) not to be at a level of explicitness that can be verbalized.

In many Melanesian systems of initiation, novices are tortured so brutally as part of the ritual process that I have described these practices as 'rites of terror' (Whitehouse 1996a). The extreme affectivity and sensual arousal occasioned by such rituals, coupled with the surprising, unexpectable nature of the objects, actions and general environments encountered, trigger vivid episodic memories, encoding many details relating to event sequence, actors' identities, and a variety of seemingly extraneous details (Whitehouse 1995; 1996a; 1996b; 2000). They also seem to give rise to loose and fluid thematic associations based on the principle of iconicity, where concrete properties of ritual choreography and paraphernalia are felt to 'stand for' more abstract processes such as plant growth, spiritual transformation, mammalian gestation, and so on. Nevertheless, it is sometimes only possible to infer these iconic processes on the basis of indirect evidence, since they may not be explicitly stated by participants. One such body of evidence might relate to the clustering of particular images in a ritual sequence, for instance images of substances that naturally increase in volume and thus appear to symbolize or instantiate mystically processes of natural fertility and growth (especially where people say that the ritual is 'good for the crops' even if they cannot tell you how or why). Another body of evidence might focus on the sequential occurrence of imagery as, for instance, ritual choreography evoking images of physical death or decay followed by images of gestation and birth, may appear to express a notion of spiritual rebirth and regeneration. Sometimes, such interpretations are supported by esoteric mythology or explicit exegetical commentaries supplied by senior ritual experts (see Juillerat 1992; Poole 1982). In other Melanesian societies, no such corpus of secret but explicit verbal information appears to be available (see Gell 1975; Barth 1975). Either way, the majority of ritual participants (e.g. novices, observers and junior initiators) seem to be unable to supply verbal explications of the meanings of ritual imagery. How are we to make sense of all this in terms of available models of the relationship between implicit and explicit memory?

The first point to make is that procedural knowledge concerning rare and climactic rituals is consciously entertained. As indicated in Figure 7.1, episodic memory is a form of explicit memory. When people recall episodes of initiatory tortures or millenarian vigils, their memories are potentially stateable. Chains of events, specifying the procedural sequences of such rituals, are not habituated or automatic, and can only be entertained as explicit knowledge. It is true that even the rarest and most exceptional (e.g. innovative) rituals are likely to incorporate units of habituated action, but the overall form of such activities will be recalled episodically, and therefore available to self-report. From the viewpoint of a young man, recently initiated, his recent ritual ordeals take the form, in memory, of a series of extraordinary (and no doubt disturbing) episodes. He can remember what happened, who did what, where, when, and to whom, as well as all kinds of assorted minutiae (aromas, sounds, visual details, thoughts, feelings, and so on). Since most of these experiences are unique, there is little or no opportunity to organize procedural knowledge for such rituals according to quasi-theoretical, generalizable principles. It is only through subsequent experiences in the role of initiator that he will be able to pick out metonymical features and generate the sort of inductively driven principles characteristic of E1 knowledge. This process of 'representational redescription' is not, however, the same as that entailed in routinized rituals.

In the first place, the initiate-turned-initiator is not on a path of converting implicit procedural knowledge into increasingly explicit representations. On the contrary, he starts with explicit procedural knowledge, and subsequent experiences of the initiatory process result in knowledge of a rather less explicit sort (E1), as yet unavailable to verbal report. He may only gradually become fully aware of the way imagery is consistently 'clustered' and its presentation 'sequenced' over a set of recurrent performances. Secondly, the RR process is retarded. Since the frequency of imagistic practices is low, it may not be until quite late in life that the initiate's understanding becomes largely stateable (E3/4), as is characteristic of ritual experts and elders in many Melanesian societies. Thirdly, the RR process in this case is not restricted to procedural schemas, but actively drives the production of exegetical knowledge. The reason for this is precisely that rituals, in the imagistic mode, cannot be reproduced as automatic, habituated actions but always require off-line, explicit processes of planning and implementation. Indeed, all recorded initiation rites in Melanesia are preceded by secret procedural discussion and conscious coordination. Because procedural knowledge in such cases is also explicit knowledge, it forms part of a cross-system code, by means of which exegesis is generated. Whereas routinized rituals can be (and often are) performed on 'autopilot', in the absence of any kind of reflexivity, imagistic practices must always be a locus of conscious thought, and it would be most surprising if participants did not, therefore, develop idiosyncratic (if tentative) exegetical notions.

These observations may help to explain the widespread lack (or relative paucity) of authoritative doctrinal discourse and exegesis with regard to imagistic practices. Unlike routinized rituals, imagistic practices do not present a vacuum (see above) for religious authorities to 'fill', nor do their elongated cycles of transmission facilitate the stable reproduction of an intricate doctrinal orthodoxy. On the other hand, a rich and revelatory religious experience is possible in the imagistic mode in the absence of authoritative dogma, since every participant is a potential exegete and, given time, a potential authority on religious matters. This explains why exegetical knowledge, with regard to imagistic practices, is highly restricted, available in its fullest form only to experienced experts. The fact that it may never be verbally transmitted, or communicated piecemeal in highly opaque, cryptic allusions and mythological narratives, should not be construed as the absence of exegetical knowledge.

Conclusion

What are the advantages of the above approach, compared with those of existing studies of the relationship between implicit and explicit knowledge in the domain of ritual? First, the approach adopted here promises a more precise and psychologically plausible account of the acquisition, development and transmission of ritual knowledge. It is no surprise that Robertson-Smith's distinction between 'practice' and 'doctrinal theory' now seems somewhat simplistic. Nevertheless, more contemporary dichotomies in social theory, for instance opposing '*habitus*' and 'dogma' (Bourdieu 1977), 'habit memory' and 'cognitive memory' (Connerton 1989), or 'hegemonic practices' and 'ideology' (Comaroff and Comaroff 1991), are scarcely more sensitive to the complex mechanisms by which cultural knowledge is reproduced 'on the ground'. As Strauss and Quinn (1997: 39) have noted, in their fine critique of recent studies of 'resistance consciousness':

the Comaroffs correlate with hegemonic representations, those representations of the world that 'are so habituated, so deeply inscribed in everyday routine, that they may no longer be seen as forms of control – or seen at all' (Comaroff and Comaroff 1991: 25). At the other pole of this continuum – complete awareness – are ideological representations, the explicitly articulated values and beliefs of a particular social group (Comaroff and Comaroff 1991: 24) . . . Much like Bourdieu's opposition between what is said and unsaid in society (dogma versus doxa) . . . several different cognitive states are lumped together at the hegemonic end where power is naturalised and in the 'liminal space' in between hegemony (uncontested) and ideology (contested ideas).

What the Comaroffs, Bourdieu and others fail to recognize is that: 'at the hegemonic end, there is a clear difference between what is unsaid because it is unknown . . .; what is unsaid because it is very well known, but as a motor habit or image rather than as a set of propositions; and what is unsaid because it would require new connections among scattered bits of knowledge people have' (Strauss and Quinn 1997: 39).

To this list could be added many more categories of unstated knowledge, including: that which is 'unspeakable' in the old-fashioned sense of being profoundly immoral and shameful; that which is secret or restricted; propositional knowledge (as opposed to motor habit) that is too widely known to be relevantly stated (e.g. principles of naive physics such as gravity and solidity). The point is that implicit and explicit knowledge take a wide variety of forms that need to be distinguished. Moreover, as the RR model suggests, we need to discriminate between degrees of explicitness – for instance between knowledge capable of being transferred between domains but not necessarily stateable, and domain-general knowledge available to self-report. And, finally, the relationship between implicit and explicit knowledge is formed in different ways, and at different rates, in relation to different cultural practices and regimes of social transmission. All these points are taken into consideration by the approach adopted here.

Secondly, the claims presented in this article are falsifiable in principle and are, for the most part, potentially testable in practice via replicable experiments. Can cases be found, in the ethnographic record, of habituated ritual actions that cannot, in principle, be performed without entertaining exegetical (why-type) knowledge? Are there cases of rare, climactic rites that can be reproduced purely on the basis of implicit motor habits? If the answer to these questions (and numerous others like them which could be posed) is 'yes', then a radical modification of the claims I have advanced would be required. Meanwhile, many of these claims can be formulated as hypotheses that, in principle at least, could be tested. For instance, one hypothesis suggested above is that the volume and frequency of internally generated speculations concerning the symbolic motivations of a ritual action performed once only will be greater than for the same ritual action that has become habituated through repetition. This hypothesis would need to be broken down into a series of more precise predictions and subjected to testing in ecologically sound and cross-culturally replicable experiments. Work of this sort is already underway (e.g. Boyer and Ramble 2001), and I am currently planning further experimental research. But the point is that we need to be pursuing empirically verifiable claims, and not simply promulgating ever more extravagant metaphors in the name of critical originality.

Finally, although our explanations should not (without persuasive justification) conflict with well-established findings in neighbouring disciplines, such as psychology, they must also contribute to the construction of distinctively anthropological knowledge, which includes making a contribution to general social/cultural theory. The arguments presented in this chapter are part of a broader, long-term project to describe and account for globally and historically recurrent correlations between patterns of codification and transmission, on the one hand, and of political structure and scale, on the other. This project goes to the heart of a long-standing tradition in social theory, beginning with Émile Durkheim and Max Weber, and providing some of the central concerns of (among others) Gregory Bateson, Victor Turner, Ernest Gellner, Jack Goody, Maurice Bloch and Fredrik Barth (see Whitehouse 1995: ch. 8; 2000). A cognitive approach can help to answer the most tantalizing questions posed by mainstream anthropology. Moreover, cognitive models can also help us to structure the questions we ask. We need, not only to produce more precise,

149

well-substantiated and empirically productive general theories, but also more reliable and systematic ethnographic data. When we look for something, it is useful to know why, but it is essential to know what to look for, and how.

In truth, we still have far more questions than answers, even in relation to the relatively narrow problems considered in this chapter. What is being advanced here is, at present, just an approach to understanding the nature of ritual knowledge, rather than an understanding of it.

References

Anderson, J. R. (1983) *The Architecture of Cognition*. Cambridge, MA: Harvard University Press.

Barth, F. (1975) *Ritual and Knowledge among the Baktaman of New Guinea*. New Haven: Yale University Press.

Bateson, G. (1972) *Steps to an Ecology of Mind: Collected Essays in Anthropology, Psychiatry, Evolution, and Epistemology*. Northvale: Jason Armson.

Bourdieu, P. (1977) *Outline of a Theory of Practice*, trans. R. Nice. Cambridge: Cambridge University Press.

Bourdieu, P. (1990) *The Logic of Practice*, trans. R. Nice. Stanford: Stanford University Press.

Boyer, P. (1993) 'Cognitive aspects of religious symbolism'. In *Cognitive Aspects of Religious Symbolism*, ed. P. Boyer, 4–47. Cambridge: Cambridge University Press.

Boyer, P. and C. Ramble (2001) 'Cognitive templates for religious concepts: cross-cultural evidence for recall of counter-intuitive representations'. *Cognitive Science* 25: 535–64.

Cohen, N. J. and L. R. Squire (1980) 'Preserved learning and retention of pattern-analyzing skill in amnesia: dissociation of knowing how and knowing that'. *Science* 21: 207–10.

Comaroff, J. and J. Comaroff (1991) *Of Revelation and Revolution: Christianity, Colonialism, and Consciousness in South Africa*, vol. 1. Chicago: University of Chicago Press.

Connerton, P. (1989) *How Societies Remember*. Cambridge: Cambridge University Press.

D'Andrade, R. G. (1995) *The Development of Cognitive Anthropology*. Cambridge: Cambridge University Press.

Edelman, G. (1992) *Bright Air, Brilliant Fire: On the Matter of the Mind*. New York: Basic Books.

Gell, A. (1975) *Metamorphosis of the Cassowaries: Umeda Society, Language, and Ritual*. London: Athlone Press.

Graf, P. and D. L. Schacter (1985) 'Implicit and explicit memory for new associations in normal and amnesic subjects'. *Journal of Experimental Psychology: Learning, Memory, and Cognition* 11: 501–18.

Graf, P., L. R. Squire and G. Mandler (1984) 'The information that amnesic patients do not forget'. *Journal of Experimental Psychology: Learning, Memory, and Cognition* 10: 164–78.

Juillerat, B. (1992) *Shooting the Sun: Ritual and Meaning in West Sepik*. Washington, DC: Smithsonian Institution Press.

Karmiloff-Smith, A. (1992) *Beyond Modularity: A Developmental Perspective on Cognitive Science*. Cambridge, MA: MIT Press.

Leach, E. R. (1954) *Political Systems of Highland Burma*, London: Bell & Son.

Luria, A. R. (1973) *The Working Brain: An Introduction to Neuropsychology*. New York: Basic Books.

Munn, N. D. (1973) 'Symbolism in ritual context: aspects of symbolic action'. In *Handbook of Social and Cultural Anthropology*, ed. J. J. Honigman. Chicago: Rand McNally.

Poole, F. J. P. (1982) 'The ritual forging of identity: aspects of person and self in Bimin-Kuskusmin male initiation'. In *Rituals of Manhood: Male Initiation in Papua New Guinea*, ed. G. H. Herdt. Berkeley: University of California Press.

Robertson-Smith, W. (1907 (1889)) *Lectures on the Religion of the Semites*. London: Adam and Charles Black.

Roediger, H. L. and T. A. Blaxton (1987) 'Retrieval modes produce dissociations in memory for surface information'. In *Memory and Cognitive Processes: The Ebbinghaus Centennial Conference*, ed. D. S. Gorfein and R. R. Hoffman. Hillsdale, NJ: Erlbaum.

Schacter, D. L. (1987) 'Implicit memory: history and current status'. *Journal of Experimental Psychology: Learning, Memory, and Cognition* 13: 501–18.

Strauss, C. and N. Quinn (1997) *A Cognitive Theory of Cultural Meaning*. Cambridge: Cambridge University Press.

Turner, V. W. (1967) *The Forest of Symbols*. Ithaca, NY: Cornell University Press.

Whitehouse, H. (1992) 'Leaders and logics, persons and polities'. *History and Anthropology* 6: 103–24.

Whitehouse, H. (1994) 'Strong words and forceful winds: religious experience and political process in Melanesia'. *Oceania* 65: 40–58.

Whitehouse, H. (1995) *Inside the Cult: Religious Innovation and Transmission in Papua New Guinea*. Oxford: Oxford University Press.

Whitehouse, H. (1996a) 'Jungles and computers: neuronal group selection and the epidemiology of representations'. *Journal of the Royal Anthropological Institute* n.s. 1: 99–116.

Whitehouse, H. (1996b) 'Rites of terror: emotion, metaphor, and memory in Melanesian initiation cults'. *Journal of the Royal Anthropological Institute* n.s. 2: 703–15.

Whitehouse, H. (1998) 'From mission to movement: the impact of Christianity on patterns of political association in Papua New Guinea'. *Journal of the Royal Anthropological Institute* n.s. 4: 43–63.

Whitehouse, H. (2000) *Arguments and Icons: Divergent Modes of Religiosity.* Oxford: Oxford University Press.

Whitehouse, H. (ed.) (2001) *The Debated Mind: Evolutionary Psychology versus Ethnography.* Oxford: Berg.

8 The Cognitive Representation of Religious Ritual Form: A Theory of Participants' Competence with Religious Ritual Systems

E. THOMAS LAWSON AND ROBERT N. MCCAULEY

Introduction

Theorizing about religious ritual systems from a cognitive viewpoint involves (1) modelling cognitive processes and their products and (2) demonstrating their influence on religious behaviour. Particularly important for such an approach to the study of religious ritual is the modelling of participants' representations of *ritual form*. In pursuit of that goal, we presented in *Rethinking Religion* a theory of religious ritual form that involved two commitments.

The theory's first commitment is that the cognitive apparatus for the representation of action in general is the same system deployed for the representation of religious ritual form. The differences between everyday action and religious ritual action turn out to be fairly minor from the standpoint of their cognitive representation. This system for the representation of action includes representations of agents. Whether we focus on an everyday action such as closing a door or a ritual action such as initiating a person into a religious group, our understanding of these forms of behaviour as actions at all turns critically on recognizing agents.

The theory's second crucial commitment (Lawson and McCauley 1990: 61) is that the roles of culturally postulated superhuman agents (CPS-agents hereafter) in participants' representations of religious rituals will prove pivotal in accounting for a wide variety of those rituals' properties. In our view religious ritual systems typically involve presumptions about CPS-agents. This theoretical commitment is orthogonal to the pervasive assumption throughout the study of religion that only meanings matter. By contrast, we hold that other things matter too (specifically, cognitive representations of religious ritual form).

153

Large conflicts lurk behind the previous sentences, but we cannot adequately address them here. For now we will only identify two of the most fundamental and comment on them briefly.

First, amazingly (by our lights anyway), our claim that (conceptual) commitments to the existence of CPS-agents is the most important recurrent feature of religion across cultures is quite controversial. With everything from Buddhism to Marxism to football in mind, various scholars in theology, religious studies, the humanities, and even the social sciences maintain that religious phenomena do not turn decisively on presumptions about CPS-agents. Perhaps this is so. In that case what we have, then, may not be a theory of religious ritual. Instead, it is only *a theory about actions that individuals and groups perform within organized communities of people who possess conceptual schemes that include presumptions about those actions' connections with the actions of agents who exhibit various counter-intuitive properties.*

If that is not religion (and religious ritual), so be it, but we suspect that this description of our theoretical object covers virtually every case that anyone would be inclined, at least pretheoretically, to count as religion, and very few of the cases they would be inclined to exclude. Overly inclusive views of religion confuse the problematic claim that only meanings matter with the even more problematic claim that all meanings matter. Hence, on these views, virtually anything may count as religion (depending upon the circumstances). Fans of such views should keep in mind, then, that *in their view* what we are advancing is *not* a theory of religious ritual.

We do not desire to engage in debates about definitions. In science explanatory theories ground central analytical concepts. Those concepts earn our allegiance because of the achievements of the theories that inspire them. These include their predictive and problem-solving power, explanatory suggestiveness, generality and empirical accountability. Whatever explanatory value construing 'religion' in such a manner exhibits turns on whether or not the theory we have elaborated provides empirically useful insights about religious ritual. (See also Pyysiäinen, this volume.)

The second conflict is more complicated. The assumption that only meaning matters conflicts with our theory's insistence that participants' representations of CPS-agents' roles in religious rituals are crucial for explaining many of their features. They conflict because the theory achieves these goals largely *independently* of the meanings either ritual participants or scholars assign to rituals.

Rituals often occasion an astonishingly wide range of interpretations not only from observers in the field but even from the participants themselves. Their own testimony reveals that the planting of this bush means one thing to the wedded couple, another thing to their neighbours, and a third thing to the ethnographer who questions them. Even when authorities intent on maintaining the status quo vigilantly police doctrines, the blooming of interpretive schemes remains a wonder to behold. While the meanings associated with rituals may vary, such variability typically has no effect on the stability of the ritual actions' underlying forms. Although they have brought nearly as many interpretations as the times and places from which they hail, pilgrims to Mecca continue to circumambulate the Ka'bah the same way year after year. Whether in Rwanda, Rio or Rome, only communicants are eligible to participate in the Mass and only priests are eligible to perform it. Not only do other things matter besides meanings; for some explanatory purposes meanings hardly matter at all.

We have just rehearsed the respect in which the details of rituals are independent of meanings either participants or scholars assign them. It is important not to confuse these proposed semantic contents of rituals with factual details about their elements. Interested parties may attribute some meaning or other to the fact that an orthodox rabbi must be a male, but that fact is not the same thing as proposals about its significance. Some points of detail may permit considerable variation, such as how high the priest elevates the host, whereas others, like the use of the bread and the wine, may not.

We think that religious ritual form and the properties of rituals it explains and predicts are overwhelmingly independent of attributed meanings. There is also a respect in which some very general features of ritual form are independent not only of meanings but even of these specifically cultural details. In other words, these very general features of religious ritual form are independent of *both* semantic *and* cultural contents. Clarifying these general features of action is valuable for distinguishing the roles CPS-agents can play in participants' representations of their religious rituals.

The action representation system

Distinguishing ritual *form* from both semantic and cultural *contents* will prove useful for many analytical and explanatory purposes. Our cognitive system for the representation of action imposes fundamental, though commonplace, constraints on ritual form. Attention to these constraints enables us to look beyond the variability of religious rituals'

155

details to some of their most general underlying properties. The point, in short, is that religious rituals (despite their often bizarre qualities) are also actions. (Ritual drummers ritually beating ritual drums are still drummers beating drums.) Consequently, this general system for the representation of action is also responsible for participants' representations of many features of the forms of their religious rituals.

From a cognitive standpoint, then, postulating special cognitive machinery to account for the representation of religious rituals is unnecessary. The requisite cognitive equipment is already available. A wide range of evidence from developmental and clinical psychology indicates that human beings normally have specific cognitive machinery for representing agents and their actions (as opposed to that deployed for the representation of other entities and events). Although this cognitive machinery is apparently task-specific, it seems – with only a few exceptions – to be virtually ubiquitous among human beings. (Baron-Cohen 1995.) This assortment of resources is what we have collectively referred to as the human 'action representation system'. (Lawson and McCauley 1990: 87–95.) This action representation system must account for humans' command of the distinctions between agents and other entities and between actions and other events. To summarize, then, we hold that the representation of religious rituals requires no special cognitive apparatus beyond the garden-variety cognitive machinery all normal human beings possess for the representation of agents and their actions.

Cognitive scientists, especially psychologists working on cognitive development, have thought a good deal about how human beings represent and distinguish *agents*. (See, for example, Leslie 1995.) Agents and their agency are clearly the pivotal concepts for the representation of action, but they are not the whole story. A basic representational framework for characterizing this special sort of event must also capture familiar presumptions about the internal structures and external relations of actions. We should note here that while cognitive scientists have proposed interesting accounts of our understanding of agency, they have had much less to say about our understanding of *actions*. We hold that whether a religious ritual action involves waving a wand to ward off witches, building a pyramid to facilitate the departure of a pharaoh to the realm of the gods, or lighting a fire to ensure the presence of a spirit, representing such actions will depend upon utilizing a dedicated cognitive system for action representation. Our theory of religious ritual offers some quite general, preliminary proposals about that system.

In *Rethinking Religion* we provided a formal system for the purpose of increasing the clarity and precision of our theory's claims about the action representation system, and therefore about the forms of the religious rituals whose representations it assembles. (A caution, however, is in order. This formal system should not be mistaken for the theory; *it is only a means for elucidating the theory's claims*.) The precision of formal systems is a valuable tool that aids in the detection of significant relationships and connections among the phenomena being modelled. Critics could complain that the formal system we introduced in *Rethinking Religion* is a very complex machine for the production of some very simple products. But, as a matter of fact, the formal system we employed and the diagrams it generates introduced a precision to our descriptions that enabled *us* to see more clearly *how* rituals' general action structures and the roles attributed to CPS-agents in particular suggest (non-obvious, unfamiliar) principles for predicting a number of those rituals' features. Assuming these principles describe, albeit quite abstractly, capacities that are psychologically real, they also constitute a first pass at an empirically testable hypothesis about the cognitive mechanisms behind participants' abilities to produce judgements about those features.

The formal system employs a set of categories and generative rules for representing action, and thereby participants' conceptions of religious ritual form. The categories signify the basic components involved in the representation of any action. They include participants, acts and the appropriate qualities, properties and conditions sufficient to distinguish them. (See for example Lawson and McCauley 1990: 120.) The rules describe basic action structures, familiar to any normal human being. They generate *structural descriptions* of people's representations of actions, including rituals. (The diagrams we mentioned in the previous paragraph, which also populate many of the pages in *Rethinking Religion*, depict such structural descriptions.) Rituals' structural descriptions portray basic action structures, which

1. include the roles (agents, acts, instruments and patients)[1] that distinguish actions (and rituals) from other events and happenings;
2. take – as ritual elements – the various entities and acts, as well as their properties, qualities and conditions, that can fulfil these formal roles in religious rituals;
3. presume that at least two of these roles must always be filled (viz.,

that every action has an *agent* and that the agent must *do* something);

4. reflect the constraint that although any item filling the role of the agent may also serve as a patient, not all items that serve as patients may also fill the agent role;
5. reveal points of variability in the form of actions such as whether they involve the use of special instruments as a condition of the act; and
6. accommodate the enabling relationships between actions, such as whether the performance of one act presupposes the performance of another.

Most talk, then, about the 'cognitive representations of ritual form' does not involve anything very complicated or unusual.

Actions typically come in one of two sorts. They either involve agents doing something or they involve agents doing something to something. In other words, some actions do not have patients and some do. In religious contexts only the second sort of action need concern us. On our theory, since all religious rituals involve agents acting upon patients and since a representation of ritual form (like any of the products of the action representation system) will reflect an asymmetry between the agent and patient roles, the structural description of a religious ritual will include three ordered slots for representing a religious ritual's three fundamental roles, viz., its *agent*, the *act* involved, and its *patient*. All of a ritual's details fall within the purviews of one or the other of these three roles. From a formal standpoint, then, accommodating all of the rest of the ritual's details involves nothing more than elaborations on the entries for these three slots.

Our claim that all religious rituals (as opposed to religious action more broadly construed) are actions in which an agent does something to a patient departs from popular assumptions about rituals. Typically, priests sacrifice goats, ritual participants burn offerings, and pilgrims circle shrines. But in religious contexts people also pray, sing, chant, stand, kneel and sit. Even though such activities may be part of religious ceremonies, such activities do not qualify as religious rituals in our theory's technical sense. All religious rituals – *in our technical sense* – are inevitably connected sooner or later with actions in which CPS-agents play a role. As noted, it follows on this account that many religious activities are not typically religious rituals in our technical sense, even though they may be present in ritual practices and qualify as religious acts. It also follows that even many actions that religious persons repeat in religious ceremonies (such as everyone standing at certain points in a religious service) will not count as rituals either.

We defend these decisions on two principal grounds. The first is what we take to be the telling coincidence of three relevant but quite different considerations bearing on distinctions among religious actions. An account of each follows.

First, invariably, religious rituals, unlike mere religious acts, bring about changes in the religious world (temporary in some cases, permanent in others) by virtue of the fact that they involve *transactions* with CPS-agents. Those interactions affect to what or whom *anyone* can subsequently apply the religious category associated with the act in question. Moreover, the performance of a religious ritual – in the sense our theory specifies – entitles anyone to apply the religious category associated with that ritual exclusively on the basis of the intersubjectively available information, as construed within the framework of the pertinent religious system. If the priest baptizes Fred, then henceforth the term 'baptized' may be used to describe Fred, regardless of Fred or the priest's states of mind when the ritual occurred. (What will matter is only that the priest qualifies as an appropriate ritual agent – which itself turns on the priest's own ritual history.) By contrast, this is not true about religious actions that are not rituals in our technical sense. If Fred prays publicly, all we can say is that Fred has appeared to pray publicly. Fred might have been feigning prayer. Only Fred knows for sure, whereas when a priest baptizes Fred (under the appropriate publicly observable conditions), anyone privy to this event and the relevant parts of the accompanying religious conceptual scheme can know that Fred has been baptized.

The second consideration differentiating religious rituals (in our technical sense) from other religious activities is what we shall call the 'insider–outsider criterion'. Although mere religious actions are typically open to outsiders, religious rituals typically are not. (Of course, who counts as an 'outsider' may change over time.) A non-Catholic is welcome to pray with Catholics but not to take Holy Communion with them. Although anyone can practice yoga, only boys of the *Brahmanic* caste can be invested with the sacred thread (Penner 1975). Anyone can chant Zulu war songs; only Zulus can be buried in the *umuzi* (village). With the exception of what we might call 'entry level' rituals (for example, for juniors or new converts), those who are not participants in the religious system are not eligible to participate in that system's rituals. The distinction between *participants in the religious system* and *participants in a religious ritual* is vital. Except, perhaps, for entry level rituals, the latter category's extension constitutes a subset of the former category's extension. This distinction, in effect, helps to explicate the notion of 'eligibility' for a ritual.

A third basis for differentiating religious rituals from other religious actions is closely related to the second. Rituals are invariably connected with other rituals. While participating in rituals turns unwaveringly on having performed other rituals, participating in these other religious actions that less obviously involve interactions with the gods does not. Below we shall develop this idea further in the discussion of *ritual embedding*.

The second ground for employing our technical sense of the term 'religious ritual' simply looks to the success of the resulting research programme the theory inspires. The theory successfully explains a wide range of those actions' features that it specifies as religious rituals. The argument, in effect, says that if the overall theory is successful on many fronts, then that fact is relevant to the defence of any of that theory's details. The introduction of technical, theoretically inspired notions that run counter to widespread assumptions is not unusual in science. Copernicus' theory did not conform to the prevailing list of the planets at the time (or to common-sense knowledge about the motionlessness of the earth). His theory *redefined* what should count as a planet. The very point of formulating systematic, testable theories in any domain is to get beyond the hodge-podge of suppositions that characterize pre-theoretic common sense.

Human participants in religious rituals, even though agents *ontologically*, can function in the role of the patients of ritual actions – as that to which something is done. This does not mean that the agent ceases being an agent but that he or she is being acted upon rather than engaging in action. So, for example, when priests baptize participants, even though the participants are agents ontologically, as participants undergoing baptism they serve as the patients in these ritual acts. In religious rituals agents with appropriate qualities and properties can do things to other agents who function as the patients of those rituals. We turn, therefore, to these qualities and properties, because a theory that only provides for a general structural description of the relationships among agents, acts and patients will prove insufficient to explicate interesting facts about ritual structure.

A structural description of a religious ritual action must include information about the *qualities* and *properties* of the participants and the actions involved. It is often not sufficient, for example, merely to represent the fact that an agent is engaged in an action upon a patient.

We should be able to represent some ritually salient qualities and properties of the agents, actions and patients. This requires that we specify, when necessary, what makes the agent eligible to perform the action, what properties a particular act must possess, as well as the qualities of the patients that make them eligible to serve in that role.

The conceptual schemes of particular religious systems will, of course, designate which qualities and properties matter. For example, in one religious tradition it might be necessary for ritual officials to be males, in another that the patient be an unmarried woman who has fasted for fourteen days, and in another that the action be performed at night. Our account of the action representation system can accommodate such cultural variations.

The cognitive representation of religious rituals will include the formal features that determine participants' judgements about the ritual's status, efficacy and relationships to other ritual acts. The efficacy of the act of baptism, for example, will have derived from the agent's legitimacy, the appropriate ritual history of the water and the eligibility of the patient. The baptism itself and the previous act of consecrating the baptismal water are qualified by the fact that the priest is eligible to carry out such ritual acts. If he is an impostor, ritual failure looms. Of course, such failures may not necessarily pose insurmountable barriers, because some religious conceptual schemes may provide ways of working around them. But they certainly are regarded as problems, because they contravene basic assumptions about the relations between various ritual actions and about those rituals' connections with CPS-agents.

Just as participants possess qualities and properties that may require specification, sometimes conditions on ritual actions do too. Particular ritual acts sometimes require special conditions for their execution; for example, carrying out some task may require particular instruments. Ritual agents often need special tools in order to do their jobs properly. These tools can be anything the tradition permits – antelope bones for divining, sharp stones for circumcising male children, red ochre for colouring corpses or long sticks for whipping initiates.

Instruments, however, should not be confused with agents. For example, a priest uses incense to sanctify a house or uses rocks of a particular shape to establish a temple site. While these instruments are not the agents, they often specify necessary conditions for the success of the agents' ritual actions. The priest may sanctify the house by means of burning incense. What we called the 'action condition' in *Rethinking Religion* can specify an element in a ritual, viz., the instrument employed by the agent (the incense) as well as qualities of the instrument the conceptual scheme defines as relevant (in this case, that the incense is burning). The complete representation is of an agent with the requisite qualities acting upon an object with the requisite qualities by using an instrument with the requisite qualities.

Sometimes such instruments contribute *fundamentally* to the outcome of the ritual. (The holy water may be fundamental to the blessing of the parishioner.) If so, it is only by virtue of their ritual connections to superhuman agency that they derive their efficacy. Water that has not been consecrated is just plain old water.

In these cases the requisite qualities of instruments are their own connections with CPS-agents through the performance of earlier rituals. Making sense of a religious ritual typically involves reference to a larger network of ritual actions. The performance of earlier rituals 'enables' the performance of the later ones. Because the priest has blessed the water in the font, participants can use it to bless themselves when they enter the vestibule of a church. These earlier rituals that fulfil necessary conditions for the performance of subsequent rituals are what we call 'enabling rituals' (or, more generally, 'enabling actions'). So, for example, a participant can partake of a first communion, because she was previously baptized. Her baptism, which establishes a more immediate connection between her and the CPS-agents than existed before, *enables* her to participate in the communion. The validity of the communion presupposes this divinely sanctioned ritual of the participant's baptism.

If there is no direct reference to a CPS-agent in a ritual's immediate structural description, then at least one of its elements must involve presumptions about *its* connections with one or more (earlier) ritual actions that eventually involves a CPS-agent in one of their immediate structural descriptions. For example, the action of initiating someone into a cohort of a certain kind requires prior actions performed on the agents involved in the initiation. No uninitiated person can initiate the 'newcomer'. The ritual practitioner performing the initiation will have to have been initiated herself. Ultimately, of course, the gods are responsible for the initiating *through* these connections with the immediate ritual agents.

Although it may not always be immediately obvious, ritual actions are systematically connected with one another. The acts involved must be performed in a certain order. Some ritual actions presuppose the performance of others. In everyday life, actions of any kind frequently presuppose the successful completion of previous actions, since those earlier actions fulfil necessary requirements for the performance of the action at hand. For example, operating a car presupposes that the driver has a valid driving licence. Carrying out a particular religious ritual action typically presupposes the prior performance of another ritual action that enables the current one to be performed.

The classic rites of passage in many religious systems offer the best illustrations. The integration of children into a community precedes their rising to adult status, which, in turn, precedes their marriages. In each case the associated rituals presuppose the successful completion of their predecessors. An example is the sequence of initiation rites among the Zulu. In order for a Zulu male to be eligible for marriage, he has to go through a number of rites of passage, starting with the naming ritual and proceeding through the ear-piercing ritual, the puberty ritual, then the 'grouping up ritual'. (See Lawson and Mc-Cauley 1990: 113–21.)

Technically, we can talk about the representation of such a connected set of rituals as *embedded* within the current ritual's structural description. Embedding is a formal notion for representing in their structural descriptions the external relations among rituals that we have described in terms of *enabling* actions. A diagram of the relationships among these successively performed rituals would start with the current ritual (the one under study), which would be depicted at the top of a tree diagram, with all of the logically (and temporally) prior rituals below, connected to it through its ritual elements. Thus the 'full' structural description of a ritual would include all of these embedded rituals.

A ritual's full structural description contrasts with an 'immediate' structural description of its surface features. A full structural description includes that immediate structural description plus the structural descriptions of all of the enabling ritual actions the current ritual presumes as well as accounts of their connections with ritual elements in that current ritual. Recall that in the case of religious ritual, enabling actions are simply (earlier) rituals whose successful completion is necessary for the successful completion of the current ritual. Thus for example, a wedding is not valid, typically, if the priest performing it has not been properly certified ritually by prior ordination. The priest's ordination enables him to perform weddings. The successful performance of the wedding presumes the ordination's success. That ordination is, therefore, an enabling ritual whose structural description must be incorporated (as a property of the priest) into this wedding's *full* structural description.

In the everyday world the exploration of such presuppositions can go on indefinitely either by tracing causal chains ('this is the cat that ate the rat that ate the cheese, etc.') or by concatenating reasons (John flipped the switch, since he wanted to see the room's contents, since he wanted to ascertain whether he could load them into the truck in the next ten minutes, since, if at all possible, he wanted to complete that job before the police arrived, since he wanted to avoid arrest, etc.). Religious rituals, while engaging the same representational resources, possess a distinctive feature which marks them off not only from action in the everyday world but also from the other sorts of religious actions, even the ritualized religious actions we mentioned above, such as standing at certain moments in a religious service. The distinctive feature of the cognitive representation of religious ritual action concerns an end point to such causal or rational explorations. In ritual representations things come to an end. Causal chains terminate; reasons find a final ground. In short, the buck stops with the gods. The introduction of actions involving CPS-agents (or agents with special, counter-intuitive qualities) into the conception of an action introduces considerations that need neither further causal explanation nor further rational justification.

Religious rituals enjoy representational closure by terminating in the deeds of CPS-agents. The actions of the gods ground religious rituals. It is from those deeds that their normative force arises. Although other human actions pretend to similar normative prestige – from law to baseball – none have access to the superhuman considerations that serve as the guarantor of cosmic (as opposed to conventional) authority in religious systems. Despite talk in the humanities and social sciences about civil religion, the religion of art or the theology of communism, such systems rarely engender such immediate authoritativeness. Our suggestion is that this is because they rarely involve such direct appeals to the specific actions of *CPS*-specific agents.

The normative force in question amounts to the assumption that we need discover no further causes, we need give no additional reasons. It should of course come as no surprise that, finally, it is what the gods do that matters in religious ritual. Our theory provides descriptions for religious ritual actions which are, in one respect, exhaustive. For the participants there is no more significant cause to locate, no more crucial reason to propose. The actions of the gods guarantee the comprehensiveness of description, because their actions are causally, rationally and motivationally *sufficient* for the ritual actions they inspire. (We rest from our labours on the sabbath, because God rested from his labours.)

These actions of the gods are the actions our theory defines as *hypothetical* religious rituals. Participants typically appeal to them as actions enabling their own religious ritual practices.

On our theory, then, explaining various fundamental features of religious rituals turns on the roles that CPS-agents play in them. In order to understand why this is the case we need to analyse what is involved in the representation of a religious ritual action.

Since all rituals are actions and only agents act, our command of the category of agency (and the inferences that accompany it) is the single most important piece of ordinary cognitive equipment deployed in the representation of religious rituals. The notion of an 'agent' is fundamental in any theory of religious ritual, because it drives our most basic expectations about the form of any action. The identification of action turns critically on the identification of agents and attributing appropriate states of mind to them. The difference between doing and happening rests in the balance. Doing something to someone differs from something happening to them. The first involves an agent acting upon a patient. The bride kissing the bridegroom differs in fundamental ways from the air-conditioner happening to go on the blink while they do so. We even distinguish between types of movements agents make. Cutting a log and tripping over a log differ in the way they are represented.

The category of agency constitutes the foundation of social intercourse and of our conceptions of responsibility, personhood and morality. Making sense even of some of the most ordinary events of human life usually requires elaborate intentional ascriptions to human beings. All of this is of course standard fare in philosophical discussion, but it has also captured the imagination of developmental psychologists, who have designed marvellously clever experiments to identify the key role that the concept of agency plays even in the mental life of very young children. (Gopnik et al. 1999.) These developmental studies show that long before infants acquire and use language they already possess the cognitive resources required for representing such basic ontological distinctions as that between agents and non-agents. These studies indicate that from early infancy human beings represent agents and the actions they perform very differently from the ways they represent other entities and events. Developmental psychologists have discovered that infants know (and therefore are capable of representing) the difference between the agent and patient of an action, as well as whether the patient is just an inanimate object or also an agent capable of acting as well. This is to say that they distinguish the vital action roles from one another as well as the sorts of entities capable of filling each.

Initially surprising, such claims have the ring of plausibility because distinguishing the nurturing mother from the unresponsive bedpost is vital for the infant's well-being. Very young children recognize that agents have goals and desires and that they are generally capable of initiating self-motion (fulfilling those desires to achieve those goals). By roughly the age of four a child grasps the notion that human agents (at least) also have minds and that their understanding of their world depends upon how their minds represent it. (Wimmer and Perner 1983; Perner et al. 1987.) Children recognize agents' intentionality. The notable point is that the same presumptions hold for the representation of CPS-agents who figure in religious rituals. Participants' intuitive assumptions about the psychology of agents purchase them vast amounts of knowledge about CPS-agents for free. (Boyer 1996.)

In terms of their basic action structures, then, nothing about the representation of religious ritual action is the least bit different from the representation of any other action. Stressing that religious rituals typically invoke ordinary cognitive resources, however, does not mean that they are not unusual. After all, we readily distinguish them from other actions. Ritual washing differs from standard bathing activities. Nevertheless, our ordinary cognitive resources – already in place in infancy – supply the framework for the representation of religious rituals. Most importantly for our purposes, the peculiarities of religious rituals do not mitigate either their basic action structures or the pivotal role of agency in their representation.

The 'specialness' of religious rituals does not turn on anomalies in their basic action structures, but overwhelmingly on the unusual agents that populate religious conceptual schemes. On most fronts CPS-agents are similar to human agents; that is why we can so readily draw inferences about their actions, their goals, their desires and their other states of mind. On a few fronts, though, they differ from human agents by virtue of their various counter-intuitive properties; that is why their implication in actions has such striking consequences.

On our theory, then, three things distinguish religious rituals from other sorts of actions. First, the specific acts carried out in religious rituals (such as sacrifices, baptisms, consecrations, and so on) are often unique to religious conceptual schemes. Second, as we noted above, what we might loosely call enquiry about the causal or rational foundations of religious rituals will always come to an end when they invoke the enabling actions of CPS-agents. At that point, such enquiry stops. There is no need or means for proceeding further, let alone the possibility of carrying on such enquiries indefinitely as is the case with any other sort of action. The third distinctive feature concerns what makes these appeals to the actions of CPS-agents so conclusive. Only with religious rituals do populations of participants carry out actions that routinely presume enabling actions by agents with these special counter-intuitive properties. (In *Rethinking Religion* we employed the marker 's' in the tree diagrams of religious rituals' structural descriptions to designate any of these special properties.)

On our theory it is the *roles* that such agents play in rituals' representations that are the critical variables that define a religious ritual's type, and therefore determine many of its important properties. In addition to its characterization of participants' cognitive representations of their religious actions, our theory also identifies two principles for organizing this information about the impact of CPS-agents' roles on participants' implicit knowledge of their rituals' forms. Those two principles clarify the significance of CPS-agency for religious ritual systems. They jointly yield a typology of religious ritual forms that systematically organizes the rituals of *any* religious system and predicts a variety of their properties. It is to these two principles that we now turn.

A cognitive account of various properties of religious rituals

With the major features of the action representation system in hand, we are now ready to discuss the principles of Superhuman Agency and Superhuman Immediacy. These principles jointly explicate the pivotal role that the concept of CPS-agency plays in religious ritual systems. By organizing the representations of particular religious rituals into a typology of ritual forms on the basis of how participants represent the contributions of CPS-agents to their religious rituals, these two principles provide a means for explaining and predicting a wide array of those rituals' properties. Both participants' intuitive judgements about those properties and their actual ritual practices corroborate this account.

The principles of Superhuman Agency and Superhuman Immediacy categorize the structural descriptions of rituals generated by participants' action representation systems. At a first level of approximation, the *Principle of Superhuman Agency* (PSA) states that whether a CPS-agent either is the agent or is most directly connected (via enabling actions) with the agent of a religious ritual – as opposed to serving in or being most directly connected with one of the other roles – is critical for distinguishing between the two salient kinds of religious rituals.

167

The first kind consists of religious rituals in which the most direct connection with the gods is through the role of the ritual's agent. We shall call these 'special agent rituals'. (We are grateful to Pascal Boyer for suggesting this term.) With special agent rituals the initial entry for a CPS-agent will be ritually connected with the role of the agent in the current ritual. What this amounts to is that one or more previous rituals connects the 'buck-stopper', i.e. the initial CPS-agent in the current ritual, to the current ritual's agent.

The second kind concerns those rituals in which the most direct connection with the gods is through either of the other two roles, i.e. through the patient or through the act itself (by way of a special instrument). In these a CPS-agent will be most directly connected by way of the second or third slots in the current ritual's structural description. Most of the rituals in this second group are what we shall call 'special patient rituals', though 'special instrument rituals' also exist. (Many rituals of divination are examples of the latter sort.)

The PSA concerns the representation of a superhuman agent's involvement in a ritual (as indicated by the location of its entry in a ritual's structural description). In assessing religious rituals' forms, the PSA focuses attention on the action role(s) of the current ritual with which CPS-agents' actions are connected. Participants represent a CPS-agent somewhere in their rituals' full structural descriptions. On our theory the crucial question is *where*. Whether the *initial* entry for a CPS-agent in the full structural description is connected with the current ritual's agent role or with one of its other roles determines both participants' judgements about a wide range of ritual properties, including ritual repeatability and reversibility as well as the potential for ritual substitutions. It also predicts these features of their corresponding ritual practices.

Especially since more than one entry for CPS-agents may arise in a religious ritual's full structural description, these descriptions of the PSA demand clarification of which appearance of a CPS-agent in a structural description qualifies as the *initial* one. Determining which connection with CPS-agents in the representation of a religious ritual constitutes the initial entry, i.e. the entry with the 'most direct connection' to the ritual at hand, is not too complicated. This is where the Principle of Superhuman Immediacy comes in. The *Principle of Superhuman Immediacy* (PSI) states that the number of enabling actions required to connect some element in the current ritual with an entry for a CPS-agent determines that entry's proximity to the current ritual. Specifically, the initial appearance of a CPS-agent in a ritual's full structural description is the entry whose connection with some element in the current ritual involves the fewest enabling actions.

These two principles identify the two most important aspects of religious ritual form. They are concerned with

1. what role(s) in the current ritual enabling rituals are connected; and
2. how many enabling rituals are required to establish that connection between an element in the current ritual and a CPS-agent.

The PSI and PSA work in tandem to delineate a typology of religious ritual actions. That typology readily clarifies a host of fundamental distinctions between the various (and indefinitely large numbers of types of religious ritual actions.

Accordingly, the principal sources of complexity in rituals' full structural descriptions concern the *number* and *locations* of embedded rituals. Recall that embedding is a formal means for representing the enabling rituals the current ritual's performance presupposes. No formal considerations set any principled limits on the possible complexity of the full structural descriptions of rituals that the action representation system can generate, though it seems a safe assumption that such things as memory limitations probably set some practical limitations.

The PSA addresses the *locations* of embedded rituals in the current ritual's full structural description. This is to say that it addresses the action roles (agent, act or patient) of the current ritual that are connected with CPS-agents' actions via enabling actions. By contrast, the PSI is concerned with the *number* of embedded rituals, i.e. with the number of enabling actions, necessary to connect some element of the current ritual with the actions of CPS-agents.

In *Rethinking Religion* we examined only the first five types of religious ritual forms (Lawson and McCauley 1990: 128–30, fig. 17) but that already introduces quite enough complexity to illustrate some important theoretical morals concerning the connections between three things, discussed below.

1. The action representation system and the well-formedness and effectiveness of religious rituals

The first of those morals concerns general considerations of action representation. Our characterizations of the action representation system and the structural descriptions it generates provide a means for precisely specifying the unique features of representations of religious rituals (among action representations generally). Our contention, of course, is that these unique features result from the distinctive items religious conceptual schemes introduce as possible entries in these representations. On one decisive front religious participants represent their rituals differently from the way they represent all of their other actions. All representations of religious rituals somewhere involve connections with the actions of CPS-agents. This is critical to participants' assessments of both their rituals' well-formedness and their efficacy. At least one such connection between some element or other of the current ritual and the action of a CPS-agent is a necessary condition for a ritual's well-formedness. Without presumptions about such a connection, participants will not judge the ritual in question to be well-formed and, if the ritual is not judged as well-formed, they will judge it as ineffective. Unless eligible agents perform correct actions on eligible patients with the right tools, participants will not judge the ritual effective. Crucially, the eligibility of at least one of the ritual participants or the rightness of a ritual instrument will depend upon enabling actions that establish connections between them and the actions of a CPS-agent.

Considerations of the well-formedness and effectiveness of religious rituals quickly demonstrate the importance of distinguishing between special agent rituals and special patient rituals. Well-formedness is only a necessary but not a sufficient condition for the effectiveness of a special patient ritual. So, for example, while the well-formedness of ritual offerings to the ancestors is necessary for these gifts' acceptability, there is no guarantee that the ancestors will accept them. (Whitehouse 1995.) Similarly, at least a casual survey suggests that the well-formedness of special agent rituals is considerably more constrained than special patient or instrument rituals, since the former exhibit much less flexibility concerning ritual substitutions (see below). (See Barrett, this volume.)

2. The PSA distinction between special agent rituals as opposed to special patient and special instrument rituals and three ritual properties

The distinction that the PSA introduces between special agent rituals as opposed to special patient and special instrument rituals (i.e. between rituals of odd- as opposed to even-numbered types in Figure 17 in Lawson and McCauley 1990: 128–30) has many important consequences. These distinctions among ritual types predict numerous properties of rituals *in any religious system*. We shall briefly discuss three.

Repeatability

Individual participants need serve as the patients of special agent rituals only once, whereas participants can and typically do perform special instrument and special patient rituals repeatedly. Consider the difference between once-in-a-lifetime initiations and the many sacrifices that ritual participants will perform as part of their religious obligations.

Our theory explains why some rituals do not require repetition in the lifetime of a ritual participant. CPS-agents act, at least indirectly through their ritually entitled middlemen, in special agent rituals. When the gods do things, they are done once and for all. By contrast, in special patient and special instrument rituals, the gods' closest connections are with the patients or the instruments of the ritual. Whatever ritually mediated connection the agent in such a ritual may enjoy with CPS-agents is comparatively less intimate. Consequently, in these rituals the agents' actions carry no such finality. They are typically done again and again. Initiation into adulthood only happens once per participant, whereas participants will make offerings to the gods over and over and over. That these rituals are repeatable hints that nothing religiously indispensable turns on any *one* of their performances.

Reversibility

Human acts have causal effects and logical and practical consequences. The effect of running a race involves crossing the finishing line. The consequence of winning a race means receiving a prize. This crucial distinction is particularly important in the case of ritual. Getting married in a wedding ritual, for example, has causal effects: bride and groom feel that they have experienced one of the most memorable days in their lives. But wedding rituals also have logical consequences in the framework of the religious system in which they occur. In a particular religious system a wedding might be a ritual which can only be performed on a pair of religious participants once in their lifetime. The gods have acted and the consequences of the ritual act are 'super-permanent'. Nevertheless, sometimes the consequences of such a non-repeated ritual need to be reversed. In everyday life couples get divorced, participants become excommunicated, ritual practitioners are defrocked. In such cases it would seem that if the consequence of a special agent ritual were once and for all (i.e. 'superpermanent'), then it would take an act of the gods to undo what they have initially done. It would seem to require performing another special agent ritual to undo the consequences of the first.

In principle, religious rituals that reverse the consequences of other special agent rituals are possible. However, such special agent rituals do not seem to exist or at least are so rare that their very absence is noteworthy. Even where they might exist they are performed very infrequently. Nevertheless people who are divorced remarry, participants who were driven from the fold are readmitted into the community, sometimes joyously (after they have met certain conditions), ritual practitioners are sometimes reinstated after being expelled. Such situations clearly require the performance of a special agent ritual. So, sometimes, what the gods do only once they need to do again! Obviously the gods can do whatever they want to! But one point shines through these puzzles: if the consequences of rituals are reversed juridically and/or ritually, only then can a ritual participant serve in the role of patient in a performance of the original special agent ritual again. Only the gods can bring about such a novel situation.

Substitutability

Our theory also explains whether a ritual will permit substitution or not. Because nothing religiously indispensable turns on any of their particular performances, ritual substitutions can arise in the even-numbered rites, i.e. the special patient and special instrument rituals. These rituals' temporary effects explain not only why these rituals are repeatable, but also why they often display greater latitude about their instruments, their patients and even their procedures. For example, ritualized washing in the desert, where water is a particularly scarce and valuable resource, can be done with sand. These rituals may also permit substitutions for patients. Some special patient rituals even substitute for CPS-agents – but *only* when they serve as the *patient* of the current ritual, not as its agent. Participants' consumption of bread and wine for the body and blood of Christ is surely the most familiar, but examples abound in the ethnographic literature.

That such substitutions for the initial appearances of CPS-agents do not arise in special agent rituals is of a piece with this. The point is that in special agent rituals the CPS-agents themselves are – so to speak – *in* on the action. Since it is the patients of these religious rituals in whom the resulting superpermanent religious changes are wrought, it stands to reason that substitutions for the patients of special agent rituals are also unlikely to occur.

3. The PSI account of the initial entry for a CPS-agent and (comparative) ritual centrality

The PSI clarifies which among (potentially) multiple entries for CPS-agents *within* a ritual's full structural description is the initial one. The different depths of these initial entries will determine what we have referred to as rituals' comparative 'centrality' to the overall religious system. On the basis of differences in the number of enabling rituals that separate the initial entry for a CPS-agent from current rituals, the PSI permits comparisons *between* rituals as to their relative centrality to the religious system. In short, the fewer enabling actions required to connect the current ritual with the action of a CPS-agent, the more central that ritual is to the religious system.

The important theoretical point is that multiple independent empirical measures correlate with a religious ritual's centrality. The most straightforward *cognitive* gauge would simply be to elicit participants' judgements about such matters. This is *not* to say that participants have explicit knowledge about this abstract property of religious rituals. They do, however, possess a reservoir of tacit knowledge pertaining to these matters. Specifically, participants can offer judgements about the *comparative* centrality of various rituals. Still, that might prove a fairly coarse measure in light of the variety of extraneous variables (e.g. performance frequency) that could influence participants' judgements. Consequently, it would be especially valuable to design experiments that tap this intuitive knowledge by means of indirect behavioural measures while controlling for these potentially confounding factors. These might range from such thinly veiled tasks as asking informants to rank their rituals' comparative dispensableness to less direct measures testing such things as participants' diverse sensitivities to variations, their default assumptions in reasoning, or their differential recollections of details.

Cognition, however, is not the only source of evidence here. Aspects of ritual practice should also provide evidence about rituals' comparative centrality. For example, participants' knowledge about ritual prerequisites generally reflects genuine constraints on ritual practice. A Zulu male really cannot use specially prepared love potions unless he has gone through a series of other rituals beforehand. (See Lawson and McCauley 1990: 113–21.) An Orthodox Jew's bar mitzvah really is a necessary condition for his becoming a rabbi. These points about ritual practice are so familiar that it is easy to lose sight of their theoretical significance. Because some of these rituals are prerequisites for others, they have less structural depth and, consequently, will prove more central to these various religious systems.

In some religious systems actual ritual practice may provide additional evidence about rituals' relative centrality. According to the insider–outsider criterion, religious rituals in our theory's technical sense are those religious activities that are only open to participants in the religious system. Further restrictions on participation in and observation of religious rituals also tend to correlate with a ritual's centrality. Participants' tolerance for variation in religious rituals is another measure. Presumably, that tolerance decreases with rituals' increasing centrality. Hence, ritual practices during periods of religious fragmentation may also supply clues about rituals' centrality. The perceived degree of upheaval within a religious system and the probability that diverging religious communities will refuse to identify with one another any longer will (if any ritual changes occur) surely correlate better with the addition, alteration or deletion of a comparatively central ritual than with one that is less central.

Conclusion

Many scholars have previously noted one or another of these patterns among ritual properties. Ours is the only theory, however, that explains and predicts all of them systematically (regardless of the religious system involved). It can do so because, finally, all of these properties turn on features of participants' representations of the forms of their religious ritual actions. We end with three important observations.

First, although we are making predictions about the types of intuitive judgements that informants are likely to make in situations, we are not claiming that such judgements require the participants' conscious reflection. In fact, evidence suggests that such judgements are usually not based on conscious knowledge, acquired by instruction and honed by reflection. As Boyer (1994) has suggested, such intuitive knowledge seems to 'come naturally'.

Second, it is worth re-emphasizing that none of this knowledge about religious rituals depends upon assigning *meanings* either to the acts participants perform or to the acts performed on them or to the qualities or properties of such acts or to the relationships among the acts. In other words, a great deal of ritual participants' (intuitive) knowledge of their religious ritual system does not depend upon their ability to provide *interpretations* or meanings for the rituals in which they participate or even for the prior rituals they presume. The dimensions of ritual knowledge that concern us can operate without reference to meaning and often do. (Baranowski 1998.) A particular ritual participant may not for example have a clue about the meaning of apostolic succession or ordination, and still know that it takes a priest to get married; another may not have the faintest idea why it is necessary to swallow a bitter herb before going courting but would not dream of approaching his prospective mate unless he had done so. (Lawson 1985.)

Sometimes all the ethnographer gets is 'we do it because our ancestors did it'. Sometimes informants appeal to specialists who possess the requisite knowledge, and sometimes informants *are* willing to engage in extended semantic commentary. It all depends. The attribution of meaning (let alone *particular* meanings) either to the ritual as a whole or to any of its parts is not a constant either between or within cultures. In any event, we expect considerable variation about the attribution of meanings. So, we are not saying that the attribution of meanings never occurs; we are only saying that *for many features of religious ritual knowledge and practice meanings simply do not matter.* In some religious systems interpretations may flourish and become resources for sophisticated theological speculation among the intellectual elite. In other religious systems the attribution of meanings remains forever beside the point. (Barth 1975.)

Finally, comparing our theory's predictions with findings uncovered in the field permits us to narrow a gap between models of participants' competences with symbolic-cultural systems and participants' actual performance with these systems. This is a gap about which many critics of competence theories (e.g. Clark 1993) have complained. But our theory does not depend exclusively on surveying participants' intuitive judgements about features of their rituals for its empirical assessment. The theory also makes predictions about ritual practices. In light of its many empirical predictions, we hope our theory will provoke ethnographers into asking new kinds of questions about religious rituals in order to see if the theory will stand up to further tests.

Note

1. We shall use the terms 'instruments' and 'patients' to refer to what in *Rethinking Religion* we referred to (less efficiently) as the ritual's 'action

175

conditions' and 'logical object' respectively. Technically these terms identify action roles. Following ordinary linguistic conventions, though, we will sometimes use them to refer to the items that serve in these roles as well.

References

Baranowski, A. (1998) 'A psychological comparison of ritual and musical meaning'. *Method and Theory in the Study of Religion* 10: 3–29.

Baron-Cohen, S. (1995) *Mindblindness: An Essay on Autism and Theory of Mind.* Cambridge, MA: MIT Press.

Barth, F. (1975) *Ritual and Knowledge among the Baktaman of New Guinea.* New Haven: Yale University Press.

Boyer, P. (1994) *The Naturalness of Religious Ideas: A Cognitive Theory of Religion.* Berkeley: University of California Press.

Boyer, P. (1996) 'Cognitive limits to conceptual relativity: the limiting case of religious categories'. In *Rethinking Linguistic Relativity,* ed. J. Gumperz and S. Levinson, 203–31. Cambridge: Cambridge University Press.

Clark, A. (1993) *Associative Engines: Connectionism, Concepts, and Representational Change.* Cambridge, MA: MIT Press.

Gopnik, A., A. N. Meltzoff and P. Kuhl (1999) *The Scientist in the Crib.* New York: Morrow.

Lawson, E. T. (1985) *Religions of Africa: Traditions in Transformation.* San Francisco: HarperCollins.

Lawson, E. T. and R. N. McCauley (1990) *Rethinking Religion: Connecting Cognition and Culture.* Cambridge: Cambridge University Press.

Leslie, A. M. (1995) 'A theory of agency'. In *Causal Cognition: A Multidisciplinary Debate,* ed. D. Sperber, D. Premack and A. J. Premack, 121–47. New York: Oxford University Press.

Penner, H. (1975) 'Creating a Brahman: a structural approach to religion'. In *Methodological Issues in Religious Studies,* ed. R. D. Baird, 49–66. Chico, CA: New Horizons Press.

Perner, J., S. R. Leekam and H. Wimmer (1987) 'Three-year-olds' difficulty with false belief'. *British Journal of Developmental Psychology* 5: 125–37.

Whitehouse, H. (1995) *Inside the Cult: Religious Innovation and Transmission in Papua New Guinea.* Oxford: Clarendon Press.

Wimmer, H. and J. Perner (1983) 'Beliefs about beliefs: representations and constraining function of wrong beliefs in young children's understanding of deception'. *Cognition* 13: 103–28.

9 'The Morphology and Function of Magic' Revisited

JESPER SØRENSEN

'Magic' is one of the most controversial concepts in both anthropology and the academic study of religion. The common opinion among scholars inspired by postmodern and relativist positions is that the concept reflects an ethnocentric division between 'religion' as a truer, higher and more profound system of belief, and 'magic' as a false, lower and more superficial practice aimed at manipulating the world in the absence of correct scientific knowledge and effective technology (see Smith 1995 and Kapferer 1997 for excellent overviews). It has, however, proven very difficult to get rid of the concept, as it seems to cover an obvious area of human activity. Following Boyer (1996), I believe a sound way out of this morass is to recognize that 'magic' and 'religion', as well as other broad concepts, are 'impure subjects', about which one cannot construct scientifically sound theories. Instead, we need to be more specific and look for structures and causal relations at a lower level in order to explain and interpret the phenomena traditionally covered by broad terms such as 'magic'. In the following, I will attempt to do so by focusing on two aspects of ritualized action: (1) the ascription of magical agency in ritual, and (2) the use of image-schematic structures to facilitate representations of ritual efficacy. This will yield information about the cognitive constraints on the morphology and function of magic.

More than seventy years ago, in 1929, E. E. Evans-Pritchard published a paper in the *American Anthropologist* on the morphology and function of magic. The paper is a comparative analysis of magic among the Trobrianders, as it is described by Bronislaw Malinowski, and of Zande magic, on the basis of Evans-Pritchard's own field studies during 1926–7. It should come as no surprise that Evans-Pritchard's primary aim in this early study is to determine the morphology of magic as a function of social structure in general, and of the relationship between exclusive ownership of magic and social power by specific groups in particular. At this time Evans-Pritchard accepts Malinowski's psychological definition, according to which the primary function of magic is the satisfaction of a need for security created by the lack of control in some aspects of human pragmatic or technical pursuits (Evans-Pritchard 1929: 621). In other words, the primary motive behind magical action is the emotions prompted by human uncertainty, which results in symbolic behaviour aimed at controlling probabilistic events. In addition to this psychological meta-theory, explaining magic as a means to control the uncontrollable, Evans-Pritchard (1929: 623) defines the overall identity of structures of magic in different cultures as consisting of the *ritual*, the *spell*, the conditions of the *performer*, and the *tradition* of magic.

Evans-Pritchard (1929: 622) confirms the overall likeness of Zande and Trobriander magic by the postulate that both the Azande and the Trobrianders would mutually recognize each other's magical rituals as specifically 'magical'. Thus he upholds 'magic' as a category of universally recognizable human behaviour, and his purpose is from this perspective to shed light on the substantial differences cultures display in the emphasis placed on the constituent elements mentioned above. This entails a critique of the view according to which magic is based on the spell as its primary and efficacious element, a view generalized by Malinowski on the basis of his own Melanesian data. Instead, Evans-Pritchard's Zande data indicate the centrality of the material element in magical rituals – the magical medicine. This difference is substantiated by a simple linguistic comparison between the Zande word for magic, *ngewa*, meaning in ordinary circumstances 'wood', with its Trobriand equivalent, *megwa*, meaning both 'spell' and 'magic' (Evans-Pritchard 1929: 626). Thus the emphasis on different elements as the container of magical agency in the ritual is locally recognized and entrenched in the conceptual systems in both cultures. By magical agency I refer to an element present in the rite, which is believed to be the primary agent responsible for the occurrence of the desired ritual result – an element which cannot be omitted if the ritual is to have any efficacy. Thus the logical agent performing the ritual action is placed in the background in order for the magical agency to be able to exercise its force. This will be further treated below. Among the Azande, magical agency is ascribed to the material elements, or medicine, used in the ritual. Thereby the importance of the accompanying spell is reduced to a mere directive device, ensuring that the proper patient will receive the magical influence. Evans-Pritchard sums up the differences between Azande and Melanesian magic in the following quote: 'In

Zande magic the taboos and the rites are subject to variation, the spell is diffuse and unformulated, the tradition is not standardized, the performance is neither public nor ceremonial; the whole act of magic is less rigidly defined and less amenable to set form than the magic acts of Melanesia' (Evans-Pritchard 1929: 632).

It is important to note that even though the Azande place greater emphasis on the material element in magic, ritualistic and linguistic elements distinguishing magical from ordinary behaviour are by no means absent, even if the exact iconic reproduction of the ritual action is not believed to be a necessary condition for their efficacy.

As mentioned, Evans-Pritchard explains the difference in the morphology of magic by its social function in relation to the respective social structures. Whereas among the Trobrianders magic plays an important role in securing the exclusive power of clans and headmen, among the Azande magic has no such power-related social function. Zande political authority is based on secular power – mainly legitimate violence – and needs no magical foundation. This again determines the basis of ownership of magic: on the Trobriand Islands magic is owned by clans, legitimized by myths explaining the origin of the magic, and transmission of the most important spells is restricted by genealogical or clan relationship. According to Evans-Pritchard, this entails a formalizing of magical spells into rigid formulas that ensure their exclusive ownership by virtue of the difficulty in learning them. Ownership of magic is one of the main arguments for political authority, and therefore the performance of important magic is restricted to the clans traditionally ruling. Thus, according to Evans-Pritchard, the morphology of magic among the Trobrianders is constrained by a desire to impede illegitimate transmission, thereby ensuring the continuation of traditional structures of power. Among the Azande, on the other hand, magic is not related to clans or genealogical lines, but owned by individuals and transmitted through commercial interaction. This embedding of magic in a commercial event-frame (Fillmore 1982) prevents spells from developing into rigid formulas that would impede their commercial exchange. Further, this entails that the legitimacy of magic is gained through 'current mythology' asserting the efficacy of magical rituals by reference to contemporary cases of successful rituals involving a particular medicine, rather than by traditional myths (a distinction related to the difference between episodic and semantic memory presented by Whitehouse 2000; this volume). It is by this means that the current 'market value' of the spell is determined (Evans-Pritchard 1929: 634, 640).

To summarize, Evans-Pritchard explains the difference of morphology in magic among the Trobrianders and the Azande by differences
in social structure in general and power structure in particular. However, the question is whether this as such is a satisfying explanation. I
think not. Malinowski states explicitly that it is not lack of knowledge
of the long and intricate spells that prevents the common Trobrianders
from uttering these spells (Malinowski 1935a: 66). They know some of
the spells very well, as these are pronounced aloud in public performances. So what keeps the common Trobriander from performing the
actions himself? I will argue that it is the essential qualities of magical
agency ascribed to the spells that prevent anyone but real magicians
(also ascribed special essential qualities) from handling the spell. The
exclusive rights of magical performance described by Malinowski are
therefore no more a question of ignorance of the correct liturgical
procedures than this is the case among Roman Catholics and the
performance of the Mass. In both cases the ritual agent or magician is
represented as endowed with special qualities enabling him to perform
the ritual not only in an appropriate manner, but also with a successful
result (cf. Lawson and McCauley 1990; this volume). Instead of
explaining these differences in the morphology of magic solely by
reference to social structure, we thus need to study differences as based
on the ritual participants' mental representations that delegate magical
agency to different elements of the ritual. Thus the causal interaction
between secular and magical power is more complex. Some rituals are
for instance believed to have efficacy because they are performed by a
person with secular power, e.g. in the healing powers ascribed to the
'monarch's touch', observed in Europe at least until the nineteenth
century (Thomas 1991).

A cognitive approach to magical action

What can a cognitive approach to magical rituals teach us? I will try to
answer this question by posing two more specific and interrelated
questions: (a) What are the cognitive constraints on the morphology of
magical rituals? and (b) What are the cognitive procedures involved in
the creation of meaningful magical practices?

The first question concerns the cognitive constraints on basic-level
categorization, concept formation and conceptual relations in magical
rituals, and their connections to similar or identical representations in
everyday life. There is an extensive literature on these subjects in the
area of 'everyday cognition' (Lakoff 1987; Mandler 1992; Carey and

Spelke 1994; Hirschfeld and Gelman 1994). Of particular interest in this context is the notion of psychological essentialism (Medin and Ortony 1989), a term used to describe the human tendency to ascribe common essence to members of a given category independent of perceptual characteristics. Elements used in magical rituals are often ascribed special essential qualities independent of their perceptual features that explain their special powers or characteristics (Boyer 1993). There is, however, *per se* no reason to claim special cognitive modules or procedures in order to explain magical and religious phenomena (Boyer 1995). This entails that categories and representations in these conceptual domains can be studied by the same methods used in the study of other conceptual domains, if one recognizes that categories and concepts used in magical rituals often have specific internal features and a complex relationship to everyday categorization and conceptualization. The question concerning the legitimate use of ritual procedures, mentioned above, is an excellent reminder of the need for a careful study of the categories and representations used, both in relation to the intuitive ontological assumptions ascribed to entities belonging to different domains (Boyer 1994), but also as semantic units. These procedures are defined relative to established cognitive and cultural models, and by novel mappings between domains. Thus, elements from several cognitive and conceptual domains are combined in the creation of frames that structure expectancy and knowledge about persons, objects and actions taking part in the ritual.

A small example may be illustrative at this point. The notion of Zande medicine, mentioned above, cannot be approached without the notion of intuitively ascribed representations of 'essence' ensuring the efficacy of the medicine. This essential quality is not reducible to the objects' outer appearance and is most likely not based on a definition based on necessary and sufficient conditions, even though it may be structured by exclusive membership (Boyer 1994). As mentioned, this automatic ascription of 'essence' is not restricted to magical or religious objects, but is a function of human basic-level categorization of both natural and to a certain extent social categories (Medin and Ortony 1989; Gelman et al. 1995; Hirschfeld 1995). Therefore magical objects are 'like' other objects despite the obvious special status and properties ascribed. What distinguishes some of the elements used in magical rituals from non-ritual elements is the semantic content or attributes of the essence (cf. Saariluoma, this volume). In the case of the Azande, medicine is believed to contain inherent magical qualities, and the ritual production of the medicine out of natural objects merely refines these inherent qualities. At the same time, the medicine takes part in commercial transactions employing a commercial event-frame (Fillmore 1982), in which a 'Seller' and a 'Buyer' 'Exchange' 'Objects' of equal 'Value'. The existence of such a frame can be illustrated by the fact that a speaker only has to say something like 'I bought medicine' in order for the whole frame to emerge as a background condition in the following discourse. The commercial event-frame in Zande magic is related to essentialist representations by the belief that medicine will lose its value, or its essential quality, if it is given away for free or sold too cheaply. This example illustrates the complex interaction of intuitive ontological assumptions on the one hand about the essential qualities of the objects, on the other about the culturally specified content and frames of interaction.

In order to describe the complex interaction of domains, categories and frames involved in the creation and performance of meaningful magical rituals, I propose to apply the theory of mental spaces and conceptual blending developed in recent years in cognitive semantics. Mappings between mentally constructed spaces are originally the idea of the linguist Gilles Fauconnier, and have subsequently been developed by several scholars (Fauconnier 1994; 1997; Fauconnier and Turner 1996; 1998; Sweetser and Fauconnier 1996). Before proceeding, I find it practical to distinguish between three interacting and mutually dependent levels of description: (1) a level governed by ontological, semantic and experiential domains both structuring and structured by basic-level categorization (both domain-specific and domain-general) and image-schemata; (2) a systemic level, organizing event-frames into mostly culturally specified sequences of action or mini-narrations; and (3) a pragmatic level, at which semantic spaces are locally constructed, enabling interaction and combination of structures from both level (1) and level (2). Basic-level categorization and event-frames are crucial for informing and structuring individual mental spaces, event-frames organize standardized sequences of causal unfolding and interaction within mental spaces, and pragmatic repertoires, such as specific rituals, facilitate interaction between spaces.

Central to the theory of mental spaces and conceptual blending is the postulate that meaning is constructed and manipulated within mental spaces and in mappings between different spaces. Mental spaces are locally constructed and contain the relevant elements needed in the discursive unfolding. Linguistic devices are used to structure reference between spaces (e.g. pronouns and anaphora), and space-builders, such as conditionals and counterfactuals, structure the logical relation between spaces (Fauconnier 1997). Thus mental spaces are locally constructed mini-domains of meaning, into which all sorts of background knowledge is imported, adding to the information explicit in the space. An important extension to the theory of mental spaces is introduced in the theory of conceptual blending. Conceptual blending encompasses both the mapping between a source and a target domain, as in the case of conceptual metaphors described for instance by George Lakoff (Lakoff 1987; 1993; Lakoff and Johnson 1980), as well as other kinds of mappings. Whereas the 'Lakovian' model is based on the uni-directionality of mappings in metaphors between 'source' and 'target' (a non-palpable concept such as 'love' understood by a more palpable concept such as 'journey'), the blended space theory proposes instead that elements from both the source and the target are projected into a new, blended space organized by a new emergent structure. Thus the conceptual blending approach allows multiple projections into a single blended space, which entails a more flexible model than the conceptual metaphor model, and by reference to the constraints imposed by the emergent structure in the blended space it explains why some and not other elements are projected into the blended space.

At least four spaces are active in the model: (1) and (2) two input spaces, including all relevant elements, frames and models, with some of these mapped from one space onto counterparts in the other; (3) a generic space, accounting for the generic aspects of the mappings between elements from the two spaces at a very abstract and schematic level, whose main organizing features I take to be image-schematic structures (Johnson 1987) and psychological essentialism (Medin and Ortony 1989); and (4) a blended space, consisting of items projected from both input spaces and an emergent structure not present in any of the input spaces (Fauconnier 1997: 149–50). Blending conceptual spaces entails that a new structure of elements emerges. The blend is thus not merely a compilation of elements belonging to the two inputs. This emergent structure is created in three interrelated manners: (a) through composition, whereby the relations between elements projected from the input spaces form a new structure; (b) through completion, whereby knowledge of background frames, and cognitive and cultural models not present in any of the input spaces, can be recruited into the blend and structure the elements therein; and (c) through elaboration, whereby items in the blend are structured through further cognitive elaborations – 'running the blend' (Fauconnier and Turner 1998).

At this point I shall mention three further characteristics of blended spaces. The first is the possibility that the structure emerging in the blended space will solidify, thereby creating a new conceptual domain. The second is that blending will enable the simultaneous manipulation of objects belonging to separate space and time, both 'real' and 'imagined'. The third characteristic is that the structure organizing a blended space need not have any likeness to the 'real' world of the participants(s), nor be judged as possible or even probable by the people using the blend. Blending is a central feature of imagination, enabling creative thinking and the construction of both possible and impossible worlds. Just think of such things as 'the unicorn', 'time-travel' or 'paradise', all notions combining elements from different semantic domains organized in a single space. All three characteristics, as we shall see, are crucial properties of blended spaces in relation to their appearance in magical and religious rituals.

An outline of a typology of magical action

A basic assumption in this outline of a typology of magical action is that conceptual blending is a fundamental procedure in ritual action, by which elements are projected into the ritual space from both a 'profane' and a 'sacred' domain. I am aware that both these concepts and especially their distinction have been under severe criticism for imposing a Western dichotomy, based on (Protestant) Christianity, onto cultures innocent of this opposition (for a historical survey of the concept see Anttonen 1992; Rappaport 1999). I do, however, find it defensible to uphold the two concepts as analytical devices because (a) most people living in cultures supposedly innocent of the dichotomy still find religious and magical concepts highly counter-intuitive, that is, violating intuitive assumptions about the world (Boyer 1994), and (b) people represent ritualized interactions with these categories as a special pragmatic repertoire different from everyday, non-ritual inter-actions (Humphrey and Laidlaw 1994). An advantage of the blended space approach is that, even though the conceptual dichotomy is upheld, the concrete ritual performance is understood as a blend between the two domains, entailing (1) that elements originating in the sacred domain always contain profane properties, (2) that these 'sacred' elements interact with strictly profane elements, and (3) that possible 'feedback' to the input spaces is facilitated, entailing in turn that otherwise profane elements can retain sacred properties outside the ritual frame, and that sacred elements can be profaned or desecrated.

This has to do both with the solidifying of structures in the blend, and with the positive or negative 'contamination' of elements inside the ritual space. Thus the ritual as such is not a part of the sacred domain, but contains elements believed to originate or gain their power from that domain (cf. the fuzzy status of the 'sacred' as a conceptual domain, Anttonen, this volume).

The first blend I will present in this typology is what I call the genetic blend. This blend is a basic constituent of the ritual frame by its treatment of the origin of the different entities appearing in the ritual, especially the origin of the ritual agency. All religious and magical rituals will have some reference to the sacred or mythic domain as the origin of ritual power, but the emphasis on which elements are endowed with these qualities will differ considerably between cultures and traditions, as already noted by Evans-Pritchard. It should be noted that the formal structure of the ritual does not necessarily stem from either of the input spaces, but can be found in a cognitive and culturally defined ritual frame used to complete the structure of the blend (such as the ritual structure proposed by Lawson and McCauley 1990).

Figure 9.1 is an elaboration of models originally designed by Fauconnier and Turner (1996; 1998). It is an abstract illustration of the possible mental projections and mappings underlying the performance of a magical ritual. In the top right-hand box is an open list of the possible elements contained in the generic space linking elements from the profane to the sacred space. The importance of this basic blend lies in the possibility of describing the origin of each single element in a given ritual by reference to its origin in either of the two input spaces, and in determining the type of counterpart connections linking elements in the two. Before turning to the elements which are by far the most important, Agent, Action and Object, I look briefly at the other items. Both Time and Location may be crucial elements in any particular ritual, by linking the concrete unfolding of the ritual in the profane space and present time to a mythic and sacred time and location. Just think of special 'holy' places, such as shrines and temples, and of the New Age belief in 'vortices' of the earth emitting special forces, or of the special auspicious times connected to astronomical or mythological events directly related to a specific time in the profane world. Participants usually play a secondary role in the establishment of magical agency, as they are not themselves wielders of this agency, but they are often required to have a special relationship to the sacred space in order for the ritual to be successful. Participants might have to be initiated or undergo ritual cleansing in order not to destroy the

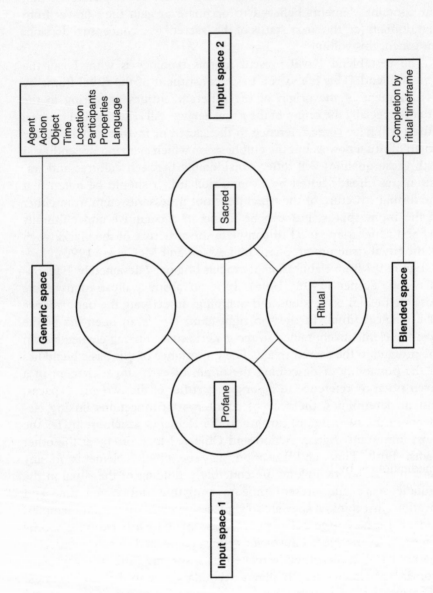

Generic space

Agent
Action
Object
Time
Location
Participants
Properties
Language

Input space 2

Sacred

Ritual

Profane

Input space 1

Blended space

Completion by
ritual timeframe

Figure 9.1

ritual. Likewise, different Properties can be represented as either blocking or promoting the connection between the sacred and the profane space. Finally, Language plays a significant role as a ritual marker distinguishing the pragmatic repertoire of ritual from non-ritual, through the employment of all sorts of linguistic devices such as prosody, iteration and archaic, ungrammatical or even nonsensical expressions. The ritualization of language (Humphrey and Laidlaw 1994) found in many magical rituals has given rise to a substantial amount of anthropological theorizing concerning the relationship between language and magic (e.g. Tambiah 1968); space, however, does not allow me to present a more thorough analysis of the relation between language and magic in the present context (see Sørensen 2000). However, as we shall see in the following, the ritualization of elements, including language, entails that the conventional or symbolic meaning of words and actions are de-emphasized, making room for image-schematic and essentialist representations, leading to iconic and indexical interpretations (I follow C. S. Peirce's (1931) distinction between icon, index and symbol). As ritualization can be performed on all types of elements present in a ritual space, language need not be distinguished as a special case, but rather offers an especially lucid example of the general process of ritualization. Thus I believe that words and phrases in magical rituals are most fruitfully studied as cases of ritual (speech-)acts or as ritual objects (e.g. talismans), rather than as semantic units (cf. Staal 1979).

Agent, Action and Object are the central elements most often ascribed magical agency, and thus seem to be the primary efficacious entities of magical rituals, either in isolation or in combination. Whether the primary efficacious, or magical, agency is invested in an Agent (e.g. by revelation), in an Action (e.g. in the iconic reproduction of certain ritual procedures), or in Objects (e.g. divine gifts or magical medicine), is by no means unimportant. Take the example in which the agency is ascribed to a human shaman, by virtue of his or her connection to the sacred domain and possession of sacred knowledge, both acquired by spirit travel in the 'mythological' world. In that case, all or some elements present in the ritual, both actions and objects, might be taken from the profane world and only invested with any ritual power through the contact with the human agent in possession of magical agency. In contrast, if magical efficacy is believed to stem from actions alone, the exact iconic reproduction of these actions will be a prerequisite for the transfer of magical agency no matter who performs them. Finally, if the magical agency is invested in objects, these can be used by several agents not imbued with any special status except by their ownership of the objects. Such mappings might explain why sacred entities are dangerous in the profane world, as they can only be handled safely in ritual spaces making a sanctioned blend of the sacred and the profane, and creating an emergent structure guiding their manipulation.

There is a clear division between Role and Value between the two spaces. To extend our shaman example, the Role is the conceptual category of 'the shaman', belonging to the sacred space and independent of its personification. There may even be a mythical model, instancing the role in the 'primordial shaman' inventing or receiving the techniques at the beginning of time. This Role is then connected to a Value, i.e. to a concrete person normally belonging to the profane space. The connection might be motivated by a genealogical link, connecting the present to previous values of the role, or it might be effected through initiation, relating the Value to the Role either exclusively in the ritual space or for good. In both cases, in order for the ritual to be successful, there is a conflation of Role and Value taking place in the ritual space. Re-entry into the profane world demands cleansing rituals restoring the profane status of the elements, or they might subsequently be represented as containing sacred qualities acquired in the ritual, thus gaining a special classificatory status.

By mixing the profane and the sacred in the ritual space, the ontological properties of elements change or become uncertain. This explains why elements otherwise belonging to the profane domain are sometimes believed to contain magical powers after the ritual has been performed, even in cases where no specific ritual actions transfer magical power to the elements in question. In the ritual space the power believed to originate in the sacred domain can 'contaminate' other entities involved in the ritual, either intentionally or as a side-effect. This ability to transfer magical power is very important in the institutionalization of magical rituals apparent in most religious traditions. Institutionalization can in this respect be interpreted as an attempt to control the ascription and manipulation of sacred power, but history is full of examples of just how difficult it is to control illicit ascription of magical agency in non-institutionalized contexts.

Genetic blending among the Trobrianders and the Azande

As will be evident from my introductory remarks, the Trobrianders and the Azande differ in their ascription of magical agency in ritual performance. Malinowski refers to two myths explaining the origin of magic among the Trobrianders. The first states that the ancestors brought magic with them when they first emerged from underground. This is related to the Trobriand myth of origin, according to which villagers are connected to their soil by emergence. Magic and people, according to this myth, are connected to the soil by a metonymic link of common origin. In the second myth, magic is a gift to humans from the culture hero Tudava in a primordial time (Malinowski 1935a: 68–75). What the two myths have in common is that magic is a cultural possession acquired in mythic or sacred times. In both cases there are on the one hand counterpart mappings between a sacred space, in which magic, in particular spells, came into the world and became the property of magicians (either through emergence or through a gift), on the other hand a present profane space with its physical magicians and uttered spells. The magicians in the two input spaces are connected by a metonymic link (the genealogical blood-line, often explicitly recited), while the ritual action (the spell) is connected to its mythic paragon by an iconic identity connector.

As illustrated in Figure 9.2, garden magic among the Trobrianders is a combination of Agent-based and Action-based magical agency. Both the magician and the spell are believed to have magical power: the magician through his metonymic relation to the ancestral magicians (who all had magical power), and the spell through its iconic identity with the primordial spell. This seems to be correlated with the population's attitude toward both spells and magicians. It is only the garden magician that is entitled to utter spells associated with the garden, and he must know the spells and recite them correctly in order for them to have any efficacy (Senft 1985). The generic space 'Agent', enabling the metonymic connection between the present and the mythic agent, is based on 'psychological essentialism' (Medin and Ortony 1989), containing specific notions about properties of human agents, common essence based on genealogical ties, and on a series of image-schemata of common origin (LINK), line of descent (PATH), and containment of essence (CONTAINER). The connection between the present action (spell) and its mythic model is based on image-schematic representations of iconic features such as pronunciation, intonation, prosody, etc. giving an abstract representation of the (speech-)act. These iconic features enable the judgement of whether a given expression has succeeded or failed in establishing a connection between the profane space and the sacred space.

Among the Azande, magical agency is ascribed to material objects

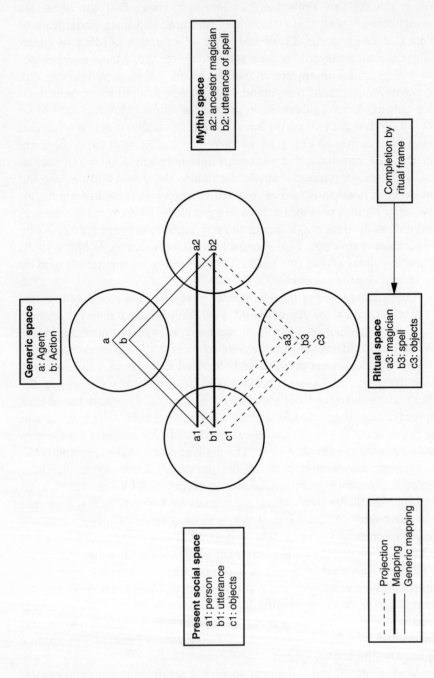

Present social space
a1: person
b1: utterance
c1: objects

Generic space
a: Agent
b: Action

a
b

a1
b1
c1

a2
b2

a3
b3
c3

Mythic space
a2: ancestor magician
b2: utterance of spell

Completion by ritual frame

Ritual space
a3: magician
b3: spell
c3: objects

- - - - - Projection
———— Mapping
════ Generic mapping

Figure 9.2

used in the ritual. The only thing a human agent needs to do is direct the essential tendencies of the medicine towards the desired target, using what Evans-Pritchard calls a 'saying-spell', distinguishing them from the Trobriand 'formula-spell' (Evans-Pritchard 1929: 625). One could object that the medicines are not natural objects, that they are cooked by human agents, and that this mixing, cooking, and the accompanying spells infuse the magical properties into the objects. However, the Azande themselves believe that the properties are essential qualities of the objects, and that the cooking and mixing merely 'heat' the medicine (making it active, a conceptual structure also found in allegations of witchcraft) and direct it toward the desired goal: 'It is this material substance which is the occult and essential element in the rite, for in the substance lies the mystical power which produces the desired end' (Evans-Pritchard 1937: 441). This interpretation is supported by the fact that most Zande spells explicitly address the medicine, telling it what kind it is, and thereby determine its expected line of actions. The material focus in Zande magic is also expressed in myths, according to which both the agent and the spell, but not the material object, can be changed without affecting the efficacy of the ritual (Evans-Pritchard 1929: 626–7). The sacred character of the material substances used in magic is also evident in the stories relating to the gathering of plants, roots and bulbs used in magical ritual. The stronger the magical medicine produced, the more dangerous it is to collect the necessary ingredients, hidden as they are in caves and surrounded by snakes and ghosts (Evans-Pritchard 1937: 215–19).

In Figure 9.3, I have chosen to represent the knowledge necessary to manufacture medicine as stemming from the profane domain, like other elements appearing in the ritual, such as the saying-spell. These are all necessary ingredients in the ritual, but are not responsible for the transfer of magical agency from the sacred to the ritual space. The mapping between an object in the profane and the sacred space is established by an identity connector, identifying an object as belonging to this class of magical objects. Contrary to the magical stones of the Aguaruna (see Brown 1985, discussed by Boyer 1994), which cannot be identified by perceptual characteristics, Zande magical objects are recognized by perceptual characteristics, such as appearance and place of growth, all functioning as indices of a common essence of magical potential residing in an object that only needs refining in order to be effective. Thus psychological essentialism, image-schemata and basic-level categorization are all active in the generic space, enabling the

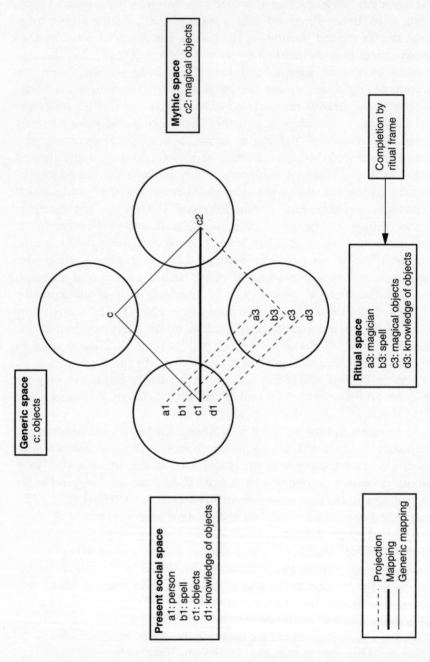

Generic space
c: objects

Mythic space
c2: magical objects

Ritual space
a3: magician
b3: spell
c3: magical objects
d3: knowledge of objects

Completion by
ritual frame

Present social space
a1: person
b1: spell
c1: objects
d1: knowledge of objects

- - - - - Projection
——— Mapping
———— Generic mapping

Figure 9.3

establishment of an identity connector between the object in the sacred and in the profane domains.

Thus the Action- and Agent-based magic of the Trobrianders can be clearly distinguished from the Object-based magic of the Azande. Even if I agree that there is often an intimate connection between political power and magical agency, I doubt whether it is as clear-cut as that proposed by Evans-Pritchard. Strong secular power seems to attract the ascription of magical agency in some cases (the monarch's touch in Europe) and not in others (the Zande prince), and the ascription of agency will therefore depend on other factors, such as the existing conceptual and cultural models connecting Agents, Actions or Objects directly to the sacred domain. Different models may coexist at the same time in the same culture with different social status, a status that may change due to social change (e.g. the status of spirit mediums at Tikopia rises significantly when the secular power and the related magical power of the chiefs diminishes due to the effects of colonization, Firth 1967). The ascription of magical agency will be influenced by both pragmatic and socio-cultural factors, and may fluctuate within cognitive constraints depending on these parameters. Thus I find it better to talk about a proclivity towards ascribing magical agency to specific elements informed by cultural models.

The schematic blend: manipulative magic among the Trobrianders and the Azande

Whereas the genetic blend described above is a prerequisite for the ascription of magical agency to a given ritual, it does not tell us much about the ritual itself. By a brief analysis of two rituals, I will try to show how the conceptual blending approach will help elucidate the characteristic feature traditionally described as sympathetic elements in magical rituals (Frazer 1993). In this context, I will restrict myself to one of the two basic types of procedures active in rituals involving representations of magical transfer, namely manipulative magic based on schematic transfer (the other being transformative magic based on essence transfer, see Sørensen 2000).

While criticizing large parts of Frazer's theory, most scholars have agreed that he was right in pointing to the explicit use of perceptual similarity in magical rituals, even if there has been considerable discussion of just how important this observation really is (for telling examples, see Mauss 1972; Rozin and Nemeroff 1990). The resemblance between similarity and metaphor has been noticed elsewhere and will not concern us in this context (Leach 1976). The primary aim of manipulative magic is to manipulate, or change, a state in one domain by interaction with elements belonging to another domain. The connections between the two domains are established by the extensive use of similarity-based counterpart connections linking elements belonging to the respective mental spaces, extracted from a given domain in a particular, local pragmatic context. As we shall see, image-schemata play an essential role in this manipulation. Manipulation can be achieved either by direct physical interaction or by indirect symbolic interaction, both interacting with elements belonging to one domain in order to manipulate a state in another domain.

The first empirical example is the central part of the Trobriand *vatuvi* spell, which plays a significant role at almost all important stages in the agricultural cycle (Malinowski 1935a: 96–8; 1935b: 255–7). This part of the spell is concerned with the protection of the garden from a variety of pests and diseases. It is a long and iterative chant, connecting several methods of physical cleansing to the expulsion from the garden of unwanted garden pests and diseases. It goes like this: 'I sweep, I sweep, I sweep away. The grubs I sweep, I sweep away; the blight I sweep, I sweep away; insects, I sweep, I sweep away . . .' etc. The verse is repeated with others verbs, such as 'blow', 'drive' and 'chase' in place of 'sweep' (Malinowski 1935a: 97). The mappings involved are represented in Figure 9.4.

This blend enables the magician to manipulate physically things that are otherwise difficult or impossible to manipulate in the real garden. It is an example of a mapping between a predominantly static domain, characterized by a very specific interaction, to a dynamic domain characterized by a very general mode of interaction. We find a high degree of iteration of all elements in the mapping, strengthening the common schematism of a movement away from the agent (and the garden), and at the same time removing unwanted inferential extensions of the expressions. Thus symbolic or conventional interpretations of the words used are de-emphasized, as these will be in internal conflict, and only very basic image-schematic properties remain. The mapping is generated by similarity-based counterpart connectors between on the one hand objects structurally related to human actions belonging to the domestic/social domain, involving expelling objects from a bounded area (CONTAINER), on the other hand similar small objects of grubs, blight, insects and beetles structured in a corresponding way to the rest of the domain of the garden – as unwanted objects inside the bounded area of the garden domain. The basic image-

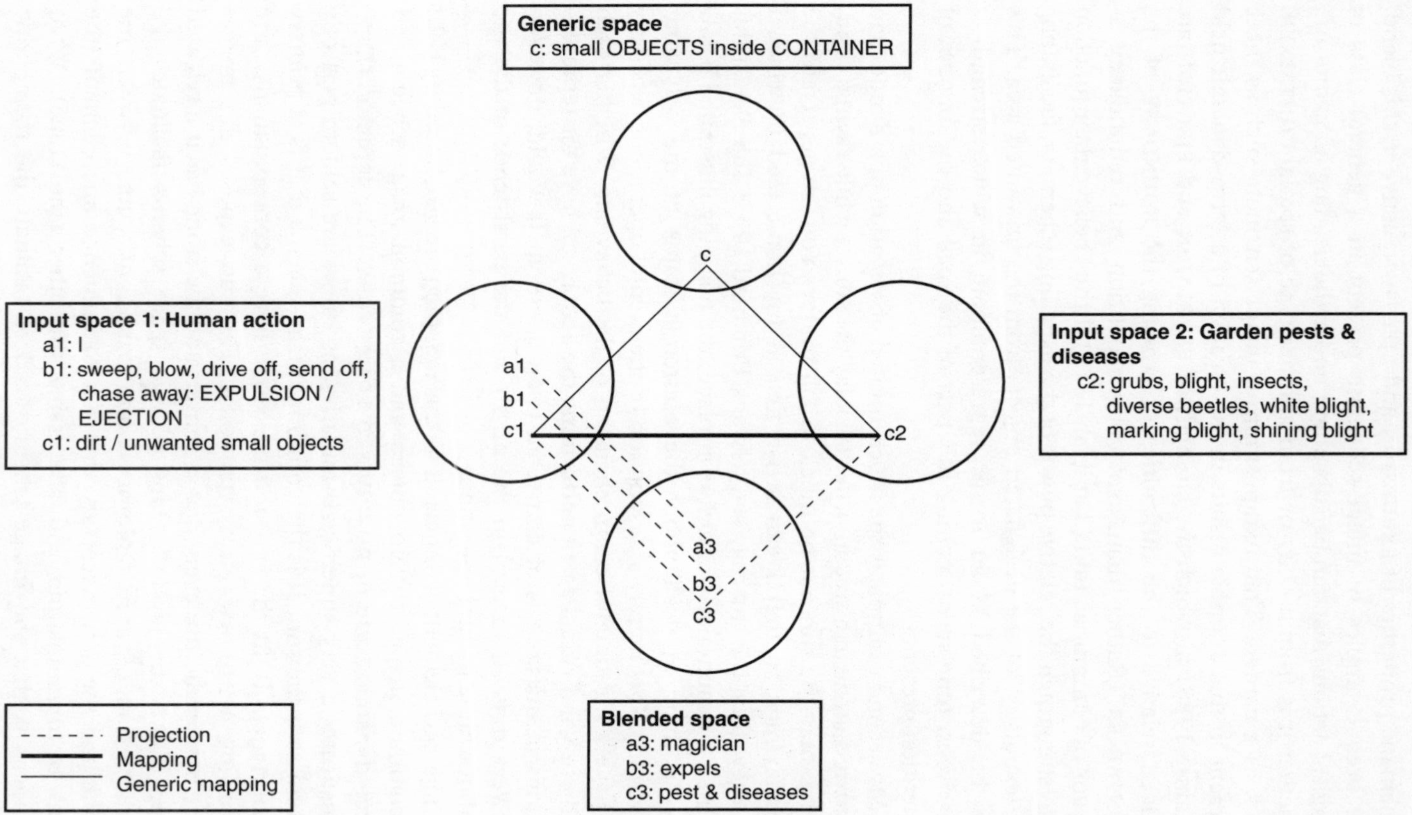
Generic space
c: small OBJECTS inside CONTAINER
Input space 1: Human action
a1: I
b1: sweep, blow, drive off, send off, chase away: EXPULSION / EJECTION
c1: dirt / unwanted small objects
Input space 2: Garden pests & diseases
c2: grubs, blight, insects, diverse beetles, white blight, marking blight, shining blight
c
a1
b1
c1
c2
a3
b3
c3
Blended space
a3: magician
b3: expels
c3: pest & diseases
Projection
Mapping
Generic mapping

Figure 9.4

schematic properties of EXPULSION and EJECTION, active in this blend, are both examples of image-schemata present in a general class of magical actions that can be subsumed under the heading of 'exorcism', whether it is from a body or from another type of spatial CONTAINER, such as a garden. The juxtaposition of image-schemata such as those present in this example results in the creation of a force-dynamic field (Talmy 1988) in which the strength of EXPULSION and EJECTION are judged relative to the difficulties of crossing the BOUNDARY of the CONTAINER. Rather than explaining repetition and redundancy as means of communication (Tambiah 1979), I thus believe their function is to strengthen the relative power of the expelling schemata, facilitating the expulsion of the designated objects from the unwanted area. This can be described as an iconic representation, in which strength is relative to time spent reciting this part of the spell and the amount of repetition present.

My second example is the much-quoted observation of a Zande man placing a stone in a tree in order to delay the sunset while saying: 'You, stone, may the sun not be quick to fall to-day. You, stone, retard the sun on high so that I can arrive first at my homestead to which I journey, then the sun may set.' (Evans-Pritchard 1937: 468–9.) At this point a precautionary remark is in place: the mapping illustrated below says nothing in itself about the epistemic status of the behaviour described. It is merely a description of the mental operations necessary to have a meaningful comprehension of the behaviour. Whether each and every individual agent performing the action will have the representations in question is of course an open question. It would, however, be very difficult to explain the origin and the persistence of the rite without these mental operations.

The two elements connected in this mapping are structured by both a common shape, ROUND object, and a common image-schema and force-dynamic pattern, DOWNWARD TRAJECTORY. The common shape constitutes a very superficial similarity, as stones are seldom perfectly round as is the sun. It is the common image-schema that is of primary importance. Both the sun and the stone have a conceptual structure involving a DOWNWARD TRAJECTORY. The sun exposes this image-schematic structure every day at sunset, and the stone has it if released from above the ground. This generic space schema facilitates the construction of a metaphoric counterpart connection between the stone and the sun, necessary in order to influence one element (the sun) by manipulating and addressing the other (the stone). What happens is that the image-schema used to facilitate the metaphoric

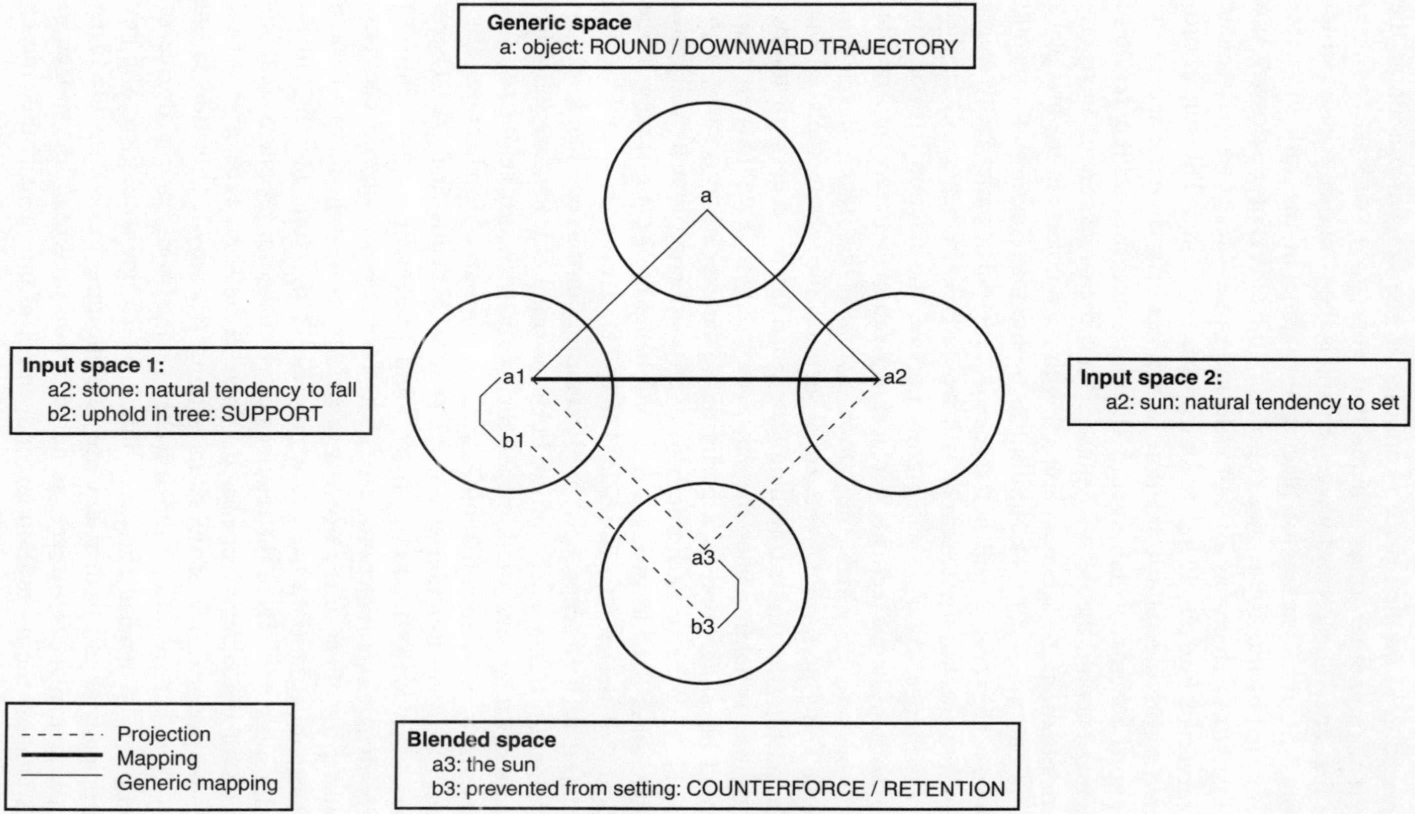
Generic space
a: object: ROUND / DOWNWARD TRAJECTORY
a
Input space 1:
a2: stone: natural tendency to fall
b2: uphold in tree: SUPPORT
a1
b1
a2
Input space 2:
a2: sun: natural tendency to set
a3
b3
Projection
Mapping
Generic mapping
Blended space
a3: the sun
b3: prevented from setting: COUNTERFORCE / RETENTION

Figure 9.5

connection in the first place is opposed in the domain containing the stone with another image-schema that works as a COUNTERFORCE to the first one. This second image-schema is the SUPPORT-schema structuring the ritual action of placing the stone in the fork of a tree performed by the agent, thus countering the effects of the DOWNWARD TRAJECTORY-schema by SUPPORTING the stone. This SUPPORT-schema is projected into the blend together with the stone. The sun is projected by its metaphoric relation to the stone, and connected to the SUPPORT-schema, which should then produce the desired result of the ritual action, the delay of sunset. Thus the ritual creates an ambivalent situation: the schema connecting the two objects in the first place is the one the ritual seeks to abolish by the introduction of a second schema. However, I will not argue that the participants really *believe* they stop the sun from setting, as it would be extremely easily falsified by experience. As Tambiah rightly notices, the relation between the sun and the stone actually replaces a relation between the traveller and the sun, in which the sun is winning the 'race' of reaching 'home'. By performing the ritual action, the agent replaces one relationship (the sun is travelling faster than the traveller) with another (the stone is holding back the sun). According to Tambiah, the ritual should be understood as a performative or expressive gesture of the traveller's desire to be home before dark, effecting that he will move faster rather than involving any strong belief by the participant in the efficacy of the ritual (Tambiah 1985: 74). I propose a middle way between such an 'expressive' understanding, on the one hand, and an explanation based solely on the belief of ritual efficacy, on the other. In the ritual an unwanted image-schema (DOWNWARD TRAJECTORY) is opposed by introducing another schema through a ritual action (SUPPORT) that will function as a COUNTERFORCE of the first one. Therefore, DOWNWARD TRAJECTORY and SUPPORT enter into a force-dynamic interaction, in which the SUPPORT-schema can only counter the effect of the DOWNWARD TRAJECTORY-schema to a limited extent, thus 'holding back' the progress of the sun. This has to do with representations of the relative power of the image-schematic tendencies of the objects concerned. There is both an expressive aspect (in the performance of the ritual action), whereby the relation to the sun is transferred from the traveller to the stone, and a degree of ascription of magical efficacy, without which one would ask why any participant would bother and use valuable time to perform the ritual in the first place. However, as noted before presenting the model, in this analysis the motivation and judgement of the agent of the efficacy or expressiveness of the ritual are secondary procedures, as the cognitive modelling presented above (or something like it) is a necessary prerequisite for the invention and persistence of the ritual as a culturally approved action.

Based on the analysis of the two examples above, I will make some more general remarks concerning the relation between image-schematic properties and manipulative magical rituals. In both examples we saw how similarity-based counterpart connections are established that subsequently enable the magician, or the ritual agent, to manipulate one domain by interaction with another domain. What is transferred from one space to another by means of the ritual blend is basic image-schemata expressing a desired causal development: the exorcising of the pests and diseases by an EXPULSION- or EJECTION-schema, and the delay of sunset by a SUPPORT-schema. Now, the last example has the interesting property that it actually substitutes the very constitutive schema used to connect the two spaces in the first place, DOWNWARD TRAJECTORY, for another schema, SUPPORT, that works as a counterforce to the constitutive schema. Based on these observations I will propose the following hypothesis concerning the role of image-schematic structures in manipulative magic: manipulative magical action is facilitated by a conceptual blending between elements belonging to two conceptual spaces, based on counterpart connections that are grounded in image-schematic correspondences. The counterpart connections enable the adding to, or even replacement of, the schemata used to establish the connection, with a more desirable image-schema transferred from one space to the other.

Conclusion

In this chapter I set out to answer two interrelated questions concerning the cognitive basis of magical ritual action, namely the cognitive constraints on the morphology of magical rituals and the cognitive procedures involved in the creation and interpretation of magical rituals. In the attempt to give a satisfactory answer to these complex and comprehensive questions, I have utilized the theory of mental spaces and conceptual blending informed by theories of human categorization and conceptualization. I have attempted to give an outline of how basic-level categorization, image-schematic structures, and event-frames supply a large amount of the structure and implicit knowledge organizing the content of mental spaces, and subsequently facilitate mapping between separate mental spaces. Viewing religious and magical ritual as a pragmatically distinct type of ritualized activity blending a profane with a sacred space, I have shown how magical agency can be ascribed to different elements used in a particular ritual. The ascription of magical agency is based on very simple representations of perceptual similarity or psychological essentialism, basic traits strengthened by ritualization, and leading to indexical and iconic interpretations of connections between the profane and the sacred space. Having established how magical agency is ascribed to elements in a ritual blending, we saw two examples of the creative use of conceptual blending inside the ritual. Both of these examples of manipulative magic exposed a strong dependence on image-schematic properties and transfers facilitating what is at the core of most definitions of magic, namely the attempt to manipulate elements in one domain by interacting with elements belonging to another domain.

References

Anttonen, V. (1992) 'Interpreting ethnic categories denoting "sacred" in a Finnish and an Ob-Ugrian context'. *Temenos* 28: 53–80.

Boyer, P. (1993) 'Pseudo-natural kinds'. In *Cognitive Aspects of Religious Symbolism*, ed. P. Boyer, 121–41. Cambridge: Cambridge University Press.

Boyer, P. (1994) *The Naturalness of Religious Ideas: A Cognitive Theory of Religion*. Berkeley: University of California Press.

Boyer, P. (1995) 'Causal understandings in cultural representations: cognitive constraints on inferences from cultural input'. In *Causal Cognition: A Multidisciplinary Debate*, ed. D. Sperber, D. Premack and A. J. Premack, 615–44. Oxford: Clarendon Press.

Boyer, P. (1996) 'Religion as an impure object: a note on cognitive order in religious representations in response to Brian Malley'. *Method and Theory in the Study of Religion* 8(2): 201–14.

Brown, M. (1985) *Tsewas' Gift: Magic and Meaning in an Amazon Society*. Washington, DC: Smithsonian Institution Press.

Carey, S. and E. Spelke (1994) 'Domain-specific knowledge and conceptual change'. In *Mapping the Mind*, ed. L. A. Hirschfeld and S. Gelman, 169–200. Cambridge: Cambridge University Press.

Evans-Pritchard, E. E. (1929) 'The morphology and function of magic'. *American Anthropologist* 3: 619–41. (Reprinted in B. P. Levack, ed., *Anthropological Studies of Witchcraft, Magic and Demonology*. London: Garland, 1992.)

Evans-Pritchard, E. E. (1937) *Witchcraft, Oracles and Magic among the Azande*. Oxford: Clarendon Press.

Fauconnier, G. (1994 (1985)) *Mental Spaces: Aspects of Meaning Construction in Natural Language*. Cambridge: Cambridge University Press.

Fauconnier, G. (1997) *Mappings in Thought and Language*. Cambridge: Cambridge University Press.

Fauconnier, G. and M. Turner (1996) 'Blending as a central process of grammar'. In *Conceptual Structure, Discourse, and Language*, ed. Adele E. Goldborg. Stanford: Stanford University Press.

Fauconnier, G. and M. Turner (1998) 'Conceptual Integration Networks', *Cognitive Science* 22(2): 133–87.

Fillmore, C. (1982) 'Frame semantics'. In *Linguistics in the Morning Calm*, ed. Linguistic Society of Korea, 111–37. Seoul: Hanshin.

Firth, R. (1967 (1954)) 'The sociology of "magic"'. In R. Firth, *Tikopia Ritual and Belief*. Boston: Beacon.

Frazer, J. G. (1993 (1911–15)) *The Golden Bough: A Study in Magic and Religion*. Hertfordshire: Wordsworth Reference.

Gelman, R., F. Durgin and L. Kaufman (1995) 'Distinguishing between animates and inanimates: not by motion alone'. In *Causal Cognition: A Multidisciplinary Debate*, ed. D. Sperber, D. Premack and A. J. Premack, 150–84. Oxford: Clarendon Press.

Hirschfeld, L. A. (1995) 'Anthropology, psychology, and the meaning of social causality'. In *Causal Cognition: A Multidisciplinary Debate*, ed. D. Sperber, D. Premack and A. J. Premack, 313–44. Oxford: Clarendon Press.

Hirschfeld, L. A. and S. Gelman (1994) 'Toward a topography of mind: an introduction to domain specificity'. In *Mapping the Mind*, ed. L. A. Hirschfeld and S. Gelman, 3–35. Cambridge: Cambridge University Press.

Humphrey, C. and J. Laidlaw (1994) *The Archetypal Actions of Ritual: A Theory of Ritual Illustrated by the Jain Rite of Worship*. Oxford: Clarendon Press.

Johnson, M. (1987) *The Body in the Mind: The Bodily Basis of Meaning, Imagination, and Reason*. London: University of Chicago Press.

Kapferer, B. (1997) *The Feast of the Sorcerer: Practices of Consciousness and Power*. Chicago: University of Chicago Press.

Lakoff, G. (1987) *Women, Fire, and Dangerous Things: What Categories Reveal about the Mind*. London: University of Chicago Press.

Lakoff, G. (1993) 'The contemporary theory of metaphor'. In *Metaphor and Thought*, ed. A. Ortony. Cambridge: Cambridge University Press.

Lakoff, G. and M. Johnson (1980) *Metaphors We Live By*. London: University of Chicago Press.

Lawson, E. T. and R. N. McCauley (1990) *Rethinking Religion: Connecting Cognition and Culture*. Cambridge: Cambridge University Press.

Leach, E. (1976) *Culture and Communication*. Cambridge: Cambridge University Press.

Malinowski, B. (1935a) *The Coral Gardens and Their Magic*, vol. 1. London: George Allen and Unwin.

Malinowski, B. (1935b) *The Coral Gardens and Their Magic*, vol. 2. London: George Allen and Unwin.

Mandler, J. (1992) 'How to build a baby. II: conceptual primitives', *Psychological Review* 99: 587–604.

Mauss, M. (1972) *A General Theory of Magic*. London: Routledge and Kegan Paul.

Medin, D. L. and A. Ortony (1989) 'Psychological essentialism'. In *Similarity and Analogical Reasoning*, ed. S. Vosniadou and A. Ortony, 179–95. Cambridge: Cambridge University Press.

Peirce, C. S. (1931–5) *Collected Papers I–IV*, ed. C. Hartstone and P. Weiss. Cambridge, MA: Belknap.

Rappaport, R. A. (1999) *Ritual and Religion in the Making of Humanity*. Cambridge: Cambridge University Press.

Rozin, P. and C. Nemeroff (1990) 'The laws of sympathetic magic: a psychological analysis of similarity and contagion'. In *Cultural Psychology: Essays on Comparative Human Development*, ed. J. W. Stigler, R. A. Shweder and G. Herdt, 205–32. Cambridge: Cambridge University Press.

Senft, G. (1985) 'Weyeis Wettermagie. Eine ethnolinguistische Untersuchung von fünf magischen Formeln eines Wettermagiers auf den Trobriand Inseln'. *Zeitschrift für Ethnologie* 110: 67–90.

Smith, J. Z. (1995) 'Trading places'. In *Ancient Magic and Ritual Power*, ed. M. Meyer and P. Mirecki. Leiden: Brill.

Sørensen, J. (2000) *Essence, Schema, and Ritual Action: Towards a Cognitive Theory of Magic*. Unpublished Ph.D. thesis, Department of the Study of Religion, University of Aarhus.

Staal, F. (1979) 'The meaninglessness of ritual'. *Numen* 26(1): 2–22.

Sweetser, E. and G. Fauconnier (1996) 'Cognitive links and domains: basic aspects of mental space theory'. In *Spaces, Worlds, and Grammar*, ed. G. Fauconnier and E. Sweetser, 1–28. Chicago and London: University of Chicago Press.

Talmy, L. (1988) 'Force dynamics in language and cognition'. *Cognitive Science* 12: 49–100.

Tambiah, S. J. (1968) 'The magical power of words'. *Man* 3: 175–208.

Tambiah, S. J. (1979) 'A performative approach to ritual'. *Proceedings of the British Academy* 65: 113–69.

Tambiah, S. J. (1985) 'Form and meaning of magical acts'. In *Culture, Thought, and Social Action: An Anthropological Perspective*, 60–87. Cambridge: Cambridge University Press.

Thomas, K. (1991 (1971)) *Religion and the Decline of Magic*. London: Penguin.

Whitehouse, H. (2000) *Arguments and Icons: Divergent Modes of Religiosity*. Oxford: Oxford University Press.

10 The Complex Worlds of Religion: Connecting Cultural and Cognitive Analysis

JEPPE SINDING JENSEN

Introduction

Cognition sets the limits and boundary conditions for the social, cultural and religious activities of humans in thought and action. Thus, cognitive studies and theorizing are crucial contributions to the explanation and understanding of social, cultural and religious activities, for cognition is the 'basic stuff' – individual and universal – upon which humanly constructed worlds become possible as higher-order phenomena. Recent cognitive analyses have contributed vastly to the cross-cultural explanations of recurrent and universal religious phenomena, and it has become quite evident, not only that, but also how and why, cognition conditions the construction of social reality, including religion. The work of cognition on religion is clear. The unavoidable question is, then, how the inverse relations may apply. What is the work of religion on cognition? Most religious traditions claim that there are unseen worlds of powerful beings and wondrous events, they prescribe arduous ritual actions and social strictures of all kinds. These and many more religious phenomena are plausible conditioners upon the complex forms of human cognition. It is also robust intuition from everyday interaction that the manners in which we act and perceive in our world(s) are conditioned by socio-cultural formations and that these affect our 'moods and motivations' in decisive ways. That intuition may be theoretically naive, but it remains an interesting question if and how we can account for the 'work' of religion upon cognition. It should be noted here at the outset that, in the present context, religion is viewed primarily as a cultural construct along a definition of culture as 'the production of meaning' (Jensen 1999). Humans produce many things by their actions, religious actions included, and prominent among these products is meaning, and all the other things semantic, such as language.

Connecting cognition and culture 'from the bottom up' poses enough problems as it is, and an attempt at reversing the direction of explanation may seem a reckless undertaking. But, then again, ever since the prehistoric 'symbolic revolution' it has been a characteristic of human cognition that it challenges itself. The questions are legion: How and how much may cognitive functions and mechanisms be 're-directed', so to speak, under the influence of culture? And if so, how could it be possible and how would it work? How are the cultural and social realms to be re-integrated in cognitive studies of complex matters such as religion? If religious thought has a certain 'naturalness' to it, is it then because natural thought is also somehow 'religious'? What would the outlines of a theory, or a collectivist methodology, of 'social cognition' be like? What are the ontological properties of socio-cultural systems? Is cognition conditioned not only by the constraints of what individual minds are able to process, but also by the ways in which that which is transmitted between minds is organized? How are the architectures of mind, language and knowledge to be linked – especially in relation to religion and the study of it?

It is the two-fold premise here that cognition is part of a cultural process and that culture is an intrinsic component of the 'human mind'. The latter idea is not exactly new; for the idea that human perception depends upon cultural prejudice is old, known since Antiquity, and widespread in folk epistemology and greatly overrated by many practitioners of the human sciences, such as anthropologists (D'Andrade 1995: 182–217; Spiro 1984). In the study of religion the idea of cultural determinism is mostly propagated in the rather problematic, so-called 'Framework Model' (Godlove 1989). Since Durkheim and Mauss (1963) maintained that categorization was social at root many sociologists and anthropologists have insisted that human thought and action were best studied in the paradigm of social determinism or social symbolism. They would perhaps admit that some 'deep'-structures of cognition might be pan-human. But these would be trivial then and of no interest to the social scientist; much like a chef not really caring about the bio-chemical properties of his ingredients. The 'surface' effects of culturally biased socialization processes are obvious and they can account for much of what is taken for granted as rational and meaningful in human behaviour. The probability of culture having some more fundamental functions in relation to cognition is an idea which has lately been proposed with more theoretical rigour, as for example by Edwin Hutchins (1995) and Bradd Shore (1996). Consequently, I suggest as a working hypothesis not only that cognitive studies contribute to an understanding of religion, but also, and inversely, that the study of religion may contribute to the study of cognition, or, at least, to certain aspects thereof. If not at those more basic levels of neurology or direct perception then at other emergent levels that relate more to the human sciences – there's more to music than just acoustics. Thus conceived, the study of religion could contribute to something other than itself – perhaps a bit like the role of linguistics in the development of cognitive studies. As human relations to self, others and the world are largely linguistically mediated it would indeed seem a truncated view to study cognition in isolation from other modes of human practice. It may also rely upon a problematic form of empiricist dualism which views cognition and culture as hardware and software, respectively, and with no intrinsic relations between them, other than the 'hardware' determining which 'software' it can run. Suppose that one of the outstanding features of human 'hardware' is that it can be (re-)configured by its own 'software'. That would turn religion into something more scientifically interesting than 'just' spurious ripples on cultural surface phenomena high above the bedrock of cognition. One of the main theoretical problems in the study of religion is the question of connecting the analyses of religion(s) in and across cognitive, cultural and social domains. In any analysis of 'things religious' it is readily apparent that the subject matter must be characterized as multi-dimensional, multi-tiered or whatever one prefers on the basis of one's vantage point or theoretical object. Certainly, descriptions, analyses and interpretations may be uni-dimensional, but only the poorer for that. The only exception to this rule is the kind of work which explicitly addresses theoretical questions in specific perspectives. However, when such 'one-track' theoretical advances have been formulated and are launched as applied tools for investigations of subject matters they should be combined in analyses. Normatively speaking, studies in the human sciences become the more informative, richer and interesting, when supplying multi-dimensional information, and such 'thick descriptions' are inevitably linked to 'thick theorizing'.

Explanation – and what comes with it

Explanatory analyses of matters religious, that is, the form of enquiry characterized by the asking of 'why'-questions, will under most conditions cross and interconnect a number of domains, levels, realms, perspectives, etc. For instance, when ritual transformations are tied to changes in social conditions, and thus correlating some domains, levels, etc., with others. Whether we are trying to formulate rules or laws for regularities in the behaviour of types of natural objects or trying to make sense of people in the retrospective accounts of the nomic-rational bases of single instances of behaviour – then we are trying to make sense through what we habitually call 'explanation'. The 'making sense' aspect of explanatory endeavours indicates the proximity of interpretation to explanation. For instance, when you explain the function of central heating thermostats to the uninitiated you do so by explaining causally what happens when such-and-such; and the neo-phyte, when content with the explanation, says: 'Oh – now I under-stand.' Trying to explain 'democracy' works in much the same fashion, although rather more contextually and less causally, for abstract and complex concepts also have functionally integrated aspects which involve logical relations and range across various domains. Thus, understanding is the purpose of explanation and so it is of interpreta-tion – making sense is a primary human feat. That human 'sense-making' is embedded and conditioned in cognitive, cultural and social contexts is perhaps but a triviality, but the interrelations between those 'realms' are far from trivial and they must be accountable for. Hence the reflections in this presentation, partly on why it is that cultural analysis as such will not disappear (to the frustrated hopes of various bands of eliminativists et al.) and partly on why the cultural and social realms, which were once 'removed' from cognitive theorizing, ought to be re-installed in a more complex research paradigm (Hutchins 1995: 353–6). The 'Grand' question in the study of religion has always been that of origin. Perhaps the question of origin will find the same answer as that concerning the cause(s) of religion – and perhaps not. It all depends on the formulation of the questions. And – more likely – it is futile to ask for the origins and/or causes of something that is 'nothing but' a more or less theoretically informed generalization of a very complex kind. Religion is not one thing, no 'natural kind' – it is a designation for a rather messy conglomerate of many things that pertain to, for example, social formations, cultural systems of symbolization and cognitive properties of the human mind (or brain?). Something tells us that if and when we want to explain 'religion' or things 'religious' then we shall have to employ, perchance, very different registers of explanation before we understand. All understanding takes place according to systems of explanation and interpretation, be they based on enclosed religious semantics or on fragmented experimental and explanatory scientific vocabularies. No understanding – explana-tory or interpretative – of anything is possible unless it is expressed in or against some system; there is no way in which we can simply understand 'just one thing' independently of all other things. Most of the systems that humans employ are of a discursive nature; they are language-like and syntax-sensitive; that is, things must be in the right place and order before they 'make sense'. Such systems come under many labels and are more or less theory-dependent: 'worlds', 'world-views', 'life-worlds', 'symbolic' or 'semantic universes', 'conceptual schemes' or 'frameworks', 'cultural systems', 'systems of symbols', and so on. In the following, I shall prefer to use 'explanatory system' as a more interesting category of the above.

When scientists design a specific combination of theoretical perspectives it implies that they view certain objects and aspects more readily, so that on a certain theoretical perspective the perceiving subject is prone to notice some properties more than others and to arrange them in some kind of order, and hopefully in a manner logically consistent with the perceived order of the theoretical architecture. In studies of human affairs, theories are the means of ascription of salience of properties, functions, rationalities, motives, etc.; that is, the theory decides what you see, and what is important is so in light of the theory. There is no chance of perceiving anything independently of all schemes; there are no theory-independent facts that we know of. Hence the deductive nature of explanatory theoretical systems. Any make-believe 'theory' which does not exhibit these properties is probably not a theory at all. In an explanatory framework for the study of religion we operate from a conglomerate of claims, inspirations, criticisms, empirical references, etc. that ought to be so designed that the various theoretical components are compatible. For instance, a theory of ritual as symbolic action necessarily ties to a general theory of symbolicity *and* to cognitive theories of mental symbolic processing *and* to a theory of rational behaviour *and* to a theory of nomic functions of social institutions . . . *and* so on, but these theories must somehow be compatible. The study of religion has had more than its fair share of 'theories' that were incompatible, or of theories where the major causal nexus requires that 'a miracle happened . . .'.

To the question of whether we can legitimately deduce from a notion of religion which is a complex and theoretically constructed generalization the answer is 'yes', precisely as long as the theories are compatible. 'Language' is also a generalization – but given theoretical consistency it is perfectly possible and legitimate to deduce from that generalization – in fact, most generalizations are born of theories. How would we know what belongs to what in a generalization if not by theory? How would one describe 'symbolism' without a theory of it? Could we correlate the theories of Ernst Cassirer or Dan Sperber with a symbolism '*an Sich*'? All explanatory analysis worthy of its name is theoretically validated and therefore also somehow deductive in nature. Definitions share a similar fate – being short versions of theories; concepts likewise, being but bits and pieces of that larger picture. If not for theories and theoretically informed concepts we should not find any interesting phenomena in 'religious' texts. Theological readings, in all traditions, applying concepts internal to the texts' own universe produce but circularity. That is a general property of religious communication, but it is not so commendable in scholarship.

Culture as object

Culture is not any collection of things, whether tangible or abstract. Rather, it is a process. It is a human cognitive process that takes place both inside and outside the minds of people. It is the process in which our everyday cultural practices are enacted. I am proposing an integrated view of human cognition in which a major component is a cognitive process . . . and cognition is a cultural process.

(Hutchins 1995: 354)

The problem of the ontology of cultural entities is a subject of ongoing investigation; they are quite often supposed to have 'mysterious' ontologies, especially for materialists, because 'What exactly is culture made of?' 'Meaning' say some? Well, that is no less 'mysterious', nor are 'conventional symbols' the materialist's favourite choice (Sperber 1996: ch. 1). If the materialist will not be satisfied it may be because the ontologies of cultural entities and 'meanings' are simply not accessible in a materialist epistemology, and the materialist is therefore probably on the wrong track. Cognitive entities, such as mental representations, have mysterious ontologies too, although some try to bypass the 'mystery' by postulating that they are 'nothing but' neuro-chemical states along a materialist explanation. 'Beliefs, intention, and preferences are mental representations' says Dan Sperber (1996: 24–5), and continues to assure us that 'Until the cognitive revolution, the ontological status of mental representations was obscure', but now, 'in psychology, the material character of mental representations has changed from the status of a mystery to that of an intelligible question.' This conviction leads Sperber (1996: 31) to assert that 'The representations which natives have of immaterial entities are themselves quite material', thereby implying that our thinking has some substance that may cause a change in a gravitational field (as is the physicist's idea of something happening). However, the attractiveness of such a 'sleight-of-hand' methodology fades in light of critiques such as those brought forward by Hilary Putnam (1988: 37–41, 92–105) on the problems of identifying and relating meaning and mental representation. Sperber's suggestions seem to produce as many new problems as they try to solve old ones. For it seems unlikely that we may count backwards from the symbolic to the physical, to 'naturalize semantics' and turn meaning into some kind of transmitter substance. Semantic naturalism is, as of yet, not able to answer the question of 'What naturalistic facts are plausible candidates to serve as metaphysically sufficient for the semantic properties of mental representations?' (Loewer 1997: 111).

The 'cognitive turn' is a real progress in the study of cultural matters, but if that turn by necessity implies a large-scale suspension of the gains of the 'linguistic turn' then 'semantic eliminativism' sets in instead of a more promising combination of the analysis of culture and cognition. All involved, whether in neurobiology, in psychology, in cognitive linguistics, etc., or perhaps even in the study of religion, should consider it an interesting mutual challenge to account for each other's insights – to work on the 'translations' so to speak. A noteworthy instance of this is the growing topic of 'mappings' – 'in thought and language' – which, in the words of Gilles Fauconnier, 'operate to build and link *mental spaces* . . . partial structures that proliferate when we think and talk . . . central to any understanding of semantic and pragmatic language interpretation and cognitive construction . . .' and he suggests that 'the domains that we need in order to understand language functioning are not in the combinatorial structure of language itself; they are in the cognitive constructions that language acts upon' (1997: 11–13).

It seems reasonable to assume that *both* cultural and cognitive entities exist, albeit not necessarily describable under the *same* form of description nor with the same methodology. It also seems reasonable to claim that cultural and cognitive entities are more or less structured and have specific properties, but whether their properties are structured similarly, or in patterns that facilitate the translation from one realm to the other, are some of the tough – and hotly debated – questions. Suffice it here to claim, as a working hypothesis, that cultural entities, such as language and religion, are structured and so are the entities of cognitive, or mental, representations. Structures come with, or presuppose, rules for combinations, in cognition as well as in the symbolic-cultural materials being cognitively processed (Jensen 2000). This may lead to a further question: Do cultural materials, say religious cosmologies, owe their nature primarily to cognitive production or do they also develop their own rules and, subsequently, 'adapt' to cognitive processing? This may seem an odd question because we normally assume that all human and social affairs are the products of intentionality – that is, of human 'work on the world' which should therefore carry the stamp of the human 'mind'. Strangely enough some of the things most difficult to handle are human products and the question is therefore not so odd: How is it that physical matter inside our heads can produce immaterial symbolic stuff that may get (with a little luck) into someone else's head? We may also ask whether (1) natural language is the product of certain properties or modules of the mind, of a specific neural architecture in the brain, or whether (2) language is as much a product 'of itself' adapting to a particular constellation of cognitive abilities? The direction of causality is quite important – and I opt for the latter position (2) for the present purpose and in what concerns the aspects relevant to the argument here, and not as the one and only solution.

There is no doubt that humans 'invented' religions – but religions have, reciprocally, invented humans and gods – also invented by humans – who were (more often than not) created by the gods – invented by . . . and so forth. Whether this should be termed 'multiple causality' or simple circularity depends on where and how the circle is broken. Scholars of religion face infinite regress – religions do not. Scholars of religion must decide upon which level of analysis should count as the metaphysical resort of reduction. And, for some purposes, retaining the notion of culture makes good sense.

Cognition and culture

It is a matter of course that cultural materials depend on there being minds. Cultural materials are only in the world because there are humans. Conversely, it is plausible to maintain that minds would not be in their state if they had no semantic, symbolic and cultural materials to process. What would the ontology and function of cognition be then? There is no way of thinking (as we conceive of thinking) without stuff to think with, and that stuff is not simply natural, for it is the intervention of the socio-cultural, symbolic and semantic (even the scientists most sceptical of semantics profess their dislikes in natural languages) that enables us to produce anything rational about the world and ourselves. Terrence Deacon emphasizes these aspects of the cognitive endeavour:

Because of our symbolic activities, we humans have access to a novel higher-order representation system that not only recodes experiences and guides the formation of skills and habits, but also provides a means of representing features of a world that no other creature experiences, the world of the abstract. We do not just live our lives in the physical world and our immediate social group, but also in a world of rules of conduct, beliefs about our histories, and hopes and fears about imagined futures. This world is governed by principles different from any that have selected for neural circuit design in the past aeons of evolution. We possess no brain regions specially adapted for handling the immense flood of experiences from this world, only those adapted for life in a concrete world of percepts and actions.

(Deacon 1997: 423)

Considering the effects of the prehistoric 'symbolic revolution' sometime in the last scores of millennia (Mithen 1996: 151–94) it could be ventured that the success of religious systems of representations of action and thought – I consciously avoid the term 'cause' here, so as not to be associated with the frailties of functionalist argumentation – is that they have managed to direct and redirect that 'immense flood of experiences from this world' to distinctive semantic and cognitive domains and thereby help control the numerous 'worlds' which humans face – the natural, the social, the psychological, etc. – by the intervention of relations with a supernatural world where contingencies are ruled out.

Religious symbolic representations take place at a relatively high level of imaginative activity. Differences of levels suggest a hierarchy of representations – most religions even suggest such hierarchies themselves; there is some unrecognized but inbuilt reflexivity at large there. However, let us consider the notion of 'hierarchy' as usable just for heuristic purposes, for we do not *really* know 'which way is up' when it comes to these matters; all we can do is to suggest plausible and provisional models: between *three* levels that, taken from the 'top', consist in: (1) computational information-processing, (2) algorithmic functions, and (3) neural machinery (Dennett 1991: 276), or between *four* levels: (1) propositions, (2) representations, (3) computational structures, and (4) neurological systems (Kamppinen 1989: 34), or between *five* levels: (1) cognitive science and linguistics, (2) neurally reducible conventional computational models, (3) structured connectionist models, (4) computational neuroscience, and (5) neuroscience

(Lakoff and Johnson 1999: 570–1). The list may, for the time being, be made longer or shorter but the overriding question concerns the existence of rule-governed relations between these levels, and the explanatory potential of the possible inferences between them.

The crucial meta-methodological question is to ascertain how cognitive insights matter for the study of cultural entities without this becoming a case of the 'Fallacy of partial description' suggesting that cultural analysis etc. should, in the end, be left to psychologists or biologists and then 'disappear'. It is, again, the issue of determining the relations between subject matters and theoretical objects. Uncontroversially, a subject matter can consist of religious representations and the theoretical object be the cognitive mechanism of the human mind, but it could equally well be the other way around – it depends entirely upon the chosen direction of theoretical reduction. Under one form of description, say physicalism, it is obvious that humans are 'nothing' but 'complex dynamic, non-linear, unstable mass-molecular systems etc.' beyond meaning, morals, intentionality and all other 'philosophical illusions' prompted by our faulty synaptic functions. Seen from that angle, human cultural products are not really interesting. The real problem is that such a statement is itself a product of human culture; anyone denying that would just be denying those same synaptic functions – and, more important, their possibility of communicating such complex statements to other synaptic systems. Humans are, among other things, powerful semantic engines with very high levels of inferential potential, and the evolution of cognition has been possible also due to the cultural materials themselves. They are not just ready-made by our brains. Conversely, we may say that they have contributed to the making of the human mind. We owe both our rationality and our ethical stance to something other than innate mechanisms of perception (e.g. Jensen 1997).

The emergence of 'World 3'

In this connection, the idea of plural ontologies and corresponding epistemologies appears more advantageous than outrageous, for it is interesting, at least heuristically. In 1979 Karl Popper proposed the existence of (at least) three worlds: 'World 1 – the physical world', 'World 2 – the mental world' and 'World 3 – the world of objective knowledge'; an unfortunate term to which I prefer 'World of Meaning', that is, as the socio-cultural semantic realm (Jensen 1999). Structurally similar conceptions of a poly-ontology can be found in Jürgen Habermas's ideas (1981: 114–26; Cooke 1997: 10, 21) about different realms of validity claims (*Geltungsansprüche*). There is much sense in this view, it is good for explanation, and it may even be true (Rescher 1997: 21). The problems concerning the interrelations and interactions between these worlds can be handled through the notion of 'supervenience'. The 'world of meaning' will then be seen as an emergent or 'supervenient' (depending upon theoretical position) world upon the mental and physical worlds. Along most interpretations the term 'supervenience' means that non-physical universals can supervene on physical universals, so that 'while nonphysical properties, kinds, and relations may not be analysable in terms of the universals of physics, the latter provide the ontological foundations on which the former rest' (Loux 1998: 44). Not all facts are gravitational facts, but all facts supervene upon gravitational facts, as for instance when biological properties supervene on chemical ones and when cultural properties supervene on cognitive ones. Thus, the notion of 'meaning' need not be considered an instance of inexplicable metaphysics. Supervenience theory is a way of tying higher-level properties to lower levels without directly reducing them ('downwards') and it explains the 'emergent properties' without having to resort to causal determination of lower-level properties. Such a theory is Donald Davidson's (1995) 'Anomalous monism' about mental events being simultaneously both mental events and physical events 'under different descriptions'; levels of events which we are unable to link causally by strict laws. The theory is fundamentally non-dualist, it is a brand of 'monism' termed 'anomalous' because of the absence of strict laws. If we combine the idea of the 'supervenience' of the non-physical upon the physical and the 'anomalous monism' of mental and physical events we are able to defend the view that socio-cultural entities supervene upon and have properties different from the properties of biological and psychological entities. Thus, I propose to expand the scope of the theories of supervenience, emergence and anomalous monism so as to suggest that social and cultural events supervene upon the mental and, further, that 'religious properties' supervene upon the cognitive and the cultural, for the reason that religions have cognitive and cultural properties and then something 'added', or 'blended' in, which makes them a particular and definable class: 'the core area of religious things, religious belief and ritual, are both cognitive and cultural' (Kamppinen 2001: 204). The notions of 'supervenience' and 'emergence' facilitate and underwrite holistic and collectivist methodologies in the human sciences. But then again, even the most individualist cognitive scientist is also a methodological holist when talking about 'global brain states'. The world of human activity is too complex to be adequately understood from just one point of view. So persuaded, Per Aage Brandt observes on language that it is

as cognitive and semiotic studies currently show, a fragile assemblage of mechanisms, inseparably related to a much broader network of semantic instances grounded in those parts of neural architecture that co-operate in creating the yieldings of consciousness, apperception, and expression accounted for by human phenomenology. It is no use either trying to settle philosophically the question of whether Meaning is the product of Language, or Language the product of Meaning, in principle, if the available evidence now supports both principles, under different, similar or even equal conditions. In a sense, the study of language then – if the reality of language is neural – leaves the Humanities and becomes a branch of biology. It stays, however, necessarily humanistic, in so far as phonetic, syntactic, and semantic forms are only accessible through introspection of human intuition, and formal information can only be obtained through negotiable interpretations.

(Brandt 1997: 147)

On cognition, culture and religion as objects

The distinctions between cognitive and cultural domains are often not at all clear. Mental states or acts such as propositional attitudes can be simultaneously viewed as individual, mental and cognitive on the one side and cultural, discursive and symbolic on the other. 'Religious cognition' exploits or employs cognitive mechanisms and representational forms, images, etc. that need not be religious or even cultural *per se*, but the point is that we are not talking, then, specifically about religion (a point made abundantly clear by Boyer 1994) but that we do so only insofar as – or when – a particular set of symbolic-cultural systems of semantics are involved in the processes or when the cognitive 'materials' are embedded in such systems of meaning and used as 'strategic' knowledge by a group of humans in their 'life-management' (see Boyer, and Pyysiäinen, this volume). Whatever else we can say about 'meaning' as the term for 'semantic content' it is a linguistic, discursive and cultural 'thing' (according to the theory of meaning involved here). The notion of meaning is inextricably linked to language, and it is thus a 'World 3' product, no matter how firm its neural grounding is. No physical stuff or individual mental event is meaningful *'an Sich'*, and that is why there are no objective or referential semantics, as the folk theory of meaning would have it. Meanings are meanings because they are ascribed by humans. Sacred mountains are sacred because humans sanctify them, and sacralization is but a discursive action. That being said there is also no doubt that without relevant cognitive processing there could be no 'sanctification' or production of meaning at all. The controversies over 'meaning' in the philosophy of language have previously been somewhat ignored by cognitive scientists, but they need to be addressed, as they increasingly are, for instance in the debate on how thought structures resemble language structures or vice versa. Semantic production obviously has a cognitive grounding as cognition includes certain modes of schematic and pre-linguistic semantics (e.g. Fauconnier 1997).

Religions are about 'other worlds'. Cognitive analysis demonstrates that these 'thought of' other worlds of religious beliefs, actions and institutions are simultaneously extensions *and* inversions of the 'lived in' physical worlds. The conceptual transformations and inversions are the more interesting from the cognitive point of view because they can be shown to systematically reverse or violate a range of assumptions of intuitive epistemologies and ontologies (e.g. Boyer 1998). Thus we have trees that remember, a pig in Valhalla of which you may eat in the evening and it is restored the next morning, and so on. Edmund Leach pointed out years ago (1976), that in the face of such claims we intuitively know that we are in the 'proximity of religion' and that, I think, goes for all humans with any familiarity with religion. The routine claim of relativist anthropological 'nay-sayers' is that 'my people do not make these distinctions' and that any insistence upon judging claims by appeal to a scientifically reasonable epistemology is but another case of Western imperialism. However, there is growing and compelling evidence to the contrary (e.g. Boyer 1998, and Barrett, this volume). This is an area where cognitive studies have contributed greatly to the clarification of very muddled issues in the study of religion.

Along with these 'other world' cognitive assumptions we also have extensions and inversions of semantic constructions. Most of the cognitive 'counter-intuitive' notions are transmitted as claims, and therefore they are linguistic and cultural 'facts'. Language is a wonderful thing, because it permits us to imagine collectively, as when children play: how would they stage plots, perform actions, cast roles and so forth if not through the imagination-creating power of language. Religious rituals are also such extensions of 'play' – with all that this includes of performative action, cognitive operations, social obligations – and all the other 'stuff' that goes into the 'making of religion' – and into religious action.

The extensively counter-factual and imagined worlds of religious cosmologies can be elaborated upon and transmitted in language – precisely because language is not directly 'of' this world. Sometimes it seems to be more of the 'other world', an intuition that can be seen as reflected in many cosmogonic myths, etc. This also means that, notwithstanding their counter-intuitive claims, religions can persist as authoritative in spite of their massive disconnectedness from the physical world (Lawson and McCauley 1990: 156). Holistic semantics explains how religion(s) can be simultaneously parasitic extensions on 'World 2' and 'World 3' and contain within their explanatory fields these worlds as well as the 'World 1' of physical matters. The reflexive, holistic character of religious discourse also allows religious representational systems to act as 'supervening' upon ordinary semantic and representational systems so that religions become 'meta-representational' as processing devices for all subvenient orders of conceptual and representational products and processes. With this conception of religion, it becomes not just the object of explanation but also an instrument of explanation, albeit without 'transcendental causality' (that it claims for itself).

On explanations of 'explanation'

In the natural sciences, explanations are generally related to analyses and questions of the 'why' kind, and they thus pertain to questions of cause and causality. If, however, the concept of explanation is restricted as belonging exclusively to the natural sciences and concerned with causality only, then the ghosts of logical empiricism have not been duly exorcized (Radnitzky 1970). There are multiple modes of explanation and, as already noted, in my view explanations are ways of making sense of relations by linking things in meaningful patterns and sequences. Explanations are thus about connections, and these may be causal, but equally well logical, functional or structural. In the perspective of the human sciences it is a meta-theoretical mistake to concede to the view that explanations are about causes only and that all other modes of explaining must measure up to a specific set of standards in the explication of covering laws in the natural sciences (Lawson and McCauley 1990: 22–31). There have been sustained battles over the status of functional explanations, also in the study of religion where many opine that religions 'fulfil needs' and others refute the premises and logic of such arguments. That controversy has also been one between defenders and opponents of religion, and in the end, it comes down to trivial problems concerning religious attitudes.

Instead, we may consider the possibility that functional explanations are about functions and not about the causes of the functions and that intentional, logical, nomic, structural and all conceivable kinds of explanations are also worthy of their name (Henderson 1993). For instance, the term 'sociological explanation' does not refer to an explanation of the causes of there being sociology or sociologists in this world, nor even about the causes of there being 'societies', but it refers to sets of intellectual procedures and practices couched or embedded or expressed in certain idioms. An explanation of a 'car' – material as it is – does not consist in an analysis of what caused the existence of cars, rather, the explanation is about 'how it works', what it is made of, how all the parts must be structured, etc. This is similar to explanations of rule-governed human activities, e.g. games or sports. James Peacock (1986: 81) uses the term 'logico-meaningful explanation' for the dominant mode of explanation in such 'configurationalist' analysis in anthropology.

Explanations link things ('explananda') in epistemologically salient orders, and they are, therefore, syntax-sensitive. The 'things' they so order are either other explanations or interpretations. That is: the elements of the explanatory syntax are interpretations, such as the symbolic generalizations of a scientific vocabulary, or other semantic and iconic 'things' which help us make sense of the world (e.g. Zemach 1989: 71). Explanations and interpretations do not belong to separate ontological or epistemological domains, nor to separate groups of sciences, they are only different aspects of cognitive and semantic processes. They are very much like sentences or stories for the simple reason that: 'Narrative imagining is our fundamental cognitive instrument for explanation' (Turner 1996: 20; Bruner 1986).

Any explanation may, in turn, be linked to other explanations, and clusters of real and/or possible explanations come together and form more complex explanatory systems of which there probably exist an indefinite number. Explanatory systems are such that they provide the means for understanding and evaluating experience and action. They also function as normative for future understanding and action, thus having both descriptive-cognitive and normative-axiological aspects (Linde 1987). Explanatory systems are employed in organizing types of meaning and explanation, not so much through direct procedures of induction or deduction but rather as a backdrop for abduction and abductive processes of reasoning (Oatley 1996).

Explanations and explanatory systems are semantic in their communicable forms. Current semantics does not rely on referential, objectivist or essentialist conceptions of meaning or on what makes things 'mean'. 'Intuitive semantics' die hard, and quite a few scholars who have discovered the defective nature of referential semantics have then thought that the consequences must be a radical relativism in what concerns semantic entities. Against this concern, holistic semantics underscores that just as the validity of scientific observations depends upon theories, so do interpretations of meanings depend upon the languages and symbolic meaning systems of which they are part. And just as the underdetermination of theory by 'fact' does not lead to total chaos neither does the interpretation-sensitivity of propositions lead to inscrutability of sense (or: 'reasonableness'). Hilary Putnam (1987: 84) once said that we are under some kind of 'primitive obligation' to be reasonable, and, philosophically speaking, that is probably the most interesting species-specific trait of our being human.

In order to be reasonable we must organize our worlds '1', '2' and '3' and make them meaningful through the application of models, metaphors, domains, blendings, mappings, etc. as communicable cultural phenomena. The terms 'model', 'metaphor', 'domain', 'blending', 'mapping' – to name just the most important – cover entities with multiple properties and functions, and they seem to be used rather indiscriminately both for cognitive, mental entities on the one side and for social, symbolic, cultural, semiotic and linguistic-semantic entities on the other. Although some degree of flexibility and theory-independence can be admitted for some concepts and this may even add to their descriptive, explanatory and/or interpretive value, it is more likely that we shall enhance the epistemological and methodological value of such terms by tying them more strongly to specific theorizing. In this context I shall stress the importance and value of these terms primarily in cultural contexts, that is, in relation to semantic-semiotic and public meaning-systems. However, analyses in cognitive linguistics demonstrate that these terms ('model', 'metaphor', . . .) cover quite specific properties, relations, functions, etc. in cognition.

The question is how and to what degree we may transfer or transform the findings from cognition into or onto the cultural and discursive realms. That is: how do we proceed from eliciting the meta-principles of cognitive ordering to the meta-principles of semantic ordering as also necessitated by the structures of the semantic universes? This is, again, the question of the relations between the sub- and supervenient levels. No strict methodological laws seem to apply – and there is always the probability that the chain of reasoning may be reversed so that the 'lower levels' may depend upon what goes on higher up in a hierarchy of systems, in so-called 'downward causation' (Andersen et al. 2000). Downward causation is responsible for what happens, when, for instance, certain cognitive properties are developed in social interaction. Humans are conditioned by what they work on, because cultural models and motivations are transformed into cognitive models and motivations. Powerful semantic metaphors condition the way we think, and a discourse – even fictitious – may strongly determine (within a range of cognitive boundary conditions, of course) our conceptions of how things are and how we feel about them. Hence the power of religion, or of any other explanatory system, to govern the lives of humans. In current cognitive research nature explains much of religion, whereas religion has traditionally explained nature and most other things. The remarkable thing is that we now go about explaining religion by mapping it onto what we think is a simpler domain, whereas in most human history religion was the 'simpler' domain – the one where 'contingency was ruled out'. The parallel structuring of religion and science are interesting, and not only for the intellectualist: both religion and science employ models, metaphors, domains, blendings and mappings in the sense-making process. Perhaps this is not really so remarkable, as both are spheres of human activity and therefore governed jointly by both cognitive and semantic constraints.

Narrative actions

When things make sense in a discursive context it is probably also because they resemble the real world '1'. That is, our ideas, thoughts, propositions and actions, etc., are all modes of practice intentionally directed towards our 'coming to grips' with the world. So, cognitive as well as discursive activities are extensions of primary 'low-level' schemas as extensions upon our sensory-bodily phenomenological experience. However, the question remains whether these primary forms of schematization are the only mechanisms responsible for the elaboration of discursive syntaxes. Basic-level schemas are in all probability primary in an evolutionary perspective but, once produced, it is quite likely that higher-level organizations of semantic principles, e.g. in syntaxes, may take on their 'own existence' and feed-back upon the lower-level representations. This is the 'downward causation' perspective. It accounts for our ability to learn from the experience of interacting with our environments ('1', '2', '3' . . . 'n'?) by means of the plasticity of our brains and minds.

Adolf Bastian suggested something along these lines more than a century ago in his theory of *Elementargedanken* as primitive physical extensions of the body, as in for example tool-making. Psychological theories focusing on religion as extension or projection of basic social experiences could find their place here – think of all the families of gods in cosmogonic myths. The point is very simple: representations of all kinds become organized according to certain principles that reflect very basic functions, and even the most basic of functions are syntactically ordered. What makes this all the more interesting is that we may thus be able to account for the causality of beliefs and representation – when one thing 'leads to the other' (Kamppinen 1989: 28–36) in causal cognition and causal semantics.

In religious worlds we constantly encounter strong narrative programmes for moral, social, ritual action where all things are bound to rules of representing and acting. One very prominent example of this is what I would call the 'Seerah' model after the biography of the prophet Muhammad which is ordered so as to be able to 'make sense' of individual Muslims' lives as well as of the community as a whole. It is built on entirely logical, syntactical principles describing and prescribing action and thought, as in a 'doctrinal' mode of action (Whitehouse 1995: 193–9). Religions are systemic, not in the sense that they are formal, deductive systems but in that more loose sense in which they act as repertoires of possible inferences of explanations and interpretations.

Ritual activities as well as religious social institutions contain models and programmes for making sense, they 'speak' in certain ways on certain occasions and become the models for other kinds of actions – some of Mircea Eliade's intuitions were not always completely off the mark. Some socio-cultural institutions become very powerful conceptual organizers, shamanism for instance, and these 'organizers' may come in highly dramatized form, in an 'imagistic' mode as Harvey Whitehouse terms it (ibid.). They have the functions of thematizing and ordering representations in collective memory or presenting patterns of action in other domains. On the basis of my own studies of matters pertaining to Islam I have chosen to term this the 'Muharram'-model, referring to the annual passion-rituals in Shia Islam, but one may substitute similar action complexes and displays in any religion one may happen to know best. What is noticeable in the case of that ritual in a complex Shi'ite Muslim social situation is that it can be demonstrated that the Iranian Shi'ite revolution was remodelled upon ritual patterns with complex, but systemic, references to the entire Shi'ite salvation history and cosmology. That is probably one of the reasons why Western scholars in the social and political sciences have had real difficulties in 'explaining' that revolution (and even more so in predicting it) as they were unaware of the symbolic logic involved. However, this prominent example demonstrates how action is related to and organized upon or around certain narrative patterns and representational logic.

Narrative knowledge

It can be argued very plausibly that not only ritual knowledge, but all human knowledge is in some way narratively organized. All that we know of or can communicate about the worlds is expressed in some kind of public medium, e.g. in formalized scientific vocabulary or in natural language. This seems to work quite well in spite of the fact that 'nothing in the world corresponds to a sentence' – semantically. As we have seen, there are things in the many non-human realms that seem to be well organized, and thus the question rather seems to be whether we shall allow for the notion of syntax in non-semantic systems or whether we should then rather talk about cybernetics. I prefer to reserve the use of the notion of syntax for semantic systems, and as far as we know, semantic systems are human contrivances.

Scientific concepts are models, metaphors, blendings and mappings, etc., in and across domains (e.g. Fauconnier 1997: 165–8). Scientific knowledge is also narrative – it is, of course, not so much presented in literary modes in the natural sciences, but still – even the most formal formulae are semantic in nature, as formulae are, in the end, highly abbreviated stories about things, their properties and functions: 'As a human product, science is more akin to the judicial-rhetorical projects than to the project of demonstrative logic', concluded Donald Polkinghorne (1983: 199) in a discussion of Jürgen Habermas's theory of practical reasoning: 'In all sciences argumentation is subject to the same conditions for the discursive redemption of truth claims. These conditions of a rationality that is not scientifically restricted can be elucidated within the framework of a logic of theoretical discourse' (Habermas 1973: 171–2). Therefore, not only cognition but also semantics set our epistemic boundary conditions. Whatever we know of all things, we know them only as what W. van O. Quine aptly termed 'cultural posits'.

In the social and human sciences it is obvious that our explanations are narratives in which we configure sets of events in 'a story-like causal nexus' (Polkinghorne 1988: 21) and as Jerome Bruner (1986: 43) noticed, 'thereby we constitute the psychological and cultural reality in which the participants in history actually live'. The question of how we come to endow experience with meaning is not just reserved for poets to answer. Many of us are familiar with the stories from Antiquity, those told by Pausanias, for instance, about oracles, rituals, peoples, etc., and these are very much narrative explanations. The idea of the epistemological importance of narratives, or of parables, is re-entering the stage, as in Mark Turner's *The Literary Mind* (1996). He argues, on the basis of convincing reasoning about cognitive processes and functions, that parable is the origin of language (and much else). There is much to suggest that experience comes to us with a narrative or dramatic shape, 'under what for want of a better word I will call "dramatic" categories' (Searle 1995: 134). Perhaps this is what religions exploit so successfully in the invasion of human brains – or, to put it in a meme-theoretical and epidemiological perspective: they supply a master-narrative according to which the stories of experience become meaningful.

Religion as culturally domain specific

Modularity theories of cognitive functions and mind propose that human cognitive networks consist of modules that have original 'proper' domains as the result of evolution but also that these, in the processes of adaptation, may be 'usurped' for novel and other use as 'actual' domains (e.g. Sperber 1996: ch. 6). A good example is music, for where as it is hardly plausible that humans would have been 'created' with a specific and 'proper' module for music, it is much more likely that we have other modules which may adapt, in combinations, so as to enable us to create and enjoy music. Nor is it plausible that evolution endowed us with a module for language – created long before language as a social, public and 'discursive' fact 'entered the stage'. In a parallel argument it is my claim here that socio-cultural systems also exhibit specifiable traits of modularity, in registers or in repertoires, so that we say, for example, that religions form 'particular registers of ideology' or contain 'certain repertoires of action programmes'. The modularity of semantic systems can explain, and be explained by, the rules governing the relations and functions between various cultural domains and, as I will suggest, this hypothesis may explain how religion as a meta-representational competence (in semantic systems) governs such things as relevance and plausibility, and from there on to motivations, emotions, attentions and memory. Thus, such an argument will also substantiate more 'pre-theoretical' notions of world-views, etc., and grant them some theoretical substance. When, for instance, Clifford Geertz repeatedly wrote about various sectors of social reality as 'cultural systems' these were presented both as aspects, 'emanations', of the same thing and also as performing distinctly different functions in social totalities. The 'religion as life-world' theory of Peter L. Berger and Thomas Luckmann also deserves to be revisited in the light of the advances in both cognitive and cultural analyses.

The narrative character of religious systems is not some peculiarity of theirs, it is a basic trait which they share with other explanatory systems. Explanations come in the form of stories, and religions come in the form of stories about, e.g., social institutions and in aetiological myths – that some folks don't know the stories is not the issue, the issue is that they are accountable for. Religion is about many things, but it can only be so because it is communicative – therefore, I shall remain convinced that the 'Essence of Religion' is communication – for the purpose of connecting individual minds and sustaining socio-cultural systems of communication. In so saying, I am well aware that I am committing myself to all the dubious assumptions of intellectualism, cognitive functionalism and a measure of teleology, but this can hardly be avoided. I find the evidence for my position compelling and the theoretical problems concerning that account must be solvable.

One of the contended issues is whether religious systems are 'really' like science. I would say no, simply because of their referential and evidential differences. But, in many other aspects, as already pointed out, yes. What must be kept in mind is the totalitarian ambition of any religious system – it claims to explain 'it all'. Religious, as well as some other cultural, explanatory systems are about much more than instrumental, strategic and cognitive knowledge about 'World 1'. Religions are, as symbolist theories go, perhaps even more 'explanations' of the 'Worlds 2 and 3' concerning human experiential-mental and socio-cultural life. We could even say that religion is about a 'World 4' consisting of supernatural or superhuman 'stuff', but let us leave that for the moment. Regardless of the number of worlds accepted we cannot disregard the explanatory potentials of religious systems, how-

ever oblique the explanatory procedures are – conscious or unconscious, whether used for illumination or manipulation etc. (Godlove
1989: 134). Symbolists, intellectualists and most other '-ists' will agree
on this – as long as it is couched in their own idiom.

One of the main reasons why religious explanatory systems work –
and continue to do so – is that they retain, through transmission, etc.,
a degree of both cultural-conventional but also of cognitive well-
formedness. If we assume that religious systems have some sort of
volition 'of their own', some kind of teleological survival strategy, then
we can assume that religious systems will adapt to various conditions,
and that these may be socio-cultural as well as psychological-cognitive.
Religions strive – that is, through the human actors committed to them
– to maintain salience, relevance and plausibility. They will also therefore strive towards maximum explanatory potential. In this connection
New Age cosmologies are a relevant example, as are the attempts at
theology–science 'dialogues'.

A theory of 'world-making': super-narratives and transcendental constraints

Now we may explore the possibilities of formulating a theory of the
formation of religious 'worlds'. Granted the validity of the aforemen-
tioned we can add, when speaking in terms of representational and/or
discursive causality, that religious worlds are kept in place by deep
organizational cognitive (bottom-up) structures and functions – call
them root-metaphors or substrata if we conceive of them as underlying.
These are then related to what I shall call 'super-narratives' – which is
preferable when operating at the cultural meta-level (top-down) in this
'imagined' many-layered theoretical construct. I am here concerned
with the total architecture of the theory. Whereas cognitive factors set
the low-level constraints we can say that the 'super-narratives' set the
highest-level 'transcendental constraints' for the formation of the entire
explanatory network. That is one plausible sketch of how 'worlds' are
made.

In that perspective religious 'worlds' are a species of 'virtual worlds',
not the only ones possible, and they belong to a species of 'virtual
worlds' that has exerted a tremendous influence upon human history –
and continues to do so. Virtual worlds set the parameters of modalities,
about what is considered true, right, possible and valuable in any
thought-of-world. After centuries of empiricism, these claims about the
importance of 'thought-of-worlds' may easily become associated with

idealism, subjectivism, relativism, etc. Fortunately, we only need to refer to the critique of positivism and find support in the recognition of theory-ladenness of scientific discourse to see what 'thought-of-realms' mean for our perception of worlds (as many as we may be involved in).

It is as if cultures, through the functions and effects of religious systems, have been endowed with a 'module' or a combination of modules that conjointly govern the multitude of lower-level domains and thus furnish or install in cultural systems a meta-representational 'module' providing certain mechanisms or structures of explanation and interpretation. Meta-representational competence governs the interpretation and implementation of conceptual information, cognitive as well as discursive – in other words: the meta-representational competence warrants the syntactical and grammatical 'well-formedness' of the ways in which symbols, meanings, etc. are related and represented, also in action. Religion is then to be considered an installation of meta-representational socio-cultural competence – one that introduces also 'The Cybernetics of the Holy' as Rappaport terms the regulatory and corrective socio-cultural processes governed by religion (1999: 429–37).

In conclusion: Religion, culture and cognition are mutually reflexive and interconnected levels of explanations. They come together because that is the only way they work. Cultural context is not just something historically specific; it is what our general humanness is made of. That is because we do not understand things 'as they are' – we only understand by 're-creating' them, in images and in narratives that follow the rules and build upon the properties of our minds. That is why children expressionistically make drawings and tell stories to make the things thus told or drawn intelligible to themselves. That is why physicists, oceanographers and all other scientists make models, maps and equations (Giere 1988). That is why most cultures have produced, and depended upon, religions as other 'worlds' that are rule-governed and non-contingent. It is also the reason why all our knowledge is in some sense narrative – this even goes for pre-linguistic schematic cognition. World-making, whether in cognition, in culture or in religion, is 'sense-making' and at the cultural level it is 'inter-subjectification' and 'objectification' – because meaning is the inter-subjective 'transmitter-substance' of culture and religion.

References

Andersen, P. B., C. Emmeche, N. O. Finnemann and P. V. Christiansen (eds) (2000) *Downward Causation: Minds, Bodies and Matter*. Aarhus: Aarhus University Press.

Boyer, P. (1994) *The Naturalness of Religious Ideas*. Berkeley: University of California Press.

Boyer, P. (1998) 'Cognitive tracks of cultural inheritance: how evolved intuitive ontology governs cultural transmission'. *American Anthropologist* 100 (4): 876–89.

Brandt, P. A. (1997) 'Domains and blendings: language in a cognitive and semiotic framework'. *Almen Semiotik* 13: 147–54.

Bruner, J. (1986) *Actual Minds, Possible Worlds*. Cambridge, MA: Harvard University Press.

Cooke, M. (1997) *Language and Reason: A Study of Habermas's Pragmatics*. Cambridge, MA: MIT Press.

D'Andrade, R. (1995) *The Development of Cognitive Anthropology*. Cambridge: Cambridge University Press.

Davidson, D. (1995) 'Thinking causes'. In *Mental Causation*, ed. J. Heil and A. Mele, 3–17. Oxford: Clarendon Press.

Deacon, T. (1997) *The Symbolic Species: The Co-evolution of Language and the Human Brain*. Harmondsworth: Penguin.

Dennett, D. (1991) *Consciousness Explained*. Harmondsworth: Penguin.

Durkheim, É. and M. Mauss (1963 (1903)) *Primitive Classification*. Chicago: University of Chicago Press.

Fauconnier, G. (1997) *Mappings in Thought and Language*. Cambridge: Cambridge University Press.

Giere, R. N. (1988) *Explaining Science: A Cognitive Approach*. Chicago: University of Chicago Press.

Godlove, T. F., Jr (1989) *Religion, Interpretation, and the Diversity of Belief: The Framework Model from Kant to Durkheim to Davidson*. Cambridge: Cambridge University Press.

Habermas, J. (1973) 'Postscript to knowledge and human interest'. *Philosophy of the Social Sciences* 3: 157–89.

Habermas, J. (1981) *Theorie des kommunikativen Handelns*, vol. 1. Frankfurt a. M.: Suhrkamp.

Henderson, D. K. (1993) *Interpretation and Explanation in the Human Sciences*. Albany, NY: SUNY Press.

Hutchins, E. (1995) *Cognition in the Wild*. Cambridge, MA: MIT Press.

Jensen, J. S. (1997) 'Social facts, metaphysics and rationality in the human sciences'. In *Rationality and the Study of Religion*, ed. J. S. Jensen and L. H. Martin, 117–35. Aarhus: Aarhus University Press.

Jensen, J. S. (1999) 'On a semantic definition of religion'. In *The Pragmatics of Defining Religion: Contexts, Concepts and Contests*, ed. J. Platvoet and

A. Molendijk, 409–31, Studies in the History of Religions (Numen Book Series), 84. Leiden: Brill.

Jensen, J. S. (2000) 'Structure'. In *Guide to the Study of Religion*, ed. W. Braun and R. T. McCutcheon, 314–33. London: Cassell.

Kamppinen, M. (1989) *Cognitive Systems and Cultural Models of Illness*. FF Communications, 224. Helsinki: Academia Scientiarum Fennica.

Kamppinen, M. (2001) 'Cognitive study of religion and Husserlian phenomenology: making better tools for the analysis of cultural systems'. In *Religion in Mind: Cognitive Perspectives on Religious Belief, Ritual and Experience*, ed. J. Anderson, 193–206. Cambridge: Cambridge University Press.

Lakoff, G. and M. Johnson (1999) *Philosophy in the Flesh: The Embodied Mind and Its Challlenge to Western Thought*. New York: Basic Books.

Lawson, E. T. and R. N. McCauley. (1990) *Rethinking Religion: Connecting Cognition and Culture*. Cambridge: Cambridge University Press.

Leach, E. (1976) *Culture and Communication: The Logic by Which Symbols Are Connected*. Cambridge: Cambridge University Press.

Linde, C. (1987) 'Explanatory systems in oral life stories'. In *Cultural Models in Language and Thought*, ed. D. Holland and N. Quinn, 343–66. Cambridge: Cambridge University Press.

Loewer, B. (1997) 'A guide to naturalizing semantics'. In *A Companion to the Philosophy of Language*, ed. B. Hale and C. Wright, 108–26. Oxford: Blackwell.

Loux, M. (1998) *Metaphysics: A Contemporary Introduction*. London: Routledge.

Mithen, S. (1996) *The Prehistory of the Mind: A Search for the Origins of Art, Religion and Science*. London: Thames & Hudson.

Oatley, K. (1996) 'Inference in narrative and science'. In *Modes of Thought: Explorations in Culture and Cognition*, ed. D. R. Olson and N. Torrance, 123–40. Cambridge: Cambridge University Press.

Peacock, J. L. (1986) *The Anthropological Lens: Harsh Light, Soft Focus*. Cambridge: Cambridge University Press.

Polkinghorne, D. (1983) *Methodology for the Human Sciences: Systems of Inquiry*. Albany, NY: SUNY Press.

Polkinghorne, D. (1988) *Narrative Knowing and the Human Sciences*. Albany, NY: SUNY Press.

Popper, K. R. (1979) *Objective Knowledge: An Evolutionary Approach*. Oxford: Clarendon Press.

Putnam, H. (1987) *The Many Faces of Realism*. LaSalle, IL: Open Court.

Putnam, H. (1988) *Representation and Reality*. Cambridge, MA: MIT Press.

Radnitzky, G. (1970) *Contemporary Schools of Metascience*. Göteborg: Akademiförlaget.

Rappaport, R. (1999) *Ritual and Religion in the Making of Humanity*. Cambridge: Cambridge University Press.

Rescher, N. (1997) *Objectivity: The Obligations of Impersonal Reason*. Notre Dame, IN: University of Notre Dame Press.

Searle, J. R. (1995) *The Construction of Social Reality*. New York: Free Press.

Shore, B. (1996) *Culture in Mind: Cognition, Culture, and the Problem of Meaning*. New York: Oxford University Press.

Sperber, D. (1996) *Explaining Culture: A Naturalistic Approach*. Oxford: Blackwell.

Spiro, M. (1984) 'Some reflections on cultural determinism and relativism with special reference to emotion and reason'. In *Culture Theory: Essays on Mind, Self, and Emotion*, ed. R. A. Shweder and R. A. LeVine, 323–46. Cambridge: Cambridge University Press.

Turner, M. (1996) *The Literary Mind: The Origins of Thought and Language*. New York: Oxford University Press.

Whitehouse, H. (1995) *Inside the Cult: Religious Innovation and Transmission in Papua New Guinea*. Oxford: Clarendon Press.

Zemach, E. M. (1989) 'On meaning and reality'. In *Relativism: Interpretation and Confrontation*, ed. M. Krausz, 51–79. Notre Dame, IN: University of Notre Dame Press.

11 Does Classification Explicate the Contents of Concepts?

PERTTI SAARILUOMA

A discussion of the content of concepts in a cognitive scientific setting can be motivated with a simple question: Do we perceive a Christian God? One can of course say that we perceive God in nature, in his deeds, in human beings, in some works of art and so on; but tradition-ally thinking, we should not be able to see God. On the other hand, we are certainly able to represent mental contents in which the concept of God is incorporated. We have an infinite number of propositions such as 'God is holy', 'God is good', etc., in which the concept of God is present. Independent of the content of beliefs, all normal people have the capability of constructing such representations of God. Since the process of constructing representations is a psychological process, it is very natural to ask what is the psychological origin of the concept of God. What are the psychological processes enabling us to mentally represent God and what kind of psychological approach should we adopt to investigate these representations?

Could it be that God is neurally implanted in our mind? This would mean that our knowledge of God originates in the contents of our inborn information content-structures. It would be somewhat compar-able to colour vision, pitch discrimination, hormonal processes or possibly the most fundamental neural mechanisms of thought (for these mechanisms, see e.g. Dehaene et al. 1999; Shulkin 1999). In this scenario, God would thus be a genetically transmitted representation. However, constructing such connections has not proven to be easy.

In historical terms the biological answer seems highly implausible. Christianity spread in a relatively short period of time over Europe; no biological change, presupposing genetic transmission, could have spread like that. Many gods have simply disappeared, so that we have very little idea about them. These arguments should make it clear that the origins of Christianity cannot be explained in terms of the brain sciences. One can naturally investigate the hypothesis that the concept of God is implanted in our neural system. However, it is very difficult to show that all people for example have experiences of god.

The problem with language is different. All normal people speak some language, and all normal people constantly use it. Language is also historically a far earlier phenomenon than Christianity. Sometimes researchers speak of a language instinct (Pinker 1994). Language ability, though not the language actually spoken, is very closely related to the biology of the human brain. There are specific brain areas which are responsible for maintaining language processing, and biological damage to these particular areas causes impairment or loss of language processing independently of culture (Ellis and Young 1995). Against this background, it also seems evident that the origin of the concept of God can hardly be exhaustively explained in terms of neurobiology or genetics.

Nevertheless, one can emotionally and conceptually experience God, be close to God and let the experience of God control one's life (Bunyan 1991). We are certainly not short of introspective descriptions, such as works of literature and music, of these experiences. This phenomenon is normally called a 'religious experience', and it is absolutely real to millions of people (James 1902/1997; Guthrie this volume). Even people who do not believe in the existence of God can have a representation of God and can have conceptions and mental contents in which God is an essential element. In attempting to understand experiences of God or representations of God in the human mind, biology provides relatively little help. Instead, we must concentrate on the human cognitive mechanisms responsible for conceptual information-processing in the mind. Without any clear conception of human conceptual cognition and thinking, it is impossible to investigate how religious representations, experiences and acts are possible, what their contents are and what they mean to individual people.

Apparently, perception is the theoretical concept that might serve as a basis in our scientific endeavour to investigate how people encode the world. Unfortunately, a closer and more reflective inspection shows that the perceptualist position is unnatural and conceptually implausible when investigating religious concepts and representations. We have simply far too many non-perceivables, i.e. concepts whose contents cannot be reduced to any percept. This means that we cannot argue that the basic mental process in the construction of cultural representations can be explained in terms of perception. We may be able to have mental representations which entail such contents as 'tomorrow', 'last century', 'memory', 'world trade', 'eternity', 'infinity' or 'electron'.

We may see that a glass is on a table or that it is not on that table, but we can hardly see that the glass is *possibly* on the table. We can perceive that someone is taking money from someone else's pockets, but we certainly cannot see that this is pickpocketing and a morally wrong deed; hence it is unclear how we might perceive theological correctness (Barrett 1999). One may also argue that religious knowledge is essentially counter-intuitive, as Pyysiäinen (this volume) argues, but how can we perceive counter-intuitive information? Finally, it would be highly metaphorical to say that we see the Christian God (Saariluoma 1995; 1997). None of these representational contents can possibly have their origin in direct perception, which is bound to the presence of a stimulus. Without a stimulus, we cannot have genuine perception; only such border cases as illusory contour or phantom limb phenomena may be sensed without the presence of a stimulus, but even these cases require very exactly definable stimulus conditions and are thus also stimulus-bound.

However, it would naturally be meaningless to say that people cannot represent or experience infinity, or God. We can and do work all the time with information contents that are non-perceivable (Saariluoma 1995; 1997). A typical example is the electron, which none of us has perceived, but which still provides a living and even wealth to many throughout this world. In this sense, God belongs to those entities which are non-perceivable but are evidently possible to experience and represent. This means that, in investigating how people conceive of religious entities, rather than perception we have to pay attention to some deeper cognitive processes.

It would thus be conceptually consistent and natural to abandon the practice of believing that our perceptual processes construct mental representations. They do not construct meanings even in those cases where the objects are visible; but our perceptions of God in perceptual objects are basically conceptual interpretations. Guthrie's examples (this volume) are very illuminating, because we do not interpret our percepts in the same way as past people. One cannot perceive anything that is not present in a physical stimulus, and all interpretations are conceptual constructions (Saariluoma 1990; 1992; 1995; in press). Instead, it would be much more logical to argue that it is necessary to distinguish between direct perception and the conceptually mediated construction of representations, or – as the process has been called – *apperception*. In this schema, apperception would naturally refer to all information-integration in the construction of representations; thus perception is just one of the sources of such information.

This difference between perception and apperception used to be very important in the psychological thinking of Leibniz, Kant and a number of other pre-experimental psychologists, but with behaviourism it lost its position outside of phenomenological circles (Kant 1781; Leibniz 1704/1979; Saariluoma 1990; 1992; 1995; in press; Stout 1896; Wundt 1880). However, the conceptual problems apparent in the case of experiencing non-perceivable mental contents make it necessary to rethink the role of conceptual contents in human information processes.

One may remark that there are numerous gods which can be thought to be directly visible or symbolically present in the perceivable environment, i.e. in the physical stimulus. In many mythologies, for example, thunder, which is highly perceivable, has been seen as a god. Nevertheless, even in such cases it is our conceptual system which integrates and interprets perceived information and gives it its god-related interpretation and contents. The mental representations of gods are outcomes of complex apperceptive processes. From the psychological point of view, it is a different thing to see something (perceive) and to see 'something as something' (apperceive), though this fact has not received sufficient attention among modern cognitive psychologists.

One may here quite logically ask whether cognitive psychology nevertheless has an explication for seeing something as something. Understanding might be a concept which accounts for seeing something as something. However, understanding presupposes a correct outcome. One cannot say that one had understood a medical book and had got a conceptual idea of its contents, but that the conception was nevertheless incorrect. The correct term is that the person did not understand the text, though he apperceived a representation of the contents of the book. He actually misunderstood the book. Thus apperception is the concept which explicates all of the construction of representations.

The difference between 'seeing' and 'seeing as' has been fundamental in philosophy in the twentieth century. It was central to Husserl (1936), but it was equally important to Wittgenstein (1958). The former refers to experiencing a physical stimulus, but the latter refers to seeing its meaning. When one reads a text in an unfamiliar language but does not understand what is said, the problem is not in perception or seeing. The problem is in encoding the meaning of the physical information, i.e. in apperceiving the message, which is essentially seeing as. In this sense, all of our experience of the sensory environment is apperceiving. What we cannot apperceive, we cannot be conscious of.

We cannot mentally represent the meanings of perceived entities and elements in the organization of physical patterns unless we can give this information an accurate apperceptive interpretation. From this point of view, religious experiences are beyond the meaning horizons of an atheist. One can of course always take a third-person or heterophenomenological view of such apperceived experiences, but this is different from first-person personal experience (Dennett 1991; Duncker 1945; Newell and Simon 1972).

Without detailed information about apperception, we can hardly have a detailed conception about how people construct representations of God and represent this and other religious entities. This means that we have to pay specific attention to the idea of the conceptual construction of mental representations (Saariluoma 1990; 1995; 2001). What are the principles of this process of apperception, and how can its principles and preconditions be investigated? Overall, understanding apperception is a large project; here it is possible to discuss only one of its necessary preconditions, which is the nature of conceptual knowledge and how we can analytically approach the contents of human concepts and representations. However, religious concepts – one of the earliest abstractions in our childhood and culturally central – provide a good platform to consider the issues of the construction and content of representations. On the whole, apperception research works to explain human actions on the ground of mental contents, their structures and construction. Such an approach can be called 'content-oriented' (Saariluoma 2001).

Concepts and classification

All scientific knowledge is ultimately intuitive (Bunge 1962; Hintikka 1999; Saariluoma 1997). There are several reasons for this; to be brief, however, I shall only mention that, since infinite lines of arguments or definitions are impossible, consequently argumentation must always have an end; for this reason alone, the foundations of any science rest on intuitions. This is as true of theoretical notions as of theories. The idea of an axiomatic system is perhaps the best explication of the intuitive limits of scientific knowledge; it is an open recognition that there is no absolute way of securing scientific knowledge.

This acknowledgement of the ultimate intuitiveness of scientific ground truths makes many phenomena in the progress of science understandable. It makes clear, for example, how almost unconscious conceptual contents may dominate the way things are seen in science

(Saariluoma 1997). Poorly understood dimensions of theoretical notions can be called conceptual postulates. Typical examples of such postulates might be 'mental capacity', 'culture', 'system', etc., concepts which have been adopted from everyday use rather than actually defined in detail. The term 'conceptual postulate' is justified because these concepts are tacitly postulated rather than accurately and fully explicated. These half-theoretical and half-intuitive concepts nevertheless have a surprisingly large and so far mostly unknown power in theory formation in modern science (Saariluoma 1997).

As far as this chapter is concerned, the conceptual postulate of greatest interest is in seeing concepts as classifiers. A number of important theories about the nature of concepts see them as classifiers, without apparently realizing that classifying cannot possibly be the primary function of concepts. Could classification really be a function that determines what concepts are by their nature? Is it perhaps rather that classifying is merely one of the many functions concepts fulfil in human thinking? This issue has received very little serious attention; as of the time of writing there has been no major discussion of the major functions of concepts. However, such intuitive silence is highly typical of conceptual postulates, which are very seldom discussed. The silence is paradoxical; open discussion would very probably transform these concepts from postulated into genuine theoretical notions and provide new grounds for empirical knowledge.

The idea of concepts as classifiers can best be seen in so-called classic theories of concepts. In these theories, the definitions and defining characteristics were aimed at providing criteria for determining which objects, events or ideas can be subsumed under a particular concept (Smith and Medin 1981). Classic psychological research on concept formation naturally accepted and echoed this view of concepts; it is quite possible that psychological research proceeded in this direction because it is by means of classification experiments that concepts are easiest to operationalize. In these experiments, subjects were asked for example to provide a criterion for an object which belongs together with certain other objects (e.g. Bruner et al. 1956; Vygotski 1934/1962). However, in prototype theories and even in the theory theory of concepts the main function of a concept is also seen to be the classification of entities (Murphy and Medin 1999; Laurence and Margolis 1999; Rosch 1978). Finally, the whole tradition of mathematical theories of concepts, from logic to neural networks and learning machines, mainly concentrates on classification (Estes 1994). Consequently, though not commonly addressed or admitted, classification or categorization provides a dominant perspective in the psychological nature of concepts.

The classification view is not invalid. People use their conceptual knowledge to classify, and large areas for instance of our scientific knowledge are based on conceptual distinctions. One could hardly think for example of botany, medicine or clinical psychology without classificatory systems, which make it possible to apply traditional knowledge rationally. One must know what one speaks about, and an ability to make delicate conceptual distinctions is often decisive for the advancement of knowledge. Thus the classificatory point of view on concepts is relevant and indeed essential. However, it has surprisingly little to contribute when one is interested in how people represent religious entities. This is why concepts should not be seen as a classificatory tool alone; we also need to pay attention to their many other functions in human thinking.

If we wish to ask how people represent such things as gods, holy places, 'sacred people', etc., the dividing of entities into gods and non-gods, holy and unholy places, or the elect and the damned does not really provide the full content of the representations. If we believe that Brutus was not saved but belongs in hell although he was noblest Roman of them all, what do we know about the ethical and real aspects of Brutus's deeds that gave him the fate he had to meet after his death? Was he worse or better than other traitors, or was he merely a politician who happened to slip into a power game? Be this as it may, knowing that Brutus does not belong to the holy as such does not express the core of his fate, his deeds or the ethical system which divides people.

This kind of discussion does not provide us with much information about what precisely the contents of the concepts are. It is one thing to be given a reference and another to understand what this reference actually is. This problem is especially serious when we are interested in apperception as the construction of mental representations and their contents. In this function, the mental content of a concept can hardly be the reference set. Indeed, what are we saying about God when we say that the mental content of God is that he belongs to the class of entities termed gods? It is clear that we need some other information than the reference set to explicate the contents of the concept 'God'.

It would be natural to think that the content of a concept is identical with the classification criterion, i.e. the definition, though it is very difficult to find a unique criterion (Wittgenstein 1958). However, even this is highly problematic. First of all, a criterion does not give much information about the content of a concept. If one takes the defining criteria of human beings to be kinship with apes and the ability to think, this still does not tell us much about what human beings are. It does not tell us for example that they are composed of cells, which are characteristic of human beings, though this naturally does not discriminate people from other animals. Human beings nevertheless have cells and characteristics, and their being composed of cells provides explanations for many things, such as illnesses. This means that there is much more information associated with the concept of a human being than is expressed in the definition needed to classify references into positive and negative cases within a certain set of referential objects.

Inference and concepts

In addition to classification, concepts have other very important functions in cognition. One of these is inference, a fact which is widely acknowledged (Boyer 1994). A typical example of such an approach to concepts is provided by conceptual role semantics (Cummins 1989). Thus, it is evident that concepts operate in some sense, or rather in some senses, in human inferential processes, but it is not always clear what the main inferential functions of concepts are. It is quite possible that they enable people to perform many kinds of inferential operations. However, before one can really speak with precision about conceptual inferences, one must have a clear idea what is inferred from concepts and how it can be done. Without our offering an explicit answer to these questions, it should be reiterated that the idea of inferential contents of concepts is necessarily absolutely intuitive.

A natural target of conceptual inferences is apparently provided by the attributes of concepts. A car, for example, has wheels, an engine and a body; these are properties that make a car what it is. Correspondingly, the concept 'car' must have representations for these properties. These expressions can be called attributes. Each concept is thus related to a number of other concepts, so that it can be considered that these other concepts form the contents of this particular concept. In general, objects, events and ideas have their properties; therefore the concepts which represent these entities must have attributes that describe the properties. Thus the content of a concept can be seen as the total set of its attributes.

This new perspective on the content of concepts is not intuitively any less justified than that of classification. Attributes entail knowledge about concepts and they describe what the concepts refer to. If we say that a human being is an animal and is capable of singing, etc., we are saying something essential about human nature; thus these attributes, like so many others, describe the content of the concept of 'human'. Discovering the attributes of a concept also means becoming aware of its content.

It is also possible to differentiate between concepts by expressing their conceptual attributes. One can make distinctions between concepts by means of attributes. Thus, a 'bachelor' is an unmarried man and a 'spinster' is an unmarried woman. In fact, all concepts can be differentiated from one another by finding one or more discriminating attributes. This process can be called the 'individuation' of a concept because it simply discriminates between one concept and another; it does not attempt to be a universal defining criterion. Thus there is nothing unnatural in thinking that attributes may reflect and express the content of a concept.

However, the knowledge that conceptual attributes are important for the content of concepts does not yet give us an explicit method for working with the content. For this purpose, we need a form of inference. This form of inference will here be termed 'Cartesian inference' in honour of René Descartes (1975), who produced perhaps the most famous example of this kind of inferential process. The problem of Cartesian inference arises to a great extent from the needs of conceptual analysis. One may assume that this process must entail some kind of inference. However, inferences are normally made on the ground of propositional premises. Nevertheless, there is the famous example of a concept-based inference in Descartes' *cogito* argument, 'I think, therefore I am.' This means that he inferred the notion of existence from the notion of thinking. This inference is possible only if a thinking thing has the attribute of existence. Without taking any position with respect to the correctness of Descartes's inference, one can accept his schema as a general mode of inference for inferring conceptual attributes.

Cartesian inference follows a simple schema:

(1) $C(A_1, \ldots, A_n) \rightarrow A_1 \mid, \ldots, \mid A_n$

In this formula C is a concept and $A_1 \ldots A_n$ represent its attributes and | corresponds to intuitive 'or'. Hence, schema (1) is to be read as follows: if concept C has attributes $A_1, \ldots, A_n$ then any or all of the attributes $A_1, \ldots, A_n$ can be inferred from concept C.

One could also use another schema:

(2) $C \rightarrow A$

This schema naturally contains the same information as (1), namely that from a concept one can infer any of its attributes.

Although Cartesian inference has only been discussed in historical contexts, it is surprisingly common in ordinary thinking. If I say that Jack is a grandfather, you know immediately that he is male and probably old. At least Jack cannot be for instance a teenager. From the notion of car one can infer its engine, from the notion of circle its radius. Such examples of inference are easy to generate. Cartesian inference is thus a central inferential tool in considering the content of concepts.

Sometimes conceptual attributes are quite explicit. The age of a grandfather is typically such an attribute. However, most conceptual attributes are much less explicit. Time-scale, for example, is a characteristic attribute of a large number of actions. We do not run infinitely but for some limited time. From the concept of 'running', we can thus infer by means of Cartesian inference that this action is time-limited. The attribute is so seldom used that it is by and large implicit. An even more difficult problem than the implicit attributes of concrete concepts can be found when the conceptual attributes of abstract concepts are discussed. What kinds of attributes can be explicated from the notion of eternity, for example? The problem is difficult, since eternity has a number of attributes, such as time and infinity.

The investigation of possible Cartesian inferences shows that Cartesian inference can be used to explicate quite different types of attributes. Let us take some examples:

(3) The tree is a pine so its needles are green.
(4) A house has windows, walls and doors.
(5) Cells have mitochondria.
(6) A square has four angles.
(7) Three is greater than two.

Clearly, all these inferential sentences express some attribute or attributes of the concept expressed by the subject. They are properties of the objects and we would expect to meet them in an entity like the one expressed by the subject. If we know an object is a cell, we also expect it to have a number of properties, such as mitochondria. If we observe a cell under a microscope and it does not have such a property we will be very surprised. At least, this will be our probable reaction if we have sufficient knowledge of biology. The knowledge associated with the concept of 'cell' clearly enables one to infer a number of attributes of cells.

Nevertheless, the main thing about the examples is that the first three propositions are empirical while the latter two (4 and 5) are more of an a priori type. In the fourth, for instance, the attribute of having four angles can be derived directly from the basic definition of a square. It is always valid. However, the first three examples need not always be valid; there are for instance dead pines, which have no needles or they are brown. This indeed means that there are valid attributes which are empirical and contingent, as well as valid a priori attributes.

There are several forms of inferences which are close to Cartesian inference. Typical examples are entailment or lexical inference, psychological and meaning postulates (Carnap 1947; Cruse 1986; Smedslund 1988). However, there are also differences between these concept-analytical tools and Cartesian inference. The major difference can be seen in the above examples (3–7). With Cartesian inference we do not infer only a priori properties. Meaning postulates cannot be constructed by combining all possible kinds of attributes. Meaning postulates follow necessarily from a concept without any empirical analysis, but this is not true of all attributes of concepts. Some of the attributes of concepts are logically contingent, and are therefore not meaning postulates. The same criterion also differentiates Cartesian inference from the psychological type inferential schemes (Smedslund 1988). The explication of necessary attributes is thus merely a special case of the general Cartesian analysis of conceptual content. In Cartesian inference, all types of attributes can be inferred from a concept. It does not distinguish between a priori and empirical attributes. Any attribute of a concept can be inferred by means of Cartesian inference, when it is defined as it is above.

The validity of Cartesian inference

The next important problem to solve with regard to Cartesian inference is its validity. One must determine under what conditions such inferences are correct. Without any rational criteria for the validity of an inference, it would naturally be useless to discuss inferences or a specific form of inference. The whole idea of drawing inferences in some definite manner is based on the idea that this form of inference is a correct way of thinking and that the outcome is true or false. However, validity is an especially difficult issue with Cartesian inference, since the attributes which are inferred may not be a priori; the outcome of the inference may be some empirical attribute. Nevertheless, this problem must be resolved in the case of Cartesian inference as with any other particular form of inference.

The first consequence of empirical attributes is that Cartesian inference, though expressed by an abstract formula as above, can hardly be any form of formal inference. Its correctness does not depend on its form. This is easy to see from the following examples:

(8) Aeroplanes have wings.
(9) Aeroplanes have muscles.

Both of the two inferences have precisely the same form, but while the first is true, the latter is false. Only birds have both wings and muscles. Consequently, the validity of a Cartesian inference depends on the conceptual attributes. If a concept does in fact have the attribute one has inferred from it, the inference is valid, but if the concept does not have such an attribute, it is invalid. It is sometimes naturally very difficult to justify the validity of a Cartesian inference. The following examples are illuminating:

(10) God has created the earth.
(11) God exists.

These inferences naturally divide people. One solution to such problem situations, in which it is hard to find sufficient evidence for the existence of a property, might be to take a modal stance. One could say that from the notion of God one can infer that God may exist.

In the previous pair of propositions, it cannot be considered that nothing certain can be inferred in the above type of situation. It is still possible that some related inferences can be made. All of us can presumably be unanimous that the inference in the next example cannot be valid:

(12) A being which has never existed has created the world.

On the ground of the above observations, it can be argued that the validity of Cartesian inference depends on the content of the concepts on which this inferential technique is used. If the concept has the required attribute, the inference is correct; otherwise it is incorrect. Thus the truth of a Cartesian inference is material by nature. It depends on what we know about things.

Indeed, like classification, Cartesian inference also expresses one way of seeing conceptual contents. The inferential content of a concept thus means a set of attributes, and these attributes give us the content of a concept. The content of concepts can be seen as the total number of attributes possessed by concepts (Saariluoma 1997). Everything that can be expressed about a concept can be included in its contents as long as it expresses a true property of a concept. Thus one may infer the existence of God from the concept of God, but this inference is not necessarily valid. Nevertheless, there are many attributes associated with the notion of God which can be hypothetically inferred from it. God is almighty and eternal.

Now a new problem arises for the validity criterion of Cartesian inference. If God does not exist, how can it be valid to infer 'almighty' from the concept of God? Obviously, something that does not exist cannot be almighty or eternal. On the other hand, it seems highly unintuitive not to be able to attribute such properties to God irrespective of the position we have with respect to God's existence. The solution to this problem is relatively clear. When we say that God is eternal, we actually mean God either as an actually existing entity or as a conception in the minds of Christians. God as a conception certainly has the property of being eternal or almighty. Thus independently of the existence or rather the type of existence God has, we can validly infer his eternality and his almightiness. The only problem is that we cannot infer that he exists as an entity independent of human conceptions. If atheists are right, the extinction of man would also mean the extinction of God, but if Christians are right, the extinction of mankind would not imply the extinction of God.

Discussions of God's existence or the manner in which God possibly exists are naturally beyond the scope of this chapter. The main thing is that we can accept the validity of our inference criterion. There is nothing unintuitive in inferring the properties God has in the human mind, in culture and in existing religious texts; we merely do not know whether the properties belong to a being which exists independently of the human mind. The attributes we infer are thus true attributes and we can retain our intuitions. It is entirely possible to infer properties of human mental representations and imaginary creatures, as long as we do not confuse the issues concerning the mode of their existence.

Concepts as constructors

A further perspective on the content of concepts could be to see concepts as the constructors of representations. They are the elements out of which we construct propositions and stories, and their content can thus be seen as the contribution they make to the representations in which they participate. This constructive point of view is very natural; concepts are indeed used to construct representations, and the construction of representations can be no less important a function for concepts than classification or inference. Concepts enable us for example to make plans and build machines. An engineer with a good knowledge of the concepts needed in constructing ships can plan them, improve old plans and come up with new ideas. No one, no matter how capable and intelligent, can do this without proper knowledge about the necessary things. Representations are rational only if they are constructed of rational conceptual knowledge. Otherwise the results are all too often poor.

If one is ignorant of some essential conceptual content, one cannot really be aware of the relevant factors. A person ignorant of spring and of botany has a very different conception of the awakening of nature after winter than that of a botanist. Walking with one's eyes open does not tell all; it is necessary to understand the meaning of the signs of spring – what has gone and what is about to come alive again. Indeed, representations are constructed of concepts, and the contents of representations are determined by the contents of those concepts. In order to understand this synthetic process of giving content to representations, we must understand what functions are served in this process by concepts.

Concepts as constructors provide us with a third perspective on their contents. It can also be considered that the content of a concept is the contribution it can make to the total content of a representation. All representations are constructed of conceptual elements because concepts are the basic content vehicles of the mind. Such a simple proposition as 'Tomorrow the sun will rise' presupposes the concepts of 'sun', 'rise' and 'tomorrow'. Like all other representations it is a combination of its basic concepts. If we have a plan of a ship, for example, even though it is a drawing, its contents are nothing but a set of propositions expressed in this analogical form. On the basis of the plan, any skilled shipyard can carry out a set of actions which will construct the ship.

While all representations are combinations of concepts, this does not mean that by integrating any set of concepts together the outcome will be a consistent and sense-making representation. There is no point in the proposition 'The thinking house yawned.' It is impossible to associate 'yawning' or 'thinking' with a house except in a metaphorical or poetical sense. However, in that case the words would also refer to non-standard conceptual representations. Both concepts, 'yawning' and 'thinking', presuppose an animal actor, 'thinking' in fact a rather advanced species. Thus the representation is inconsistent and impossible. Representations must make sense, i.e. they must be senseful. Each part must have a reason to be included in the whole and no element can be inconsistent with the other elements. This means that the whole of representations must be explainable in functional terms (Saariluoma 1990; 1992; 1995; 1997; see also Jensen, Chapter 10 this volume).

The theoretical concepts of sense-making or sensefulness and consistency, however, are not simple. How do we know that a given concept forms an inconsistent representation? The previous example provides a good hint for a solution. Inconsistencies can be explicated by analysing attributes. Let me take an example of two propositions:

(13) I am in connection with God.
(14) I am in connection with God through a mobile phone.

The question, obviously, is why the first sentence seems standard and makes sense, but the latter does not. The reason seems to be that God is supposed to be almighty and therefore the mobile phone is unnecessary (see also Barrett, this volume). Furthermore, in a historical sense mobile phones are rather new inventions, while people have had representations of being connected with God for ages.

The attributes of concepts are important when we consider the content of concepts. Clearly, attributes limit the possibility of using concepts in constructing representations. It is inappropriate, except in a metaphorical sense, to say 'the grass thinks'. It is quite possible to say that grass is green, full of life and grows, but still it does not think. Grass is not an entity with the capability of thinking. Its concept does not possess such an attribute, because it is not an intentional entity. Therefore we cannot build true representations with deeply thinking grass, though we could build an analogous representation with a deeply thinking physician. Even a deeply thinking ape would be a problematic construction, and very probably only an imaginary and projective metaphor.

Nevertheless, the point of the above example is easy to understand. The attributes of concepts define limits to the use of the concepts as constructors of representations. They can be applied only in contexts in which their conceptual attributes do not lead to representational inconsistencies. The space of possible correct representations is of course infinite, but this does not mean that we can apply concepts at will. Representations with random contents lead to impossibilities and senseless representations such as 'non-existent past stones will hit the clouds in the depths of a lake'. The contents of attributes constrain the construction of the representational context in which one can use concepts, and serve as criteria for sensefulness. This contextual constraining, however, makes it understandable that concepts can be seen as the constructors of representations and that their contents are essential in this construction process.

Conceptual change

One very interesting property of concepts is their historical change. People find new properties of the referred entities and thus they give new attributes to the concepts. They may also abandon certain attributes in favour of certain others. Some centuries ago it was common to think that different types of illnesses and disasters were sent by gods. They were signs of their anger. Today illnesses are seen, for example, as the consequences of micro-organisms, and they are cured accordingly. Even floods, droughts and other similar disasters are commonly seen as consequences of human acts rather than punishments sent by gods. This means that the attributes of droughts, for example, have essentially changed in the minds of people. In a similar way, most of our concepts seem to slowly change in the course of time (Thagard 1992).

Another important perspective on content is opened up by individual development (Carey 1985; Vosniadou and Brewer 1992). The concepts of a child are different from those of an adult. The contents of an expert are different from those of a novice (Chi 1992). There is thus clear evidence to support the fact that concepts change, that they are fluid by nature. The fluid nature of concepts may apparently seem to open the door to an arbitrariness of conceptual contents. One may think, for example, that if the attributes of concepts can change, this means that the whole of our conceptual system is in a constant and irrational state of fluctuation. If anyone can suggest new attributes, how can our conceptual system have any stability? The dynamism of the conceptual system would seem to lead to irrational conceptual worlds. Therefore, one could argue, the idea of dynamic attributes must go against the true nature of concepts as the stable elements in our scientific worlds.

At first sight the principle of the stability of conceptual contents seems very rational. We have concepts such as 'being' or 'infinity', whose contents cannot possibly have changed. How can the notion of belongingness acquire a different form? In addition, it is totally counter-intuitive that one could suggest any new contents for even the most ordinary concepts. They do not change if some of their attributes change, because most of the attributes are firmly grounded in the structure of the concept.

The latter point is true, but still it does not prevent concepts from changing. It just makes the change slower. To get an accurate grasp of these intuitions, it is necessary to discuss the criteria for something being an attribute of a concept. What are the criteria for something being an attribute of some concept, and why cannot some other attribute belong to that concept? Why cannot the concept of 'stone' have an attribute of singing or running? They do not have these attributes simply for the reason that stones do not have the corresponding properties. They simply do not sing or run, and it would be false to think that they could do either.

Attributes must thus be true properties of concepts. The criterion for something being an attribute of a concept is its truth. This observation naturally immediately removes all arbitrariness from a concept. An attribute of a concept must be a true property of the entity represented. Otherwise the attribute is false and cannot be an attribute of the concept. This truth criterion solves the problem of conceptual change in a very logical manner. The precondition for conceptual change is truth; that is why concepts cannot change in an uncontrollable manner.

If only true attributes are accepted as attributes of concepts, then the effect of the introduction of new attributes on the content of concepts is very slow, because most of the attributes remain intact. Of course concepts may slowly change and they do change. Continuity, for example, has changed greatly in our conception of infinity. Thus there is nothing wrong in conceptual change, but it is a natural process both in the development of an individual and in the historical process (Carey 1991; Thagard 1992). It is simply part of human cultural evolution. We develop new conceptions and we incorporate these ideas into our conceptual system. The change is real and unavoidable.

Concepts, contents and construction

We have discussed at least three different ways to approach the content of concepts, based on the three different cognitive functions concepts have in human information processing, and correspondingly three different notions of the content of concepts. The first had to do with referential content; in other words, the references of a concept were seen as its content. This view can also be called classificatory. The second had to do with attributive or inferential content, the discussion of which ended with the introduction of the total set of attributes of a concept. Finally, the last point of view was termed 'constructive content', which refers to the content contribution made by a concept to a particular representation. This last perspective on content can also be called the use of a concept.

These three perspectives on concepts, and above all on the cognitive functions associated with them, allow us to present a combinative theory of the role of concepts in cognition. The goal of such a theory is naturally to provide tools for humanistic and cultural investigation, which must rely on cognitive theories. Another motivation for presenting a theory of concepts and conceptual processing is that this is the only way to unify the three views of the content of concepts. This means that it is necessary to reflect once more on the three perspectives and see how they function together.

In cognitive terms, the main function of concepts is to serve as elements in mental representations. All human actions are directed and controlled by mental representations, and the constructive function is therefore the major one in this theory of concepts. Inferential and classificatory functions are secondary and serve the processes of the construction of representations. Consequently, the theory can be called a constructive theory of concepts.

The idea of construction presupposes that concepts actually have two states in the mind. One is potential and it is characterized by total content. We have a very large set of concepts in our long-term memories. There we find a large storage of concepts, with large sets of associated attributes. These attributes may even be mutually incompatible. Nevertheless, the potential mass of concepts is the basis of all representation construction. What its content allows can be incorporated with sensory knowledge into representations.

However, when a concept is incorporated into a representation, all of its attributes cannot be relevant. The simplest argument to support this point can be based on the contradictory attributes in the total contents of a concept. It is clear that from the notion of a car, for example, we can infer both black and white, but a car cannot be simultaneously wholly black and wholly white. It also cannot be without colour. Consequently, the total content of a concept cannot be incorporated into any representation imaginable, but only into those in which it makes sense.

In fact, in propositions we mostly have a rather narrow content of the total concept. If we say that the human body flies, we are not actually interested in whether it has an autonomous nervous system and millions of other attributes. We are only interested in the fact that it flies. This is practically the only relevant dimension. The weight and aerodynamics of the body may also have some importance, but the ability to read a book can hardly be important. The active set of attributes which are relevant in some representational context can be called the 'use' of a concept (Saariluoma 1997). The use of a concept is the set of attributes which are relevant when a concept is incorporated into a particular representation. As is well known, Wittgenstein (1958) equated the meaning of a word with its use, so that the meaning of a word was co-extensive with its use. Wittgenstein, however, had no concept of representation or representational contents. But use can also be found in so-called conceptual role semantics (Cummins 1989; Harman 1987).

The actual content of a concept is thus its use. The content of God is precisely what it contributes to some particular representation. This explains how it is possible that the Christian God has been at once a source of beauty and cruelty, salvation and hatred, self-sacrifice and egoism. In different action contexts, different aspects of the notion have become dominant in its use. In individual terms, all people have personal attributes in their notion of God, although social practice naturally creates numerous similarities between the representations of this concept in the minds of individuals. It is the context – textual, representational, social, cultural and historical – which makes the constraints for the actual construction of representation determine the particular use.

The inferential functions of concepts and especially Cartesian inference are essential because they enable us to investigate the content of concepts, both potential and actual. Presumably, the processes making inference possible are not very distant from the processes which enable us to abstract use from total content. It is a process whereby a set of conceptual attributes is selected and abstracted. It is an analytical operation, while the actual construction is synthetic.

At this stage, one must ask what is the function of the referential content. The answer is that it can provide us with the criteria for content. As already mentioned, only true attributes make sense in representations. But how do we know that some attribute is true? The answer seems to be by comparing attributes with the properties of references. Only such attributes make sense which can have a referential property. Thus, investigation of the reference set is the very source of attributes and the content of concepts in the attributive and representational sense.

One further problem must be discussed here; the constructive approach presupposes a special procedure for clarifying the borders of concepts (Saariluoma 1997). This is the differentiation of concepts from each other. The reason for asking such a question is the importance of distinguishing between entities and naturally also between the corresponding concepts. The constructive approach to concepts assumes that concepts always have their actual content defined in some context. The individuation of concepts is here not assumed to be as absolute as in classic essentialism. It is relative to a definitional context. This means that the individuation of a concept normally distinguishes it from a definite set of concepts, i.e. a definitional domain group, and not from all imaginable concepts in all imaginable contexts. Thus the criteria may vary between different contexts. This kind of slightly pragmatic and dynamic position can be termed 'contextual essentialism' (Saariluoma 1997).

The notion of perception may serve as an example. In consciousness research, the major attribute of perception is conscious experience. Perception is the experienced mental content. In space perception research, depth-cue systems and mechanisms are vital. They are, however, completely unconscious. In this way, the goal of the research and the research context determines the relevance criteria for different attributes of perception, which can be either conscious or unconscious. In some contexts, some attributes are more important than others; the change of context may change the importance of some particular attributes. In fact, the differences are essentially connected with the use of concepts. More accurately, to understand the use of a concept one must often be able to distinguish the current use from other possible uses. In this, contextual discrimination is essential.

Contextual essentialism assumes further that definitions do not express the content of the concept. In principle, the content of a concept is precisely what can be attributed to it, i.e. propositionally stated about it. Of course, everything that can be attributed is not equally relevant or equally frequently important, but this is not essential here. The contents of a notion entail all its attributes and their organization. Thus the notion of unipolar depression may contain various operational and structural issues, such as a negative conception of the self and the future (Beck 1976). However, the notion of

Classification and the Contents of Concepts

depression does not entail the attribute that it could greatly contribute to happiness in the world.

Contextual essentialism and attribute organization provide a clear account of most definitional theories. Wittgenstein's problem (1958) of family resemblance, for example, can be solved in terms of conceptual essentialism. One manifestation of a concept can be seen as one location, while some other manifestation has some other, partly similar, system of attributes. The notion of a game may in one manifestation refer to non-serious playing such as Monopoly, while in another it may refer to soccer, which may sometimes be taken very seriously indeed. The concept of a game may also refer to political or stock market intrigues, which have relatively little to do with Monopoly in terms of the seriousness of the consequences, but very much if the context is one of honest productive work. Thus the different manifestations simply mean a minor transformation of location in the multidimensional spaces spanned around them.

The use of a concept refers to the relevance of subcontent in different contexts. By the 'subcontent' of a concept I refer to the set of attributes that are relevant in a particular context. The notion of subcontent is important in characterizing the use of a concept; the use of a particular concept is precisely its subcontent, which is relevant in some definable context (Saariluoma 1997). The weight of a mental patient may be important in making a diagnosis of depression, but it may be much less relevant when searching for the cognitive dimensions of the illness or the capabilities of the patient.

To understand a concept is to know its attributes and how they are organized, the definition of the concept, and its use in different contexts. Of course, no one can understand and explicate a complex concept completely. Moreover, it is impossible to determine automatically either the attributes of a concept or their organization. This is why research into concepts is so difficult, but also why conceptual research is so badly needed. Without such research the clarity of a conceptual system and its foundations cannot be improved.

One final question which needs to be discussed here is the relationship between the three perspectives. What makes them unified? The answer is simply that they are three aspects of one and the same constructive process. The potential contents of concepts are constructed, at least in part, on the basis of their actual contents. Each time a new actual attribute is given to a concept in the construction of actual representations, it may also be added to the total content

249

of the concept. If I learn that Mike knows French, this attribute is added to his concept in my long-term memory. On the other hand, the total content constrains the construction of actual representations. Classification and inference are subprocesses of construction. In this way, the basic human capacity to construct representations becomes the hub around which the conceptual process revolves.

The place of the constructive approach

The constructive theory of concepts presented here has its own characteristics and goals. It has been developed for apperception research; it therefore emphasizes those properties of concepts which are important in the construction of representations. The main function of concepts is seen as the construction of representations, rather than the classification of entities. The theory has a number of features which resemble certain other theories of concepts. It is therefore useful to discuss briefly the relations of the constructivist theory of concepts and certain other relevant theories of concepts and semantics.

In modern cognitive semantics, the major theories of concepts are presumably classic theories, prototype theory, image theory, atomic theory, theory theory and conceptual role semantics (e.g. Fodor 1991; Harman 1987; Laurence and Margolis 1999; Miller and Johnson-Laird 1976; Murphy and Medin 1999; Paivio 1971; 1986; Rosch 1978). Each of these theories shares certain features in common with the constructivist view of concepts, but they also have some differences. The theories themselves are of course also partly overlapping.

There are two major differences between the constructive theory of concepts and the classic theory. In the latter, definitions play a central role in determining the content of concepts, while in the former definitions are merely one case of use and do not have an essential role in determining or explicating the content of a concept (Saariluoma 1997). Definition is not essential even in discriminating a given concept from others, since this is based on individuation, i.e. on finding a context-dependent set of features needed for discrimination (Saariluoma 1997). Finally, the use of a concept depends on its representational environment and thus its content may vary constantly within the limits of the total content.

The difference from prototype theories is also essential. Prototype theories are psychological theories, and they presumably show that more common and frequently used representations are processed faster. This is not very surprising, if we consider matters from the point of view of automatization (e.g. Shiffrin 1988). However, prototype theory does not really have much to do with the content of concepts. While the penguin is not as prototypical a bird as the sparrow, the content of the concept of a 'penguin' is not smaller. Prototype theories thus focus on very different aspects of concepts from constructive theory.

Image theory, as discussed here, is part of Paivio's (1971; 1986) dual coding hypothesis, which assumes that mental images have an essential role in the construction of meaning in words. Again, there is much evidence for the importance of images in the psychological processing of many types of words, but image theory is not actually a theory of conceptual contents. It is rather a theory of information format. (Saariluoma 1997.)

The next approach is conceptual atomism, which assumes that there exists a basic set of primitive notions and that all representations are constructed of these elements. At first sight the principle of compositionality seems to emphasize the constructive role of concepts. However, constructive theory does not accept the metaphor of the atom. Concepts are living entities and they are all formed in the context of other representations. Some are sensory, such as 'red', while others are more experiential, such as 'possible'; but all of them have other concepts as defining attributes. 'Yellow' is a colour and it exists. It is also used in new cars and other objects. All of these facts characterize 'yellow' and belong to its contents. Furthermore, the use of concepts can vary and therefore the content they contribute to representations also varies. The constructive theory of concepts thus takes a much more dynamic view of concepts than does conceptual atomism. (Saariluoma 1997.)

Constructive theory also shares many features in common with theory theory. It assumes that concepts are nodes in a network of concepts. Indeed, it is possible to demonstrate that many concepts are associated with certain theory theory type attributes. However, concepts have many other types of attributes as well, and it is unclear whether all concepts have some defining theory. From the constructive point of view, theory theory relies on one, or at most a few, of all the possible uses of a concept. Certainly a concept such as 'whale' has important non-theoretical attributes, such as visible size, and yet these attributes are essential in many contexts. Thus the attributes discussed by the theory theory merely represent a special case of the constructive theory of concepts outlined here.

The last approach discussed here will be conceptual role semantics. It is apparently a very similar theory to the constructive approach. Its leading idea is that the meaning of a concept is its role or use in a representation (Cummins 1989; Harman 1987). Like the constructive approach, it is interested primarily in mental representations, i.e. in the construction of thought, and not in its expression in some language (Harman 1987). However, these similarities should not conceal some very fundamental differences.

One difference between conceptual role semantics and the constructive approach is in the way they consider that the contents of representations and concepts are used. In conceptual role semantics, the content of a concept is determined by its functional role in a representation. The constructive view assumes two different dimensions of conceptual contents. First, it postulates the content of a concept in the human long-term memory, i.e. the total content. In addition, the constructive approach also postulates the use of a concept or its actual content, which is created when it is combined to represent something specific. The difference between actual and potential justifies the use of the term constructive.

The second difference is the constructive process itself. According to the constructive theory of concepts, the actual contents of concepts are constructed on the spot. This assumption makes the theory highly dynamic and versatile. The uses of concepts can be abstractive, so that many of the attributes can be ignored. This means that the content of a concept can only be understood by knowing the potential use a person has for this concept and the actual construction process, i.e. what kind of other concepts are needed, and how and for what purposes they are integrated. It is of course usually possible to operate on a much more general level. One can discuss Vienna without ever having been there. The topics of discourse will of course be limited compared to a native of Vienna, but for many uses this is not important. Also, as a hearer one can construct numerous basic-level representations and imagine how to get around the Ring. Representations are conceptual constructions and it is possible to construct them on several content levels. Thanks to this dynamism and process orientation, the constructive view is essentially different from conceptual role semantics as a theory of concepts.

The practice of conceptual analysis

At this point, concrete examples may be needed. If we are interested in investigating a religious text, for example, we may encounter a situation in which all types of contents are needed to construct an interpretation of an accurate representational content. The key notions of the previous sections make it possible to define some major properties of practical conceptual analyses. One of the main tasks in cultural research is often to understand what meaning contents characterize cultures, and in this work conceptual analyses naturally have an important role. This role is to determine the correct use and interpretation of concepts, conceptual relations, etc. This means the precise determination of the information content of a semiotic presentation. In investigating religious concepts, this major task can hardly be anything different from what the analysis of information content must be by its very nature. The problem is to find a suitable practice to carry out the analysis and explication of information content.

Naturally, in this work conceptual analysis is the major goal of the whole discussion. All the information content in human representations is reducible to conceptual content. The contents of concepts, and how they are combined, are crucial points when we think of the content of any complex representation such as a proposition, a text, a discourse, a mental representation or a culture. Concepts form the elements which provide us with the exact meaning of symbolic expressions and the exact contents of the corresponding mental representations. Only by means of conceptual analyses do we know, in a given representation, what is pain, fatherhood, duty or God.

Conceptual analysis is the essence of investigating any cultural entity, from God to the papers of war councils. Cultural entities have meanings, or more precisely meaning contents, and what the expressions in a given linguistic or symbolic object refer to depends decisively on the way concepts are used in constructing the corresponding mental representations. However, only by determining the exact use of the concepts incorporated into these representations can one become aware of the contents of representations. This is why the search for the precise attributes of the concepts used is vital; and the method of working with concepts is conceptual analysis. Naturally, Cartesian inference forms one of the main processes in such analytical investigation.

One and the same set of signs can turn out to mean very different things when its conceptual content has been clarified. A sentence like 'God blessed their marriage' may have a very different content for a Catholic compared to a Lutheran, for a town-dweller compared to a farmer, for people of the twentieth century compared to people from the nineteenth. The use of the terms is different; in particular the whole differs decisively between different people. For a devout Catholic, marriage should endure no matter what, but in Lutheran societies attitudes towards divorce are more liberal. The meaning of the proposition has to be read with an understanding of the context and the set of attributes associated in this context with the incorporated concepts.

In order to make sense of concepts, one must be able to individuate the content of concepts in their current contexts. This means in practice the explication and analyses of their use and the attributes which determine it. In this type of work, Cartesian inference is normally a necessary tool. Explicitly or implicitly, these analyses enable us to make the crucial distinctions. One can for example differentiate the Leibnizian notion of Theodicy from that of Kant by the empirical attributes Kant gave to this concept (Lorentz 1998). For Leibniz the problem of why there is evil in the world when God is almighty and good was resolved by rationalistic optimism. The world is the best of all possible worlds. This notion of Theodicy is very difficult to apply to the world experienced. However, God has given us the moral duty to follow just principles and thus realize in his creative work his goodness. Clearly, the two notions have different attributes and thus they also provide different solutions to the original problem. Characteristically, solving these differences in detail (which is not the goal of this chapter) presupposes a Cartesian analysis of the attributes, which is common in conceptual analysis in the field of cultural research.

The determination of conceptual contents is not defining, because defining means finding a crucial attribute, but individuating, which means explicating the relevant attributes. One must say which set of attributes is decisive for talking about the holy, God, ritual, the sacral, etc. in the relevant context. Thus, when certain contextual preconditions have been fulfilled it is possible to take the killing of another human as sacrifice and worship, as is the case for example in certain South American cultures. Today, it is difficult to find any context in which such sacrifices would be acceptable. This means that in one context one can take an action to be holy, while in another it certainly is not that.

These examples should illustrate how one can use Cartesian inference in defining the content of representations. It provides us with a tool that enables us to explicate the hidden meaning content in representations. It allows us to recognize and accurately individuate the differences between various cultural representations, even when their immediate expression is the same. It also makes it possible to investigate changes in cultural and religious meanings in the course of history. Clearly, the symbolic meanings for instance in many works of art do not have the same content today that they did earlier. There have in fact been periods during which many artists important today have hardly been understood at all.

Apperceiving cultural entities

It is now time to return to the beginning. This is the question of apperceiving God. We know from empirical investigation that people experience God in very different ways, and also that in different contexts they have very different Gods. God may be merciful or punitive. God may mean relief from pain or imprisonment. Like human beings, God creates and destroys. Indeed, there are as many Gods as there are kinds of people. From the current point of view the crucial difference between Gods is in the set of attributes people associate with the notion of God. This essentially means investigation of the set of conscious and tacit attributes people ascribe to God in different situations.

The main goals of apperception research are in understanding individuals and their experiences. This can be seen in the curious fact that apperception was one of Kant's (1781) basic psychological notions, while the historically and culturally oriented Hegel barely mentions it. Cultures do not apperceive. Only individual members of these cultures can do so. There is, however, no culture outside of these individual experiences; it is for this reason that one cannot justly eliminate the cognitive–apperceptive and individualistic point of view in investigating cultural entities.

Individuals represent the world as they can, and how they represent it depends on the content of their concepts. Thus, understanding and explaining how people in a culture see a thing as something presupposes reconstructing the content of their concepts. To early Greeks, however intellectual, an abstract entity such as the Christian God was incomprehensible. They could not conceive of such a cultural dimension as monotheism and the related relation to God, because this way of apperceiving things developed much later in their culture. Similarly, the idea of a personal relation to God was not part of the medieval Catholic experience. It was not thought about in churches or in schools, and thus it never penetrated the general cultural experience. Consequently, large numbers of people did not see the world as for instance a modern Lutheran sees it.

One thing which apperception research effectively explains is that we cannot be conscious of something whose concepts and conceptual attributes are unknown to us. The reason is that in the absence of

255

suitable conceptual content it is impossible to construct mental representations of these references. Medieval people did not know that slowly appearing masts on the horizon were a sign of the roundness of the earth. They were unable to become conscious of the roundness, even though they regularly observed the phenomenon. They were no more aware of the form of earth than a novice understands the beauty of a chess master's moves or an ordinary person an unfamiliar language.

Apperception makes human beings conscious of reality; thus its properties necessarily give us understanding of the processes and contents of cultural experience and change. To become conscious of something we must have the relevant conceptual knowledge. If we do not have this knowledge, we also lose the conscious experience. A person with no idea of God as an existing and actively participating entity, a kind of Nietzschean conception so to speak, can hardly experience the involvement of God in current history. It is not the kind of representation such a person consciously makes about reality. On the other hand, to a person with a concept of God that contains the attribute of active participation, the role of God may be very evident. While the former would never think of his/her sins causing the death of his/her child in a traffic accident, the latter may experience deep guilt in the matter.

The conscious world is the world our apperception can construct for us. Nevertheless, it can construct only that type of representation which the attributes of personal concepts make possible. Spring is different for the botanist and the layperson. The latter does not necessarily see the stages and interaction of the ecosystem which are easily represented by the botanist. This means that the poet is no longer conscious of the information provided by nature. Likewise, a modern medical doctor can hardly encode all the religious systems relevant to medieval medicine. The content of the new medical culture is very different from the old and the contents of Western medicine are very different from the earliest ones. Almost all scientific notions have similarly changed over the years and with them our way of seeing things.

Apperceiving God or religious entities is thus reducible to the conceptual contents people have. A good example of 'seeing as' rather than mere seeing is Guthrie's analysis (this volume) of how people project godlike attributes onto their percepts of nature. This explains the individual variation which is typical of religious concepts. People make their own interpretations of religious concepts, although some core conceptions are shared socially. In order to understand how the views of people differ, conceptual analysis is necessary. Sometimes this may be difficult because concepts have intuitive and even unconscious attributes. The phenomenon is an everyday problem in clinical psychology. Patients may be totally unaware of numerous aspects of their behaviour, because so many behavioural schemes remain outside their consciousness (e.g. Beck 1976).

Without any additional notions of conceptual contents we are naturally powerless when investigating how people apperceive religious issues. What kind of models they have about God and rites, for example, is not simply an issue of reference. It is an issue of what kind of meaning structures we have built onto the concept. For us the entities are as we represent them and the way we represent them depends on the contents of concepts. The importance of culture for the individual is in the fact that concepts are learned in interaction with the environment. Both the way people see things and the form these concepts take on in individual mental representations make it possible for them to experience reality as they do. The brain forms the representation vehicle, i.e. the material basis for this process of learning, experiencing and apperceiving the world, but the material and cultural environment gives a content to this experience. Since the individual brain alone cannot control developments in the life-environment, mental contents cannot be explained in biological terms (Saariluoma 1999). The brain of a Buddhist need not be essentially different from that of a Christian. Or rather, the possible differences cannot explain the religions of individuals. Consequently, we do not perceive God. We have had numerous experiences related to religion in our lives, we learn religious concepts, and each of us constructs our own concept of God out of that culturally transmitted information. This is why we have so many experiences of God, so many sects, religious movements and, indeed, religions.

References

Barrett, J. (1999) 'Theological correctness'. *Method and Theory in the Study of Religion* 11: 325–39.

Beck, A. (1976) *Cognitive Therapy of Emotional Disorders*. Harmondsworth: Penguin.

Boyer, P. (1994) *The Naturalness of Religious Ideas: A Cognitive Theory of Religion*. Berkeley: University of California Press.

Bruner, J., J. Goodnow and G. Austin (1956) *A Study of Thinking*. New York: Wiley.

Bunge, M. (1962) *Intuition and Science*. Westport, CO: Greenwood.

Bunyan, J. (1991) *The Pilgrim's Progress*. New York: New American Library.

Cann, R. (1993) *Formal Semantics*. Cambridge: Cambridge University Press.

Carey, S. (1985) *Conceptual Change in Childhood*. Cambridge, MA: MIT Press.

Carey, S. (1991) 'Knowledge acquisition: enrichment or conceptual change'. In S. Carey and R. Gelman (eds), *The Epigenesis of Mind: Essays on Biology and Cognition*. Hillsdale, NJ: Erlbaum.

Carnap, R. (1947) *Meaning and Necessity*. Chicago: University of Chicago Press.

Chi, M. (1992) 'Conceptual change within and across ontological categories: examples from learning and discovery in science'. In *Cognitive Models of Science*, ed. R. Giere, 129–86. Minneapolis: University of Minnesota Press.

Cruse, D. A. (1986) *Lexical Semantics*. Cambridge: Cambridge University Press.

Cummins, R. (1989) *Meaning and Mental Representation*. Cambridge, MA: MIT Press.

Dehaene, S., J. Jonides, E. E. Smith and M. Spitzer (1999) 'Thinking and problem solving'. In *Fundamentals of Neuroscience*, ed. M. J. Zigmond, F. E. Bloom, S. C. Landis, J. L. Roberts and L. R. Squire. San Diego: Academic Press.

Dennett, D. C. (1991) *Consciousness Explained*. London: Butler & Tanner.

Descartes, R. (1975) *Collected Works*, vols 1, 2. Cambridge: Cambridge University Press.

Duncker, K. (1945) *On Problem Solving*, Psychological Monographs, 270. Washington, DC: APA.

Ellis, A. and A. Young (1995) *Handbook of Cognitive Neuropsychology*. Hove: Psychology Press.

Estes, W. L. (1994) *Concepts and Categories*. Oxford: Oxford University Press.

Fodor, J. A. (1991) *A Theory of Content and Other Essays*. Cambridge: MIT Press.

Harman, G. (1987) 'Nonsolipsistic conceptual role semantics'. In *Semantics of Natural Language*, ed. E. LePore, 55–81. New York: Academic Press.

Hintikka, J. (1999) 'The emperor's new intuitions'. *Journal of Philosophy* 96: 127–47.

Husserl, E. (1936) *The Crises of European Science and Transcendental Phenomenology*. Evanston, IL: Northwestern University Press.

James, W. (1902/1997) *Varieties of Religious Experience*. London: Macmillan.

Kant, I. (1781) *Kritik der Reinen Vernunft*. Stuttgart: Philip Reclam.

Laurence, S. and E. Margolis (1999) 'Concepts and cognitive science'. In *Concepts*, ed. E. Margolis and S. Laurence. Cambridge, MA: MIT Press.

Leibniz, G. (1704/1979) *New Essays on Human Understanding*. Cambridge: Cambridge University Press.

Lorentz, S. (1998) 'Theodicee'. In *Historisches Wörterbuch der Philosophie*, ed. J. Ritter and K. Gruender. Darmstadt: Wissenschaftliche Buchgesellschaft.

Miller, G. A. and Johnson-Laird, P. N. (1976) *Language and Perception*. Cambridge: Cambridge University Press.

Murphy, D. and D. Medin (1999 (1985)) 'The role of theories in conceptual coherence'. In *Concepts*, ed. E. Margolis and S. Laurence. Cambridge, MA: MIT Press.

Newell, A. and H. A. Simon (1972) *Human Problem Solving*. Englewood Cliffs, NJ: Prentice-Hall.

Paivio, A. (1971) *Imagery and Verbal Processes*. New York: Holt.

Paivio, A. (1986) *Mental Representations*. New York: Oxford University Press.

Pinker, S. (1994) *The Language Instinct*. Harmondsworth: Penguin.

Rosch, E. (1978) 'Principles of categorization'. In *Cognition and Categorization*, ed. E. Rosch and B. B. Lloyd. Hillsdale, NJ: Erlbaum.

Saariluoma, P. (1990) 'Apperception and restructuring in chess players' problem solving'. In *Lines of Thought: Reflections on the Psychology of Thinking*, ed. K. J. Gilhooly, M. T. G. Keane, R. H. Logie and G. Erdos, 41–57. London: Wiley.

Saariluoma, P. (1992) 'Error in chess: an apperception restructuring view'. *Psychological Research* 54: 17–26.

Saariluoma, P. (1995) *Chess Players' Thinking*. London: Routledge.

Saariluoma, P. (1997) *Foundational Analysis*. London: Routledge.

Saariluoma, P. (1999) 'Neuroscientific psychology and mental contents'. *Life Long Education in Europe* 4: 34–9.

Saariluoma, P. (2001) 'Chess and content-oriented psychology of thinking'. *Psicologia* 22: 143–64.

Shiffrin, R. M. (1988) 'Attention'. In *Stevens' Handbook of Experimental Psychology*, vol. 2: *Learning and Cognition*, ed. R. C. Atkinson, R. J. Herrnstein, G. Lindzey and R. D. Luce, 731–811. New York: Wiley.

Shulkin, J. (1999) *Neuroendocrine Regulation of Behaviour.* Cambridge: Cambridge University Press.

Smedslund, J. (1988), *Psycho-Logic*. New York: Springer.

Smith, E. and D. Medin (1981) *Categories and Concepts*. Cambridge, MA: Harvard University Press.

Stout, G. F. (1896) *Analytic Psychology*. New York: Macmillan.

Thagard, P. (1992) *Conceptual Revolutions*. Princeton: Princeton University Press.

Vosniadou, S. and W. Brewer (1992) 'Mental models of the earth: a study of conceptual change'. *Cognitive Psychology* 24: 535–85.

Vygotski, L. (1934/1962) *Thought and Language*. Cambridge, MA: MIT Press.

Wittgenstein, L. (1958) *Philosophical Investigations*. Oxford: Blackwell.

Wundt, W. (1880) *Logik*, vol. 1. Stuttgart: Enke.

12 Explaining Religion: Cognitive and Evolutionary Mechanisms

MATTI KAMPPINEN

Introduction

The current research design in cognitive theory of religion is to account for cultural properties in terms of cognitive and evolutionary mechanisms. This explanatory strategy is a classic case of relating emergent properties to lower-level mechanisms. In what follows I will examine what is at stake when we account for something on the basis of something else. Accordingly, I will analyse the notions of description, subsumption and explanation, especially in the light of their ontological commitments. I will argue that proper explanation should refer to the unobserved mechanisms functioning behind observable patterns. As a case in point I will refer to cognitive explanations supplemented by evolutionary principles. More precisely, I will single out two evolutionary principles, the Law of Extremes and the Law of Middle Things, that have proven and will prove especially fruitful in accounting for things religious. The overall conclusion is that if scientific progress will have its way in the study of religion, then pseudo-scientific labelling practices devoid of any explanatory power will become first endangered, then extinct. The heavy metaphysics of this exercise will be balanced by examples from the cognitive anthropology of religion. The conclusions I have reached contradict several schools in the anthropology of religion, especially those engaged in cultural description. Since most of my own work has been carried out in the very same descriptive spirit, I appear to contradict even my earlier self. I find the premises and the inferences credible, and the conclusions inevitable. Contradiction over time is natural personal development, I guess.

The relevance of philosophy in the study of religion

Empirical scientists are usually busy with collecting and interpreting the data, and writing reports on how the world is. This is understandable, since that is what they are paid for. Philosophical reflections on scientific activities are left for leisure activities, retired colleagues or fellow philosophers. Philosophical reflections cover the use and foundations of methods, models and inferences. One of the central aims in the philosophy of science is to analyse and reconstruct the ontological commitments of scientific theories. What kinds of entities – objects, processes, systems, mechanisms – are postulated by them? What would the world be like if the theories were true?

Addressing philosophical questions in empirical science is not welcomed by all scientists. A colleague of mine, a physicist, puts the scientist's attitude towards philosophical reflections as follows: Damn the torpedoes, full speed ahead! Still, philosophical reflections serve many important functions: they can be used in explicating and justifying the practices, they serve in clarifying the nature of the discipline for newcomers, and most importantly, they bring to light the rational structure and foundations of what we are doing. And, just in case the foundations are not rational, philosophical tools help to dismantle and rebuild the conceptual groundwork.

One traditional philosophical issue in any field of research concerns models of explanation. How are the objects of study rendered intelligible? What kinds of mechanisms, lawful connections and patterns are referred to in explaining the data? To put it briefly, what are the ontological commitments of explanations?

The varieties of explanation

There exists a considerable variety of explanations in different fields of scientific research. They range from the classical deductive-nomological model articulated by Carl Hempel (1966) to the contextualizations of cultural traits practised by postmodern anthropologists. James Clifford (1986), the well-known postmodern anthropologist, once formulated the goal of anthropology as 'constructing links between phenomena'.

Looking back at the history of science and its philosophy, it is obvious that different disciplines have functioned as exemplary models of explanation. The deductive-nomological model was inspired by classical physics, while functional accounts in early cultural anthropology were loosely based on biological explanations. The currently dominant metaphor is the computer and its rule-governed, systemic behaviour. Anything can be recast in terms of information processing. (It is worth mentioning, as an aside, that the prevalent use of computers in all areas of scientific modelling probably induces the idea that in order to be scientifically respectable an entity has to relate to a computer model.) Another source of analogy strongly present in the current philosophy of science is evolutionary theory.

Source models, be they from physics, computer science or evolutionary theory, have their strongest impact on pre-paradigmatic (or, as some would say, even pre-scientific) disciplines such as – to name a couple – sociology and the study of religion. Exemplary models structure scientific argumentation, shifting burdens of proof to those who use other models of explanation and understanding.

Understanding, description, subsumption and explanation

Let us now move to a more detailed picture, and examine the distinction between understanding, description, subsumption and explanation as developed by Mario Bunge, especially in his books *Scientific Research 1–2* (1967), *Understanding the World* (1983) and *Finding Philosophy in Social Science* (1996).

Understanding is the shared goal of all cognitive beings: scientists, laypeople and priests alike aim at grasping the reality and at navigating in the world of uncertainty. Understanding is not an all-or-nothing operation. It comes in several degrees and modes. As cognitive anthropologists of religion we are familiar with cultural variations of understanding, with how our objects of study conceptualize the world. Scientific understanding (which interests us here) involves the systematic use of theories and their assessment in the light of empirical or conceptual data. (At times it happens that our study object challenges our interpretations on the basis of his/her theories, but that is another, long story.) Another hallmark of scientific understanding – especially important for the study of religion – is that each field of research should have systematic connections to neighbouring fields of research, such as psychology and biology. This criterion of scientific understanding requires that findings at the level of cultural systems have some interpretation at the levels of psychology and biology. Scientific understanding is here understood as a cover-term that can be divided up into explanation, forecasting and backcasting (or historical accounts).

Scientific understanding begins with intellectual problems, hypotheses and their testable consequences, backed by theories, and data, which serve the function of assessing the hypotheses. Descriptions make up a crucial part of this research cycle.

Description is an ordered set of factual statements, such as 'There are witch doctors and patients in the Amazon,' or 'The healing process where projectiles are extracted from the patient utilizes the cognitive model of boundaries.' Such descriptions alone add little to scientific understanding. Even the Geertzian thick descriptions are of little value on their own. Their proper place is to provide data for further interpretation and, finally, explanation. It should be mentioned, as an aside, that the folklore-oriented and archive-dominated study of religion practised in Scandinavia is more often than not satisfied with descriptions. Many of our students and even colleagues in the field of comparative religion are happy with labelling cultural entities and writing up coherent accounts. Those infected with postmodern intertextuality, naturally, are satisfied even with stories that are not necessarily coherent.

More ambition is added as we move from description to subsumption.

Subsumption is a methodological category widely used in anthropology of religion. In subsumption, a given fact is subsumed under a general pattern. For example, the above description, 'The healing process where projectiles are extracted from the patient utilizes the cognitive model of boundaries,' can be subsumed under a more general pattern: 'The cognitive model of boundaries is used when people are dealing with extended objects that possess the inside, the outside and the line between.'

The general scheme for subsumption is as follows:

Pattern	For all x, if Fx then Gx.
Circumstance	Fb.
Given fact	Gb.

Subsumption is used for explanatory purposes, even though it is not an explanation proper. The general pattern may be a law-like statement or a classificatory statement, but it does not identify the real mechanism responsible for the *explanandum*. Both Piagetian developmental psychology and Fowler's psychology of religion are filled with statements about general patterns. For example, the statement 'Peter believes in an anthropomorphic God because he is seven years old' exemplifies a subsumption. Likewise the statement 'Perceptions of extraterrestrial aliens are anthropomorphic because intentional systems in general are anthropomorphized' is a subsumption.

In the case of classificatory generalization, the subsumption scheme looks as follows:

Premise 1   Entities in the class X have properties A, B and C.
Premise 2   Entity b belongs to the class X.
Conclusion   Entity b has the properties A, B and C.

Or, if we are inductively inferring the further properties of an entity b on the basis of our general pattern, we get the following:

Premise 1   Entities in class X have properties A, B and C.
Premise 2   Entity b has properties A and B.
Induction   Entity b has the property C as well.

As in the case of description, subsumption too invites many students of religion to do bad science by means of labelling. Subsuming empirical findings under some broad cultural category is perhaps interesting, but it is not the scientific study of religion at its best.

Explanation proper enters the stage when we are able to identify the mechanism responsible for the facts. Whereas subsumptions give answers to *what* and *how* questions only, explanations answer both *how* and *why* questions. The gist of explanation is in identifying the theoretical mechanism responsible for the general pattern. Theoretical mechanisms are postulated entities, whose conditions and impacts are specified by the theory and further identified by indicator hypotheses.

Explanatory mechanisms exist on lower levels of reality in relation to the *explanandum*. Thus, for example, the pattern 'Peter believes in an anthropomorphic God because he is seven years old' should be supplemented by an account of the mechanism that makes Peter perceive God in this way. The lower-level mechanisms in this case could be multiple. The multipurpose cognitive mechanisms involved in the developmental ontogenesis of categorizations, discussed by Keil (1989), for example, exist at a lower level than the ontologization tendency identified by Boyer (1994). The lower the level of the mechanism recruited for explanatory purposes, the more systematic power it has. That is, it can be used in explaining several kinds of cultural properties: not only religion but gossip and football as well. Moving on to neurobiological mechanisms is bound to give even deeper explanations.

The general pattern of explanation can be put as follows:

Pattern 1   For all x, if Fx then Mx.
Pattern 2   For all x, if Mx then Gx.

Circumstance   Fb.
Given fact   Gb.

Here M symbolizes the mechanism, and F and G are properties under explanation. The mechanism M belongs to a lower level, whereas the properties F and G reside on the higher level.

The most prominent difference between description, subsumption and explanation lies in their ontological commitment. Descriptions and subsumptions are almost non-committal, positing as they do only things, properties and relations between them. Explanations postulate the existence of a hierarchical level structure of reality, where the links between levels are the major object of scientific research.

Evolutionary explanation

Cognitive explanations should be supplemented with evolutionary accounts. The role of evolutionary explanations is becoming more and more prominent in the study of religion. One of the leading theorists in the field of general evolutionary theory is Daniel C. Dennett.

Evolutionary thinking has pervaded Dennett's work. *Content and Consciousness* (1969), *Brainstorms* (1982) and *The Intentional Stance* (1987) proposed a general theory of mind, where cognitive mechanisms and contents were constrained by environmental factors. In Dennett's scheme, organisms try out different courses of action, and the selective forces of the environment choose the viable ones. With humans, and other complicated cognitive systems, there is the possibility of first testing the actions in the inner environment, then proceeding to act in the outer environment. Human cognitive systems are complex enough so that our ideas can die instead of us, which was a major leap in the general evolution of organisms. This evolutionary standpoint, where systems are understood with reference to their inner and outer environments, was one of the constituents of Dennett's Intentional System Theory: intentional systems are belief-generating systems that test their ideas in the inner and outer environments. In *Consciousness Explained* (1992), Dennett took a more explicit evolutionary turn. Consciousness itself, according to him, is a collection of *memes*, units of meaning competing for existence. The Multiple Drafts model of consciousness compares the human mind to a gene pool, where constant struggle, change and combinatory possibilities rule. The idea that the individual consciousness is a system of memes realized in human brains invites one to think of meaning systems as something supra-individual, social and shared. Cultural meaning systems, or religions for that matter, have seriously attracted Dennett's interest only in his 1995 book, *Darwin's Dangerous Idea: Evolution and the Meanings of Life.* I think that, of all Dennett's works, this is the one that no student of religion should ignore.

Let us look at the principles of evolutionary explanations and how they serve the purpose of explaining religion. To begin with, evolutionary theory can be used in two different, although complementary, styles in explaining things religious.

First, we may want to look at how religion functions in biological systems, that is, what are its causes and effects in terms of evolutionary biology. The general pattern of this approach is as follows:

Given fact   Organic property P exists.
Pattern   Anything that exists must be evolutionarily viable.
Conclusion   Property P is evolutionarily viable.

Here 'organic' means that the property is exemplified by an organism. Religions, on this construal, are organic properties and have their evolutionary reasons for being. This type of explanation usually serves as the starting point in research where the next step is to find out the ways in which property P is connected to such basic ecological variables as food, fighting and reproduction. This style of evolutionary explanation is exemplified in the work of Marvin Harris (Harris 1979).

The *second* style of utilizing evolutionary explanations in the study of religion is by means of analogical inference, where evolutionary principles are transferred to the realm of cultural properties. This inference runs as follows:

Premise   Biological and cultural realms are structurally
               similar.
Premise   Principle C holds for the biological realm.
Conclusion   Principle C holds for the cultural realm.

Here the gist of the argument is that explanatory patterns can be transferred from one region of reality to another. On this construal, the cultural reality is pervaded by the same evolutionary laws as the rest of the universe. This argument has been formulated nicely by Daniel Dennett (1995), as well as by Stuart Kauffman in his book *At Home in the Universe: The Search for the Laws of Self-Organization and Complexity* (1995), which is a popularized version of his *The Origins of*

Order: Self-Organization and Selection in Evolution (1993). For begin-
ners, it may be useful to start with books that were inspired by
Kauffman's ideas: Michael Crichton's *The Lost World*, the sequel to
Jurassic Park.

Hunting for memes

What are the properties most profitably transferred into the realm of
religion and culture? The notion of meme is extremely useful – cultural
traits self-organize into systems and compete with each other for
existential space (Dennett 1995). They invade human minds and other
media just for the sake of flourishing in abundance. During the process
of invasion, they adapt themselves to the surrounding cultural systems,
which are constrained by biological and other material boundary conditions. Let us take an example from the folk religion of the Peruvian
Amazon (Kamppinen 1989). There the dominating Catholic framework has permitted the existence of such traditional supernatural
entities as *yacuruna* (the water people), *sacharuna* (the forest people),
and *tunchi* (an aerial spirit). These indigenous beings have been recast
as *espíritus*, which is a broad and ill-defined category in the Catholic
system. It allows the existence of both good and bad spirits, which is in
tune with the traditional conception. The Protestant movements, such
as the Pentecostals, who are trying to establish a foothold in the area,
have problems with these entities. Their system recognizes only evil
spirits; when these two systems meet, the meme for *tunchi* will either
radically transform itself or cease to exist. Another example from the
Peruvian Amazon: the character of Marx coexists side by side with
Jesus in local versions of liberation theology. In these hybrid systems of
meaning, Jesus is recast as the first communist, thus making peaceful
coexistence possible.

The Law of Extremes

Another example of a promising evolutionary principle is the Law of
Extremes (so-called). That is, in the absence of hindering conditions,
traits in the Space of Possible Designs will grow to extreme proportions.
The emergence of extreme forms is built into evolutionary systems. In
the realm of biology, extreme solutions are usually favoured by some
selective force. For example, the overly decorated tails of Australian
birds of paradise, like the common peacock's tail, are favoured by
sexual selection: the more colour and size, the better your chance of

mating and passing on your genes. Extremes in the nose department, such as the elephant's trunk, are again extremes favoured by the distribution of resources in the natural habitat of their carriers.

Cultural systems detached from the conditions of reproduction and biological survival may grow to surprisingly extreme proportions, since they are not restricted by biological boundary conditions. Excessive wealth, overworking, decorating and mutilating one's body are features that have grown to extremes. 'Extreme' in these contexts is defined by what is standard among primates.

In the realm of religion the Law of Extremes appears to have produced at least two pivotal traits: the notions of the 'sacred' and of 'God'. What is sacred? Fundamentally, it is a classification. Distinguishing between different types of entities has been a valuable capability among animals. Different classifications were of different importance for early human beings, for example. Distinguishing between two edible fruits involves less intensive cognitive activity than distinguishing between an edible fruit and a charging wolf. The sacred, as it is exemplified in religions, is nothing but emotionally intensive practices of classification.

The notion of God has reached its extreme forms in the written theologies of Christianity and Hinduism. The anthropomorphic principle has produced human-like entities who have been stripped of their human qualities one by one and who have developed into extreme entities, consisting for example of pure actuality. So, from an evolutionary perspective, what is the Christian God of Thomas Aquinas? It is an extreme human being – a product of systems long since detached from biological conditions. Some of God's properties, such as omnipotence and pure love, have generated problems, for the simple reason that they have not been taken to all the possible extremes. In some versions of Hinduism and Islam, the notion of God has been transformed into an entity that is beyond description. This is a sure way to shelter it from any competing and invading memes.

The Law of Middle Things

The paths of evolutionary dynamics may head in directions that are not compatible with the requirements of cognitive systems. It is this fact that is responsible for what we may call the Law of Middle Things: whenever there is an extreme form of some conceptual system, there is bound to be a continuum of forms that are less extreme, yet different from the human realm. The sacred, in other words a classification that is the deepest divide imaginable, is not suitable for everyday life. In Protestant movements in the Turku area in Finland, for example, there are degrees and varieties of sacredness. The café called *Mix*, run by Pentecostals, is intended for youngsters. It is not an ordinary café, but it is not as sacred a place as their Salem, the real meeting place. The small crosses worn around the neck by some Christians are also less sacred than the ones you find in churches or in the Vatican. The God of Aquinas proved to be too abstract even for Aquinas himself. His 'middle things' were angels, whose less-than-godly properties were essential when he tried to connect human beings with the eternal God. A special theme he treated in *Summa Theologica* was time. Humans live in the world of change and running time, whereas God resides in an eternal present, where nothing changes or moves. What to make of such an idea? What is it like to be God or even to be near him? God's eternity is beyond comprehension. Angels, on the other hand, live in what Aquinas called *aevum*, the angelic time, which resembles human time but has no end, is slower and so on (Aquinas 1952).

The end

Having travelled from the philosophy of science to evolutionary explanations and encounters with angels, it is time to look at the lessons of the story.

Cognitive and evolutionary explanations are of more scientific value than pure descriptions or subsumptions. These explanations refer to different levels of reality, explain the observed in terms of the unobserved and utilize lawful patterns that have been proven valuable in other, neighbouring fields of research.

The cognitive and evolutionary turn in the study of religion is occurring right at this moment. When the dust has settled, much of the descriptive and labelling work done in the study of religion will be put in its proper place: to provide materials for cognitive and evolutionary explanations. Cultural analysis as such – meaning the classifying and labelling of cultural items without explanation proper – will disappear, if scientific progress will have its way in the study of religion.

My prediction assumes that the rational and the good will prevail. The theory of memes gives us an alternative perspective, a frightening prospect. Mediocre science, especially if connected to national traditions and identities, is a successful meme. It may prevail over the rational. The memes don't care – as long as they can infect weak minds and replicate themselves.

References

Aquinas, St Thomas (1952) *Summa Theologica*, trans. Fathers of the English Dominican Province. Chicago: Encyclopaedia Britannica.

Boyer, P. (1994) *The Naturalness of Religious Ideas*. Berkeley: University of California Press.

Bunge, M. (1967) *Scientific Research 1–2*. Berlin: Springer.

Bunge, M. (1983) *Understanding the World*. Dordrecht: Reidel.

Bunge, M. (1996) *Finding Philosophy in Social Science*. New Haven: Yale University Press.

Clifford, J. (1986) 'Introduction: partial truths'. In *Writing Culture*, ed. J. Clifford and G. Marcus. Berkeley: University of California Press.

Crichton, M. (1990) *Jurassic Park*. New York: Ballantine Books.

Crichton, M. (1995) *The Lost World*. New York: Knopf.

Dennett, D. C. (1969) *Content and Consciousness*. London: Routledge & Kegan Paul.

Dennett, D. C. (1982) *Brainstorms*. Cambridge, MA: MIT Press.

Dennett, D. C. (1987) *The Intentional Stance*. Cambridge, MA: MIT Press.

Dennett, D. C. (1991) *Consciousness Explained*. Boston: Little, Brown.

Dennett, D. C. (1995) *Darwin's Dangerous Idea*. New York: Simon & Schuster.

Harris, M. (1979) *Cultural Materialism*. New York: Random House.

Hempel, C. G. (1966) *Philosophy of Natural Science*. Englewood Cliffs, NJ: Prentice-Hall.

Kamppinen, M. (1989) *Cognitive Systems and Cultural Models of Illness*. Helsinki: Academia Scientiarum Fennica.

Kauffman, S. (1993) *The Origins of Order*. New York: Oxford University Press.

Kauffman, S. (1995) *At Home in the Universe*. New York: Oxford University Press.

Keil, F. (1989) *Concepts, Kinds, and Conceptual Development*. Cambridge, MA: MIT Press.

Name Index

Subject Index